Freedom and Political Order

Freedom and Political Order

Traditional American Thought and Practice

Linda C. Raeder

LEXINGTON BOOKS
Lanham • Boulder • New York • London

Published by Lexington Books
An imprint of The Rowman & Littlefield Publishing Group, Inc.
4501 Forbes Boulevard, Suite 200, Lanham, Maryland 20706
www.rowman.com

Unit A, Whitacre Mews, 26-34 Stannary Street, London SE11 4AB

British Library Cataloguing in Publication Information Available

Library of Congress Cataloging-in-Publication Data

Names: Raeder, Linda C., author.
Title: Freedom and political order : traditional American thought and practice / Linda C. Raeder.
Description: Lanham : Lexington Books, [2018] | Includes bibliographical references and index.
Identifiers: LCCN 2017058170 (print) | LCCN 2017051361 (ebook) | ISBN 9781498566056 (electronic) | ISBN 9781498566049 (hardcover : alk. paper) |
Subjects: LCSH: United States—Politics and government. | Political science. Classification: LCC JK31 (print) | LCC JK31 .R33 2018 (ebook) | DDC 320.0973—dc23
LC record available at https://lccn.loc.gov/2017058170

In loving memory of my father, Howard M. Maxwell

Contents

Acknowledgments

I am indebted above all to the many students at Palm Beach Atlantic University who participated in my courses in political philosophy over the past sixteen years. This work would not appear in its present form without the knowledge and understanding I have gained through my experience teaching undergraduates at PBA, and especially those enrolled in my Freedom and American Society and Roots of American Order courses. I would like to thank all those students who shared their perspectives and insights over the years and provided indispensable feedback to the ideas presented in this work.

I am further indebted to the PBA administration, particularly President Bill Fleming and Dr. Ken Mahanes, both of whom have provided unwavering support and encouragement for my scholarship and teaching. My colleagues in the Politics Department, Dr. Francisco Plaza and Dr. James Todd, have also earned my deepest gratitude, not only for their graciousness and collegiality, but also for the penetrating insight and maturity of vision that mark their scholarship and teaching. I am especially thankful for their willingness to read and comment on the manuscript over the course of its development.

Thank you as well to my mother, Evelyn Pokorny Maxwell, for her steadfast love, support, and strength, and my dear animal companions, Max, Sophie, Callie, and the Muscovies, who make day-to-day existence a continual joy.

Introduction

Freedom has traditionally been regarded as the foundational value of American political order, enshrined and celebrated in its most significant national symbols. The centrality of liberty to American identity is attested not only by the enduring appeal of revolutionary rhetoric—"Give me Liberty or Give Me Death" . . . "Live Free or Die"—but also the legendary American sacrifice offered on its behalf.[1] Over the past century, however, the characteristic American commitment to liberty has been challenged by the ascendancy of various beliefs and values unsympathetic and even hostile to individual freedom. The widespread embrace of such beliefs among significant portions of the American populace, including both cultural elites and the general public, has not extinguished but certainly dampened traditional American fervor for the "sacred fire of liberty."[2] For many members of contemporary society, the existential passion that impelled founding patriots to pledge "life, fortune, and sacred honor" in support of American liberty is more a relic of history than a matter of personal experience. Such a development has contributed, among other consequences, to a gradual and ongoing transformation of American political order into a form scarcely recognizable by traditional standards and greatly at odds with the vision of the Founders.

The purpose of this study is to explore the meaning of freedom in the American experience and its relation to other characteristically American values and institutions. Although such an exploration necessarily touches upon relevant historical experience, it extends beyond a history of freedom toward wider fields of inquiry, including and especially, moral and political philosophy. Political philosophers throughout the ages have been concerned with a question of great and perennial significance to human experience: what are the rules that ought to govern human relations in society or, less formally stated, how should human beings treat one another? Such a question is unavoidable for human beings, one that has confronted and must confront every society known to man. Its necessity derives from the nature of things, from the fact that human existence is essentially social or political existence (existence within the polis). The rare Robinson Crusoe aside, "No man is an island," and from birth to death every person encounters other human beings with whom he must interact. Every society has thus established rules regarding the ethical treatment of human beings, rules embodied in the various moral, legal, and political orders developed within human history. The formal discipline of political philosophy aims to explore and identify the proper substance of such rules.

The philosophy of freedom elaborated herein is the traditional American response to the perennial question of politics so conceived. The free society as developed within the American experience is an integrated whole that comprises various distinct but related dimensions, political, moral, legal, and economic. Freedom touches upon myriad dimensions of human experience, and the full measure of its significance can only be gained by a similarly multifaceted exploration of the topic. A study of freedom in American society must therefore consider not only the meaning of freedom but also its relation to wider social experience, including the relation between and among freedom, government, law, economics, morality, and religion. Such a study must also explore the various modern and postmodern threats to freedom as traditionally conceived and practiced by the American people.

An exploration of the topic of freedom is by nature a work of scholarship. The present study, however, is not intended exclusively for professional scholars or academics but also for both the general public and students of American government and society. Contemporary university students may find the work of particular value. The overwhelming majority of incoming college students in the typical American university possess little substantive knowledge of the nature of American institutions and traditions. Such a conclusion is based on more than sixteen years of experience teaching courses in political philosophy and American government to university students in the United States. Our students are generally intelligent, decent, honest, and earnest, but they are woefully ignorant of human experience in general and the American experience in particular. Few college students possess even general knowledge of American history and even less familiarity with the conceptual tools of political and economic theory. Few students can name one president who served during the 1960s or the four Allied powers during World War II. Almost none can translate the meaning of *E pluribus unum*. The vast majority have little if any conception of the nature or substance of the U.S. Constitution, including even general concepts such as federalism and separation of powers. Many cannot identify the document that contains the Bill of Rights let alone the constitutional and legal protections devised to secure the individual rights of the American people. Instead they have generally been taught that America has long been an unsavory and perhaps immoral nation. The historical "knowledge" possessed by contemporary students is typically limited to the slaveholding of the American Founders and their oppression of Native Americans and women. It would be comforting to believe this is an exaggeration, but, sadly, it is not. Deracination is not too strong a term to describe the plight of the rising generation.

Thomas Jefferson once pointedly warned that "a nation that expects to be ignorant and free . . . expects what never was and never will be."[3] The present work thus aims not only to bring to light the fundamental values and institutions of traditional American society but, in so doing, assist in their preservation. Many members of contemporary American society are coming to recognize what scholars and students of the American experience have apprehended for decades—the American constitutional order is crumbling, if not already crumbled. America, they fear, is coming more and more to resemble the late Roman Republic that inspired Cicero's famous lament:

> Long before our own time, the customs of our ancestors moulded admirable men, and in turn these eminent men upheld the ways and institutions of their forebears. Our age, however, inherited the Republic like some beautiful painting of bygone days, its colors already fading through great age; and not only has neglected to freshen the colors of the picture, but has not even taken the trouble to preserve its configuration and, so to speak, its general outlines. For what is now left of the "ancient customs" on which . . . "the commonwealth of Rome" was "founded firm"? They have been, as we see, so completely buried in oblivion that they are not only no longer practiced, but are already unknown. And what shall I say of the men? For our customs have perished for want of men to stand by them, and we are now called to an account, so that we stand impeached like men accused of capital crimes, compelled to plead our own cause. For it is through our own faults, not by any accident, that we retain only the form of the commonwealth, but have long since lost its substance. [4]

Cicero places the blame for the decline of the Roman tradition squarely on the shoulders of the Roman people. The decline of American constitutional order must be attributed to the same source—the American people. Cause-and-effect operates in social as in physical experience. For more than a century many members of American society embraced and propagated beliefs and values that have led to the present state of affairs. Philosophers have long recognized the determinative role of belief with respect to social experience; to paraphrase David Hume, in the end "opinion governs all."[5] In the end, the path of cultural and political development follows the path of belief and conviction. A recognition of the symbiotic relation between abstract ideas and values and concrete social experience is crucial to understanding both the course of events and the appropriate means of rectifying past errors. Such a recognition has the further benefit of inspiring hope for the future of American society. There is no historical necessity or inevitability, no "law of history" that determines the course of American development independent of the beliefs, values, and practice of the American people. The preservation of American constitutionalism in general and individual freedom in particular is indeed possible. Such a felicitous outcome, however, depends not only upon a widespread comprehension of the nature and preconditions of the free society, but, perhaps of even greater importance, a renewed *willingness* to preserve traditional American values and institutions, not merely in form but also in substance. The preservation of the free society ultimately depends upon the will to observe both the letter of the law—the written Constitution—and its spirit—the so-called unwritten constitution of the American people, the inherited moral and cultural values presupposed by American institutions and the American way of life more broadly conceived.[6] The hope remains that a sufficient portion of the American people is willing to do just that.

NOTES

1. "Is life so dear, or peace so sweet, as to be purchased at the price of chains and slavery? Forbid it, Almighty God! I know not what course others may take; but as for me, give me liberty, or give me death!"—Patrick Henry (1736–1799), speech given at St. John's Church, Richmond, VA, March 23, 1775. Avalon Project, Documents in Law, History and Diplomacy (New Haven: Yale Law School).

2. "The preservation of the sacred fire of liberty, and the destiny of the republican model of government, are justly considered deeply, perhaps as finally, staked on the experiment entrusted to the hands of the American people." George Washington, "First Inaugural Address," April 30, 1789. U.S. Government Printing Office, 1961.

3. ". . . [I]f a nation expects to be ignorant & free, in a state of civilisation, it expects what never was & never will be. The functionaries of every government have propensities to command at will the liberty & property of their constituents. [T]here is no safe deposit for these but with the people themselves; nor can they be safe with them without information. [W]here the press is free and every man able to read, all is safe." Thomas Jefferson, Letter to Charles Yancy, Jan. 6, 1816, *The Papers of Thomas Jefferson,* vol. 9, Sept. 1815–April 1816, ed J. Jefferson Looney (Princeton: Princeton University Press, 2012), 328–31.

4. Cicero, *The Republic,* trans. Niall Rudd (New York: Oxford University Press, 1998), 81 (hereinafter cited as *Republic*).

5. "Though men be much governed by interest, yet even interest itself, and all human affairs, are entirely governed by opinion." David Hume, cited in F. A. Hayek, *Law, Legislation, and Liberty,* Vol. 1, *Rules and Order* (Chicago: University of Chicago Press, 1973), 168, n39. Hereinafter cited as *Rules and Order.*

6. Claes G. Ryn, "Political Philosophy and the Unwritten Constitution" (*Modern Age*: 1992, 303–9). Hereinafter cited as "Unwritten Constitution."

ONE

Freedom and Law

One evening, when I was yet in my nurse's arms, I wanted to touch the tea urn, which was boiling merrily. . . . My nurse would have taken me away from the urn but my mother said 'Let him touch it.' So I touched it—and that was my first lesson in the meaning of liberty.—John Ruskin[1]

. . . Where there is no law, there is no freedom.—John Locke[2]

More than two millennia have passed since Confucius issued a warning of special relevance to contemporary American society: "when words lose their meaning," he cautioned, "people lose their freedom."[3] The wisdom of the ancient sage clearly has been confirmed by modern experience. For good cause did George Orwell and others sound a similar alarm in the twentieth century, the so-called Age of Totalitarianism definitively shaped by the militant ideological movements of the era. The ascendancy of communism, socialism, fascism, and other forms of political collectivism entailed a tragic loss of freedom for millions upon millions of human beings, a loss accompanied and facilitated by pervasive corruption of language. Such corruption affected not only the totalitarian regimes but also Western society more generally, including American society. The result has been a transformation of the meaning of various concepts central to the American moral and political heritage. Terms such as freedom, law, rights, justice, equality, tolerance, democracy, and others have gradually assumed novel meanings and constructions greatly at odds with traditional American ideals. The American Founders were, of course, chief carriers of such ideals, including and especially the ideal of individual freedom. The U.S. Constitution explicitly aims, among other goals, to secure the "blessings of liberty." Its authors chose their words carefully and employed them meaningfully. An exploration of the traditional American ideal of freedom and its significance for the American experience thus requires, first and foremost, a clarification of that meaning.

The terms liberty and freedom, which will be employed interchangeably throughout this work, are of ancient lineage. Attempts at definition are complicated by the diverse meanings attached to the concept by various peoples and cultures over time. While a detailed historical account of the myriad experiences signified by the terms "liberty" or "freedom" is beyond the scope of this work, a cursory overview will indicate not only the variety of such usage but also its persistence as a potent and compelling symbol throughout the development of Western civilization. The earliest extant symbol for liberty (Latin, *libertas*) has been traced to the city-state of Sumer.[4] The ancient Greeks spoke of liberty, as did the Romans, Germanic peoples, and Fathers of the Christian Church. Members of Western medieval society inherited, and would further elaborate, a tradition well informed by the concept of liberty, a tradition bequeathed in turn to their modern descendants, including, of course, Americans of the founding era.

The Greeks employed the term liberty or freedom (*eleutheria*) in several distinct senses. It could denote the status of a free man as opposed to a slave. It was also commonly used in a sense more or less equivalent to the modern concept of democracy, that is, the ability of citizens to participate in the determination of law and other dimensions of political rule. Greek liberty so conceived generally involved the ability to vote and hold political office, as well as exercise what modern peoples refer to as political self-determination or home rule. A Greek polis was free in the latter sense insofar as its members established laws for their own community and were not subject to foreign rule; Athenian freedom would be violated by Spartan hegemony. The nineteenth-century writer Benjamin Constant famously classified such classical Greek views as the "ancient conception of liberty."[5] The Romans also valued *libertas* and developed both a form of republican government (election of political representatives and leaders) and a conception of rights (*jus*) acquired by positive law (citizenship) and secured by the rule of law.[6] The Fathers of the Christian Church inherited the wealth of Greco-Roman thought, including the conception of liberty, which was characteristically reinterpreted as relating to interior disposition ("inner" or "spiritual" liberty) rather than political or legal status, as in Greece and Rome.[7] The Germanic tribes that rose to prominence upon the decline of the Western Roman Empire also held a conception of freedom (*Freiheit*), from which developed the Gothic terms *freis* (free) and *freihals* (freedom). The literal translation of *freihals*, "free-neck," indicates the status of a person who "does not bend the neck or wear the collar of servitude." As etymologist Winfred Lehmann explains, *freihals* thus refers to "one who is possessor of his own neck as opposed to a slave who is the property of his master."[8] The term liberty is found in a wide variety of medieval sources and employed in a wide variety of senses, ranging from corporate or community privileges and immunities to "right and liberties granted by God and nature."[9]

The ideal of *Freiheit*, freedom, is deeply rooted in the historical experience of Western peoples. Over the course of history, the concept of freedom spread beyond the confines of Western civilization and, indeed, is presently proclaimed, in some fashion, by virtually every regime on earth. The near-universal proclamation of freedom, however, does not necessarily represent the actual achievement of freedom, certainly as generally conceived in the American tradition, throughout the world. Freedom in many societies is more often nominal than actual, partly because the words freedom and liberty continue to be employed in a confusing variety of senses. Modern freedom is sometimes defined in the manner of the ancient Greeks, that is, as democracy or home rule. It is sometimes identified with self-mastery—a person is said to be free if not enslaved to his lower desires or impulses. Religious thinkers often regard freedom so conceived as a metaphysical attribute—the aforementioned inner freedom that enables a person to overcome "slavery to sin."[10] Another common view conceives freedom as the ability to do whatever one wants to do, conflating freedom with what an older tradition termed license. Yet others, especially cultural Marxists and fellow travelers, identify freedom with self-realization, that is, the ability or power of the individual to achieve his goals and fulfill his potential. Freedom as self-realization is generally associated with the related Marxian notion of "freedom from necessity," a type of "positive" freedom whose achievement is said to require the presence (provision) of certain factors, typically of a material nature. As the twentieth-century Nobel Laureate and social theorist F. A. Hayek explains,

> The new freedom promised [by Marxists] . . . was to be freedom from necessity, release from the compulsion of the circumstances which inevitably limit the range of choice of all of us, although for some very much more than for others. Before man could be truly free, the "despotism of physical want" had to be broken, the "restraints of the economic system" relaxed. Freedom in this sense is . . . another name for power or wealth.[11]

AMERICAN FREEDOM

None of the aforementioned conceptions adequately capture a particular kind of freedom supremely significant for American political thought and practice. The freedom for which many American patriots and revolutionaries were willing to pledge life, fortune, and honor involved a conception distinct from democracy, inner or metaphysical freedom, license, and the positive liberty associated with other political traditions. Americans of the revolutionary and founding era would come to embrace a kind of freedom that constitutes a unique class and is signified by correspondingly unique designations, namely, *freedom-under-law* or *nega-*

tive liberty. The American colonists did not originate such a conception but rather carried a moral and political tradition proximately rooted in English experience and, more distantly, in several thousand years of cultural development. The contributions they would make to individual freedom and related values did not emerge *de novo* but were firmly rooted in history, the "lamp of experience," in the celebrated phrase of Patrick Henry.[12] The Americans' self-styled establishment of a *novus ordo seclorum* ("A New Order of the Ages") was only possible because they built upon a foundation of knowledge laid by previous generations in their own struggles to secure freedom.

The prevailing American conception of negative liberty was particularly indebted to the political creed of the Englishmen whom Edmund Burke called the "ancient, constitutional" or "Old Whigs" and who themselves had built upon a tradition extending into antiquity.[13] English philosopher John Locke (1632–1704) succinctly formulated the conception of freedom-under-law mutually embraced by the Americans and their Old-Whig forebears: "Freedom is . . . to have a standing rule to live by, common to every one of that society, . . . a liberty to follow [one's] own will in all things, where that rule prescribes not; and not to be subject to the inconstant, uncertain, arbitrary will of another man."[14] Jefferson formulated the prevailing meaning of "rightful liberty" as "unobstructed action according to our will within limits drawn around us by the equal rights of others."[15] As Hayek restated the Old-Whig view, "[t]o the great apostles of political freedom the word had meant freedom from coercion, freedom from the arbitrary power of other men, release from the ties which left the individual no choice but obedience to the orders of a superior to whom he was attached."[16]

The Old Whigs expanded upon an understanding of English liberty as old as the Magna Carta of 1215. As Justice Clarence Thomas explained, liberty to the English mind was originally understood to involve freedom from arbitrary physical restraint or imprisonment by government, that is, "the power of loco-motion, of changing situation, or removing one's person to whatsoever place one's own inclination may direct; without imprisonment or restraint, unless by due course of law."[17] As he further notes,

> Chapter 39 of the original Magna Carta provided, "No free man shall be taken, imprisoned, disseised, outlawed, banished, or in any way destroyed, nor will We proceed against or prosecute him, except by the lawful judgment of his peers and by the law of the land."[18] . . . [T]his provision was later reissued in 1225 with modest changes to its wording as follows: "No freeman shall be taken, or imprisoned, or be disseised of his freehold, or liberties, or free customs, or be outlawed, or exiled, or any otherwise destroyed; nor will we not pass upon him, nor condemn him, but by lawful judgment of his peers or by the law of the land."[19] After Magna Carta became subject to renewed interest in the

> 17th century . . . William Blackstone referred to this provision as protecting the "absolute rights of every Englishman." And he formulated those absolute rights as "the right of personal security," which included the right to life; "the right of personal liberty"; and "the right of private property."[20] [Blackstone defined the "right of personal liberty" as freedom from physical restraint or imprisonment, as above.][21]

The originally narrow legal understanding of liberty as freedom from arbitrary physical restraint broadened over time to include the demand for freedom from arbitrary coercion more generally. Accordingly, the traditional Anglo-American ideal of freedom, freedom-under-law, may be formally defined as the ability to act in the absence of (arbitrary) coercion, in other words, to act in a truly *voluntary* manner. On such a view, an individual is free if and only if his beliefs and actions stem from voluntary or uncoerced choice. Freedom so conceived is realized so long as the individual is not forced to think or act in a manner contrary to his own free will, desire, or purpose, within the bounds of law.[22]

Such a conception is sometimes distinguished from the classical Greek or "ancient" conception of liberty by its corresponding designation as "modern liberty."[23] While modern freedom, as we shall see, is related to ancient freedom in an important manner, the ability to think or act in the absence of coercion is conceptually distinct from the ability to participate in the political process, the most common meaning of freedom in classical Greece. Modern freedom—freedom-under-law—is further distinct from inner freedom (self-mastery of lower impulses) and metaphysical freedom (the inherent human capacity for choice). Nor does its achievement, in contrast to the positive freedom promoted by cultural Marxism and related perspectives, entail positive material action on the part of other human beings. The realization of modern freedom requires not provision or presence of one factor or another, such as sufficient material resources to fulfill one's goals, but rather absence, more particularly, the absence of arbitrary coercion or force.

Accordingly, Anglo-American freedom-under-law law is conventionally classified as a kind of "negative" liberty, corresponding to, yet sharply distinguished from, the "positive" liberty valorized by other traditions. In all instances, as Justice Thomas observes, the "American legal tradition has regarded liberty as involving individual freedom from . . . action, not as a right to a particular . . . entitlement."[24] The negative freedom central to traditional American order is realized not by positive action on the part of other persons (including persons organized as "government") but rather the exercise of self-restraint, that is, willingness to refrain from employing arbitrary coercive force toward achievement of one's goals. To be free is to follow one's own will and pursue one's own purposes, and this requires the absence of arbitrary coercion on the part of other members of society. So long as such a condition is met, freedom is said to exist. One of the chief purposes of the American Founders and their contemporaries was precisely to secure freedom so conceived, to secure for each and every individual a sphere of truly voluntary belief and action.

The conception of individual freedom-under-law implicit in the constitutional constructs of the revolutionary era was not the only kind of liberty secured therein. The American colonists and founders also aimed to establish so-called *republican liberty*, understood to involve a non-monarchical government whose authority derives exclusively from the people and which is ultimately accountable to them through the process of election. Negative freedom of the individual also remained in tension with older conceptions rooted in colonial experience, especially the identification of freedom with local and communal self-government. The latter conception is sometimes referred to as *corporate* or political liberty—the right of self-government to which sovereign moral and political entities—in the American case, the several states that constitute the United States of America—are entitled. The nature and purpose of corporate liberty, as well as the related constitutional doctrine of *dual sovereignty*, will be examined more fully in a later chapter. As we shall see, individual, corporate, and republican liberty were ultimately reconciled in the mutually supporting relationship embodied in the federal structure of government established by the U.S. Constitution.

Individual Freedom in Practice

Freedom conceived as the absence of coercion is a generalized quality of human action. Regardless of the particular context, the exercise of freedom always involves the ability to think or act in accord with one's own voluntary choices and purposes and not those coercively imposed by another person or persons. Human beings, of course, act within various social dimensions, private and public, from home to the workplace, but in all instances human action is oriented toward realization of a purpose or goal. However chaotic or irrational it may appear to a casual observer or however little the individual is consciously aware of his intentions, human action is never random but always purposive.[25] The question relevant to the issue of individual freedom is *whose* purpose is to be achieved, that of the acting individual or that of another person who wields coercive power over the individual.

The traditional conception of freedom-under-law and its relevance to human experience are readily illustrated by concrete example. Imagine the hypothetical situation of a lone individual strolling along a city sidewalk who is suddenly confronted by a gun-wielding assailant demanding his wallet. The victim rapidly scans the environment to determine if help is on the immediate horizon; seeing no such possibility, he hands over his wallet to the assailant. The question is whether the victim's response is an act of freedom, and the answer will depend on the definition of freedom employed in the analysis. From the perspective of metaphysical or inner freedom, surrendering the wallet is self-evidently an act of freedom. Every human being knows that he is not an automaton or robot. Every human being knows that the mere fact of having a gun at one's head does not compel relinquishment of personal property on demand; every human being is aware of his personal capacity to say "no." If further evidence were needed, history provides innumerable examples of persons who have resisted predatory or coercive threats, even to the point of death.

Most Americans will nevertheless be uncomfortable with such a conclusion. An individual who surrenders his wallet at gunpoint does not feel that he has done so freely but rather feels violated in some fashion. He feels, more particularly, that his liberty has been violated. Such a reaction is not only normal but validated by universal experience within American courts of law. Imagine in the present case that the gun-wielder is apprehended and the case brought to trial. Further imagine that our hypothetical defendant argues for his acquittal on the grounds of metaphysical freedom. The victim, he explains to the jury, could have refused to relinquish the wallet but did not; he rather chose to hand it over to the defendant. Justice, he concludes, thus demands a verdict of "not guilty." Although it is absurd to suggest that any American jury would accept such a defense, it must be admitted that the defendant has a point: the victim did choose to part with his wallet. Such action was neither inevitable nor beyond his control. The victim clearly had a choice—to surrender the wallet or not—and freedom involves precisely the capacity for choice. In the metaphysical sense, then, the victim did act freely, and the defendant has made a reasonable case for his acquittal.

Such a conclusion, however, flies in the face of common sense; every American recognizes, however inchoately, that handing over one's wallet at the point of a gun is not an act of freedom. In this instance, as in many others, common sense proves a reliable guide. The behavior of the victim under the circumstances described is not an act of freedom in the qualified sense presupposed by American legal and political institutions. As we have seen, the victim did exercise a kind of freedom—metaphysical or inner freedom, the existential capacity for choice—but such is not the kind of freedom American law aims to secure. The American system of justice aims to secure not metaphysical freedom, which indeed is beyond the reach of human law, but rather freedom conceived as voluntary action, that is, freedom from arbitrary coercion. Such a qualified freedom—negative freedom-under-law—was indeed violated by the assailant with the gun, as daily affirmed by every court in the land.

The manner in which the victim's freedom was violated by his assailant may be further clarified by a detailed analysis of the situation. The assailant pointed a gun at the victim and demanded his wallet. The victim handed it over, by choice (he could have refused to do so). His choice to surrender the wallet, however, was not free or voluntary but rather coerced or forced. By wielding coercive force (threatening the victim at gunpoint), the assailant gained control not over the victim's existential capacity for choice but rather over his *range* of choice. More particularly, the assailant's action narrowed the victim's options to the following two possibilities: one, surrender the wallet and reduce the risk of further harm to his person; or, two, refuse to surrender the wallet and increase the risk of further personal harm, potentially to the point of death. The victim himself would not voluntarily choose either of these two options but all other choices are foreclosed by the threat of imminent violence.

Under such constrained circumstances, many if not most people will surrender the wallet. No victim, however, *wants* to surrender his wallet or *wants* to resist an assailant's demand and face possible further harm. It can be assumed, on the contrary, that any person in the victim's position would want to keep his wallet and walk away unharmed. The victim, however, is not permitted to act as he wants, as he would freely or voluntarily choose. He is instead induced by the assailant's coercive intimidation to act as the assailant wants, that is, surrender the wallet. The threat of violence forces the victim to choose between two evils: either turn over the wallet or risk even greater harm. All other choices are eliminated by the point of a gun; the victim chooses but his choice is coerced. The assailant's successful use of coercion subjects the victim to his will and achieves the assailant's express purpose—to obtain the victim's wallet. The victim's own purpose, to keep his wallet, is thwarted. His freedom—his ability to act in a voluntary manner and in pursuit of his own purposes—is violated. Common sense is validated.

Coercion

Americans of the founding generation aimed to minimize the potential for violation of individual freedom so conceived. American legal and political institutions aim to protect a so-called private sphere wherein individuals are able to think and act in a truly voluntary manner, a goal that can only be achieved by successful constraint of arbitrary coercion. The interdependence of freedom and coercion means that a careful analysis of freedom requires an equally careful examination of the concept of coercion, beginning with formal definition of the term. Coercion has been broadly defined as "such control of the environment or circumstances of a person by another that, in order to avoid greater evil, he is forced to act not according to a coherent plan of his own but to serve the ends of another."[26] More particularly, coercion exists whenever one person (the coercer) exercises his ability to determine the consequences of another person's (the coerced) choice with the deliberate aim of inducing the coerced to act as the coercer wills rather than as the coerced himself wills.[27] The previous example is a classic illustration of coercion proper. The assailant who points a gun at a victim and demands his wallet has thereby acquired the power to determine the consequences of the victim's choice. A victim who chooses to relinquish his wallet consequently reduces the risk of further harm; a victim who chooses not to relinquish the wallet consequently increases the risk of greater harm than loss of a wallet. The coercer's ability to control the consequences of the victim's choice effectively restricts that choice to one of two evils (lose his wallet or perhaps his life). Under such circumstances, the victim is unable to act freely or voluntarily but rather constrained or coerced to make a choice contrary to his own free will.

It should be emphasized that the exercise of coercion proper, and thus the violation of freedom, requires the conscious and willful intent of the person(s) wielding coercive force. In other words, the violation of one person's freedom requires the existence of another human being who deliberately aims to coerce the former so that he will act as the latter wishes. An act of coercion thus requires the active presence of at least two conscious and intentional human beings. For that reason, it is meaningless to say that a person is coerced either by general circumstances or abstract entities incapable of conscious intent, such as the weather or nature more generally. Politically and legally relevant coercion can only be exercised by a conscious and willful human being who intentionally aims to induce another human being to act against his own free will and as the coercer wills.

The preservation of individual freedom thus demands, among other conditions, a careful use of language. The common human propensity toward anthropomorphism is especially problematic, leading to misleading if not false statements that obscure rather than clarify the status of freedom in society. Who among us, for instance, has never implicitly blamed prevailing circumstances for our inability to carry out our plans, complaining, say, that "I was forced to stay home because of the bad storm." Strictly speaking, however, such a statement is untrue: the decision to stay home was not a forced or coerced choice but rather a voluntary choice. Every human being encounters numerous constraints, obstacles to the realization of personal goals, throughout the course of life, but not all of them constitute coercion and thus a violation of freedom. Many constraints, such as the violent storm, are attributable not to human intention but rather the impersonal "nature of things." As previously mentioned, legally and politically relevant coercion, by contrast, always requires the deliberate intent to coerce. Only human beings possess conscious intention and will, which means that coercion, the violation of individual freedom, always and necessarily involves the existence of a human coercer. The situation under discussion clearly fails to meet the necessary condition of coercion proper: obviously no human agent had either the intent or the power to create the storm and, moreover, for the express purpose of forcing the complainer to act against his own free will and submit instead to the coercer's will. Nature (the storm) neither intended nor desired to influence his choice; impersonal phenomena cannot and do not possess conscious minds, intent, or desire. Mindful of the human propensity to anthropomorphize impersonal phenomena, the formal definition of freedom may be further qualified as "the ability to act in the absence of coercion of man by man."[28]

Coercion is ubiquitous in human existence, encountered by most human beings in myriad personal situations throughout the normal course of life. Moreover, coercion can be exercised in various ways and also range widely in degree of severity, from outright physical violence through threats and intimidation to subtle psychological pressure of one kind or another. Coercion is pervasive in life because it is a solution to a common human problem. Every person inevitably encounters belief and behavior in other persons that, for one reason or another, he would like to change. There are essentially two and only two methods of inducing other persons to think and act as we ourselves would prefer, especially when this differs from their own preferences, namely, *persuasion* and *coercion*. Persuasion involves the attempt to influence another person's belief and action by discussion and discourse, by appeal to his rationality, self-interest, moral values, and so on. The strategy of persuasion, however, is fraught with difficulty; not only is it often time-consuming but, worse yet, often ineffective. One can spend countless hours and enormous energy in the attempt to persuade another person, and all for naught; the other person can simply choose to ignore such counsel and persist in the objectionable belief or behavior. Such frustration, however, is a price of freedom. A person who values individual freedom will honor the right of another person to make voluntary choices regarding both belief and practice, to be reached by persuasion or not at all, even when the outcome conflicts with the former's own preferences. Freedom requires that individual members of society tolerate belief and behavior in their fellow men that they themselves may personally dislike or even condemn. Such toleration is often difficult for human beings, the majority of whom are rarely angels or saints.

The difficulty of influencing other persons by means of persuasion can thus lead to the adoption of its only alternative, the less honorable strategy of coercion. To illustrate the dynamic typically involved, imagine a situation in which a university student decides for one reason or another to drop out of college. His mother learns of her son's plans and is unhappy with his choice; she wants him to remain in school. She thus seeks to change his mind and begins with efforts of persuasion. Perhaps she speaks to him of the foolishness and short-sightedness of such a decision and makes passionate appeals to his reason, self-interest, and long-term well-being. Mother's efforts, however, fall on deaf ears; the son's resolve to leave school is untouched by her arguments. In response to his recalcitrance, Mom thus purposefully changes strategy. She now pleads with her son, "If you drop out of school, you will break my heart."[29]

An analysis of Mother's behavior in light of the definitions of freedom and coercion reveals her final plea as a clear if subtle attempt at coercion. Freedom involves voluntary or uncoerced action. The son's free or voluntary choice is to drop out of school; this is what he himself wants to do. Mom wants him to make a different choice but was unsuccessful in her attempt at persuasion. If she is not willing to accept her son's decision, her only other option is to attempt to force her son to act as she wishes, that is, stay in school. She does so, in our example, by making a delicate but deliberate threat intended to induce her son to act as she wishes, against his own desire. Her threat of potential heartbreak effectively determines the consequences of her son's choice and narrows the range of options available to him to two undesirables, from his point of view: he can either stay in school to please his mother, against his own wishes, or drop out, as he himself wishes, but live with the burden of his mother's broken heart. He does not want to choose either option; it can be assumed that he wants to leave school and also have a happy mother.

Such an option, however, has been foreclosed by Mom's threat. By establishing the consequence of heartbreak, she has restricted his options in such a way as to lead him, she hopes, to follow her will rather than his own. Mom's threat has compromised her son's ability to act in a strictly voluntary manner, in accord with his own free will; such, indeed, is its purpose and the purpose of every act of coercion. Mother's threat is formally indistinguishable from that posed by the gun-wielding assailant; both examples meet all relevant criteria of coercion proper. Such a recognition may be discomfiting—no one wants to regard one's mother as a coercer—but it simply underscores the aforementioned pervasiveness of coercion in human experience. Examples of similar coercive strategies, enacted by persons of every imaginable description, could be multiplied almost endlessly; they are the stuff of everyday existence. The great majority of human beings have almost certainly experienced coercive pressure of one form or another, and many of them have probably exerted such pressure as well, for the reasons discussed.

Mother's example points not only to the ubiquity of coercion in human existence but also the wide degree of severity that may be employed in various coercive acts, ranging from a threat of heartbreak ("soft coercion") to, say, death by crucifixion ("hard coercion"). Individual response to coercion also varies widely across persons. Attempts by one person to coerce another are not always or necessarily successful. Whether or not an individual submits to coercive pressure undoubtedly relates to personal qualities such as strength of character and conviction. Extremely timid individuals may be cowed or coerced by so much as a hostile glance; an insecure child may remain in college merely in response to the tone of his mother's voice. Other individuals, by contrast, will resist even the most violent and barbaric forms of coercion. Early Christian martyrs are representative. At various points in Roman history, citizens, including those who converted to Christianity, were required by law to participate in the Roman imperial cult, which involved an acknowledgment of the emperor as divine. By enacting such a law, Roman authority deliberately limited the choices of early Christians to two undesirables—either violate their religious commitments (idolatry) or suffer legal penalties, perhaps to the point of gruesome death. Martyrs were those individuals who withstood such coercive pressure and died, as they believed, for God. History testifies to the human capacity to resist even the most draconian forms of coercion. Indeed, it is not necessary to look to ancient history for evidence of the human capacity to resist such coercion. In recent years, the world has been witness to the horrific slaughter of Christians by the forces of radical Islamic fundamentalism. The Christian faithful beheaded on the shores of Tripoli have as certain a claim to the heroic status of martyrdom as any Christian crucified by the Romans.

Coercion, then, is a more or less inevitable aspect of human existence and individual liberty thus ever susceptible of violation.[30] Despite the general and well-founded prejudice against coercion, however, it is neither possible nor desirable to completely eliminate coercion from human experience. Its absolute prohibition would mean, for instance, that Mom is forbidden to warn her son of her potential heartbreak if he should leave the university. Coercion could only be eliminated from human experience by destroying its source, that is, human nature in conjunction with the limited options human beings face in shaping their fellows' beliefs and behavior. Unless all human beings can somehow be made to share identical opinions, transformed into robots or zombies by political terror or some other Orwellian means, coercion will always be a feature of human existence. Human beings will always be tempted to resort to coercive pressure, however subtle, since the only alternative, as we have seen, is the often difficult and unreliable means of persuasion.

The inevitability of coercive pressure, however, does not render individuals helpless before it. As previously mentioned, human history has demonstrated time and again the individual capacity to resist coercive tactics, whether employed by family, friends, and loved ones or strangers and government. In any event, so long as human nature remains imperfect and human options limited, coercion will remain an aspect of social existence. For this reason, the free society is not, and cannot be, a society of *perfect* freedom. Freedom requires the absence of coercion and perfect freedom would require the perfect absence of coercion, which, given the human condition, is impossible. Such freedom as can be achieved in human society will inevitably be an imperfect freedom.

The recognition of such a fact, however, is not necessarily a cause for concern. While it may seem counterintuitive, the perfect absence of coercion—perfect freedom—is not only impossible but also undesirable. It is undesirable because coercion is not always and everywhere an evil but can also be a force for good. Coercion is best regarded as a neutral tool or strategy that can be employed for a variety of purposes, both moral purposes ("good" coercion) and immoral purposes ("bad" coercion). The philosophy of freedom central to traditional American political ideals does not contemplate the perfect elimination of coercion from society. It rather aims toward the more realistic and modest goal of *minimizing* certain forms of coercion—"bad" or immoral coercion—so far as humanly possible. Particular forms of coercion have come to be regarded as profoundly inimical to human well-being and thus impermissible in civilized society. Paradoxically, however, such pernicious forms of coercion can only be minimized or contained by "fighting fire with fire," that is, employing the fire of "good" coercion to fight the fire of "bad" coercion. Coercion is a double-edged sword. On the one hand, its exercise can diminish freedom, diminish voluntary choice; on the other, its exercise is indispensable to the preservation not only of freedom or voluntary choice but also the comprehensive social order within which all human action, free or otherwise, necessarily takes place. The resolution of this seeming paradox will emerge more clearly as we explore the next crucial dimension of individual freedom: the means whereby it has historically been secured in Anglo-American society. We shall see that the exercise of freedom, as well as other traditional individual rights, inescapably involves the concomitant exercise of coercion.

FREEDOM AND LAW

Ideals are essential guides to human action and few are more beautiful or inspiring than the ideal of freedom. The practicing idealist, however, will desire more than abstract guidance; he will yearn for the realization or instantiation of his ideals. In the case of freedom, such involves the establishment of conditions that enable individuals to actually exercise voluntary choice in their daily activities. This is only possible, as we have seen, if other persons refrain from employing coercion, whether in the form of threats, intimidation, or outright violence, to achieve their ends. The ubiquity and inevitability of coercion in human existence thus pose special challenges to the realization of freedom. The American Founders were not blind to such difficulties. They were moral realists who accepted human beings as they are, including their propensity to resort to coercion toward fulfillment of their goals. Despite such challenges, however, they firmly believed that human freedom is more than a utopian dream. The Founders reached not for an unachievable eradication of coercion—not for perfect freedom—but rather, as said, a more realistic and attainable goal—the minimization of coercion in the interest of securing a wide sphere of freedom for every individual. Imperfect man will never realize perfect freedom, or perfection of any kind, but that does not mean freedom is a mere chimera. Its realization may be imperfect but is not impossible.

Americans of the founding era regarded certain forms of coercion as especially dangerous to individual freedom. Their particular concern was to prevent what they called *arbitrary* coercion, that is, coercion "not in accordance with recognized general laws."[31] As philosopher Mortimer Adler succinctly stated the traditional view, freedom demanded ". . . emancipation from the arbitrary rule of other men."[32] The concept of arbitrary coercion is classically illustrated by the gun-wielding assailant of our former example, whose actions represent precisely the kind of willful or "ruleless" coercion that cannot be tolerated in human society. A society that permits any person with a gun to coerce any innocent person at will, without consequence, could not long endure let alone flourish. The peaceful and innocent would be ever at the mercy of the violent and brutal. There could be no civilization, no commerce, no art, science, human fellowship or justice, no security of person or property. There could be no freedom, no possibility of voluntary choice in pursuit of individual purposes. Individuals would rather face chronic vulnerability to forceful subjection to the whims of any person willing to employ coercion to achieve his goals. The unbridled exercise of arbitrary coercive force would, indeed, give rise to moral and social chaos, a state of perfect injustice in which "the strong do what they can and the weak suffer what they must," to paraphrase the Greek historian Thucydides. Might would make right. The unchecked exercise of might would reduce society, in the celebrated words of Thomas Hobbes, to a perpetual "war of all against all."[33] To avoid such a possibility, every society known to man has aimed to reduce, to one degree or another, the incidence of arbitrary and predatory coercion against peaceful persons. Every society, moreover, has employed essentially the same means to achieve that end: *law* of one form or another, whether unwritten law embodied in custom, judge-made law as embodied in the English common law, or explicit positive law enacted by statute. America is no exception to this rule. Indeed, and on the contrary, traditional America is not only the world's greatest champion of individual liberty but also of the means whereby such liberty is secured, namely, the rule of law.

The Ideal of the Rule of Law

The traditional Anglo-American ideal of freedom is capable of realization but only imperfectly. The impossibility of perfect freedom, as we have seen, follows not only from the impossibility of eradicating the human propensity for coercion but also the indispensable role played by coercion in the preservation of freedom itself. Freedom and other traditional American rights are secured by the rule of law, and every human law, as we shall see, employs coercion to achieve its end. The indispensability of law in a free society thus ensures the perpetual existence of coercion, that is, the necessary qualification and limitation of freedom.

Locke classically summarized the Old Whig conception of the intrinsic relation between freedom and law inherited by the American colonists: *"the end of law,"* he says, *"is not to abolish or restrain, but to preserve and enlarge freedom. For in all the states of created beings capable of law, where there is no law, there is no freedom."*[34] The Lockean and American conviction of the dependence of freedom on law may strike contemporary Americans as somewhat puzzling or even outrageous. Many so-called laws in contemporary American society do in fact restrict and not enlarge the individual's ability to act in a voluntary manner, that is, restrict and not enlarge freedom. One may legitimately feel one's freedom violated, for instance, by legislation that prohibits the use of "trans fats" in the commercial preparation of food, as mandated by recent legislation in New York City.[35] One may readily feel one's freedom violated when forced by the federal government to purchase health insurance whether one wants to or not, as mandated by recent federal health-care legislation.[36] One may feel one's freedom violated when forced by "law" to purchase a fluorescent light bulb rather than the incandescent bulb one would voluntarily choose.[37] One's voluntary choice may be to eat greasy French fries or do without health insurance, but such choices are foreclosed by contemporary legislation. Legislation of this nature does restrict the individual's ability to engage in voluntary activity and thus, contrary to Locke, does restrict and not enlarge the range of human freedom as traditionally conceived in American society.

Locke, however, was not wrong to assert the inseparability of freedom and law. The aforementioned examples point not to his error but rather the increasingly routine violation of individual freedom in contemporary American society. They further point to the modern corruption of language which, as mentioned, has transformed the meaning of various terms central to traditional American political discourse. The concept of "law" is emphatically among such terms. It is widely employed in contemporary discourse in a sense markedly different from that presupposed by Locke and the Founders. The loss of the traditional meaning of law raises serious concerns regarding the prospects for freedom in view of the fact that the rule of law, as developed over the course of Western and Anglo-American history, comprises the institutional means of securing individual freedom and other traditional rights. The Americans spoke of establishing a *"government of laws, not of men"* and championed the ideal of freedom-under-law; Locke pointedly asserted that "where there is no law, there is no freedom."[38] All such conceptions presuppose particular understandings of both freedom and law that were more or less universal throughout the seventeenth and eighteenth centuries but have become opaque or unfamiliar to later generations. The recovery and revitalization of American freedom thus requires, among other remedies, a recovery and revitalization of the traditional conception of law that implicitly informs both American political principles and practice.

A clarification of the traditional meaning of law begins with a recognition that law as historically conceived within the Western tradition is conceptually distinct from both *legislation* and *public policy*.[39] Although such entities are widely, if misleadingly, termed law in contemporary discourse, the political and legal tradition inherited by the Americans clearly distinguished law from legislation throughout most of its development. Such is evidenced by the distinct words for the two concepts found in many Western languages: *jus* and *lex* (Latin); *Recht* and *Gesetz* (German); *droit* and *loi* (French); *diretto* and *legge* (Italian); and so on. Legislation, as distinguished from law proper, comprises the rules, edicts, decrees, regulations, orders, directives, policy measures, commands, and other enactments of a legally constituted governmental entity ("legislature"). The federal Congress in Washington and the legislatures of the fifty American states are representative. Legislation, in other words, is classified by the *source* of the rule or policy—an official legislature so described.

Law proper, by contrast, is defined not by the source of a rule but rather its *attributes*. A law is a particular *kind* of rule—a general rule governing relations either between private persons (*private law*) or between private persons and government (*public law*) and possessing each of the following attributes:

1. It is a general (abstract) standing rule, employed by individuals as a means or instrument toward pursuit of their particular purposes.
2. It is known, certain, and prospective, intended to be more or less permanent and apply to an indefinite number of similar situations over time. Accordingly, it is impossible to know who will be affected by the rule.
3. It typically takes the form of a negative prohibition ("thou shalt not").
4. It applies equally to all persons (the ideal of equality-before-the-law or *isonomia* [Greek, "same laws" or "equality of laws to all manner of persons"]).[40]

A true law, law proper, is a rule that simultaneously possesses each such attribute, which altogether ensure that law is both impersonal and impartial. The Anglo-American vision of a "government of laws, not of men," as well as its ideal of the rule of law more generally, presuppose a conception of law more or less in line with such an understanding and distinct from legislation and other directives emanating from political authority.

Law, Freedom, and Coercion

Threats to individual freedom may arise from two possible sources—private persons and public officials, fellow citizens and government. Accordingly, the Anglo-American tradition developed means of securing freedom against potential violation arising from either source. Locke's confident claim that "where there is no law, there is no freedom" accurately captures traditional Anglo-American thought and practice: freedom is secured against both private citizens and public officials by identical means, the rule of law. Law, moreover, is conceived in the sense described, that is, a general standing rule, usually negative or prohibitory in form, permanent, equal, universal, and proscriptive. Law proper, in the dimension of private law, is a purpose-independent rule of just conduct that structures the means private persons are permitted to employ in pursuit of their ends. Public law may share various attributes of law proper but may also comprise specific directives given to agents of government.

The traditional relation between law and freedom may be clarified by revisiting the example initially employed to illustrate the meaning of freedom—the gun-wielding assailant demanding the victim's wallet. Such action, as we have seen, violates the freedom of the victim. The coercer employs force deliberately to narrow the victim's range of choice such that he is induced to act not as he himself freely wills but rather as the coercer wills. The victim's ability to act in a voluntary manner, his freedom, is compromised. To value freedom is to value a society wherein individuals can rest secure in the expectation that they will not be forced by an agent wielding the power of coercion to think or act contrary to their own free will.

Such a society is only possible if arbitrary violations of individual freedom are somehow prevented or at least restricted. The historical means developed to achieve that goal are precisely as Locke indicated, the establishment of law. The law forbids such action as pointing a gun at another person and demanding his wallet, and such is a true law, possessing all the requisite attributes of law proper. First, it is a general standing rule. The legal rule prohibiting threats at gunpoint does not expire upon its execution but remains in force to govern any and all future instances of similar behavior. Second, it is negative or prohibitory in form—"thou shalt not" put a gun to someone's head and demand his wallet. Third, it is universally applicable. There are no exceptions to the rule; anyone who engages in the prohibited activity will be penalized, not merely particular individuals or groups. Finally, it is, in intention, perpetual: the obligation to refrain from threatening another person at gunpoint does not expire at some predetermined date.

Such a rule is also purpose-independent, in other words, individuals governed by the law are not forced to pursue a particular positive purpose established by authority. Law proper simply structures the *means* that individuals may employ in achieving their self-chosen purposes; it is silent with respect to ends. The law, for instance, does not forbid an individual from aiming to obtain another person's wallet. It only informs him that he must find some other means to achieve that end than threatening its owner at gunpoint. The only "purpose" of such a law is the general and universal protection of every individual's rights to liberty and property. As previously observed, a society without laws prohibiting the kind of coercion employed by the gun-wielding assailant could not know freedom. No individual could be free if any person with a gun could demand his private possessions with impunity but rather would be subject to the arbitrary will of the stronger or better-armed person at every turn. As Locke explains,

> . . . [L]iberty is to be free from restraint and violence from others which cannot be, where there is no law: but freedom is not . . . a liberty for every man to do what he lists: (for who could be free, when every other man's humour [*sic*] might domineer over him?) but a liberty to dispose, and order, as he lists, his person, actions, possessions, and his whole property, within the allowance of those laws under which he is; and therein not to be subject to the arbitrary will of another, but freely follow his own.[41]

In the absence of law, no individual could enjoy the security of a legally circumscribed private sphere within which he is protected against arbitrary interference with his voluntary choices.

We previously noted the irony of the fact that law should prove the means to enlarge freedom, that is, to minimize coercion in society. The seeming paradox arises from the fact that law, the means of preventing arbitrary coercion, is itself coercive: a law is not a suggestion but an enforceable rule to which is attached a coercive penalty of one sort or another. A person who threatens another at gunpoint will lose his liberty (jail). A person who drives over the speed limit will have to pay a fine. A person who murders an innocent person will lose either his liberty (prison) or his life (capital punishment). Penalties, of course, are supposed to fit the crime, but every human law involves a coercive penalty enforced by government.

That is only to say that every human law employs coercion to achieve its end. Indeed, law proper provides yet another classic example of coercion proper, intrinsically embodying all the defining attributes of coercion. Law, like any form of coercion, deliberately aims to narrow an individual's range of choice in such a way that he will be induced to act as the coercer (in this case, the lawmaker) wills rather than as he himself wills. The lawmaker, like any coercer, establishes consequences of the individual's choice that force him to choose between two undesirable options. A law establishing criminal penalties for murder, for instance, puts a symbolic gun to a potential murderer's head. It says to him, in effect, "here are your choices: either refrain from murder and live in freedom or engage in murder and face imprisonment or death." Thus the law against murder, like any form of coercion, narrows the potential murderer's range of choice to two evils, from his point of view. His voluntary choice would no doubt be to murder with impunity. The law, however, forecloses such an option, constraining him to choose between the two aforementioned options, neither of which he would freely choose (he does not want either to refrain from murder or face imprisonment or death). The potential murderer's freedom, his ability to act in a truly voluntary manner, is certainly restricted by a law prohibiting murder. Such, however, is precisely its goal. The unconstrained exercise of his freedom would entail the death of the potential victim, the innocent and peaceful person whose rights, in this case, the right to life, the law aims to protect.

Moreover, the establishment of a law against murder, like any form of coercion, represents a deliberate attempt by the lawmaker (coercer) to influence the choice made by another person (the potential murderer) in such a way that he will act as the coercer desires (not kill) rather than as he himself desires (kill). The lawmaker-coercer does so by determining the consequences of a potential murderer's choice through the attachment of legal penalties, negative consequences or disincentives, to certain actions. The coercive sanction of law thus presupposes human rationality. It assumes that would-be murderers will take probable legal consequences into account before engaging in an act of murder. It assumes that would-be criminals, like all human beings, are reasonable beings who can respond rationally to incentives and disincentives and consider the consequences of their actions.

Every human law is an act of coercion proper, both in form and manner of operation. Coercion is coercion, whether employed by lawful authority for lawful purposes, by criminals for unlawful purposes, or by a mother attempting to change her son's mind. Coercion is coercion, whether relatively benign or draconian. The difference between lawful and unlawful coercion, between "good" and "bad" coercion, relates not to form, substance, or manner of operation but rather the morality of the purpose for which the neutral tool of coercion is employed. Lawful or good coercion is employed to serve good or moral purposes, such as protecting innocent persons from murder at the hands of a criminal predator. Unlawful, bad, or arbitrary coercion is paradigmatically illustrated by the criminal predator's action against peaceful persons. The good coercion of law aims precisely to protect the freedom and other rights of peaceful persons by preventing or minimizing the bad coercion exercised by potential criminals and fellow travelers. The Anglo-American tradition, as previously remarked, fights fire with fire: "Where there is no [coercive] law, there is no freedom."

Law, Command, and Knowledge

Law, then, is the institutional means developed over the course of Anglo-American history to secure freedom and other individual rights. Law, moreover, is crucial to traditional American order not only for the specific role it plays in the protection of individual rights but, more generally, for its contribution to human flourishing and the growth of civilization. The overwhelming importance of the rule of law with respect to American social order may be illustrated by a concrete if homely example: general traffic regulations or "rules of the road" (speed limits, stop signs, and so on). Such an example will bring to light the significance of law for both the ordering of human action in general and the advance of knowledge in particular.

The rules of the road possess all requisite attributes of law proper. First, such rules, like law more generally, are impersonal: the lawmaker has no way of knowing the particular persons they will affect. The rules refer to normal situations in which any person may find himself (the desire to drive somewhere), and they apply to everyone. Each individual will use the general traffic rules as a means or instrument in pursuit of his own individual purposes. One person may use them to drive to work, another to take a road trip across the country. Law proper, as we have seen, does not concern the particular goals of individuals—no one is forced by law to drive, say, to Chicago—but only the means they may employ to achieve them. Whatever a person's voluntarily chosen destination, the law establishes certain restrictions on the means he may use to reach that destination. The law provides the driver with advance knowledge that he will be required to reach his destination in a certain manner, for instance, within the speed limit, and he will incorporate such knowledge into his personal plans. Second, the rules of the road are abstract or general rules universally applicable to all persons, void of reference to particular people and enforced without exception. Generality and universality are essential elements of the rule of law because one of its crucial social functions is to ensure *security of expectation*. Such security involves the ability of one person to predict the behavior of other persons (to correctly anticipate that others will behave as "expected"), and such is only possible if the rule is known to apply in all cases. Indeed, it has been argued that the certainty and universality of law may even be more important than its particular substantive content. It may not matter, for instance, whether members of society drive on the left or the right side of the road; what matters is that all of them drive on the same side.[42] The rules of the road, then, classically exemplify the meaning of law implicit in the doctrine of the rule of law. The law that orders a free society consists of a body of general, abstract, universally applicable rules, permanent, prospective, and equal. Such rules never involve the goals or ends of human action but only the means that persons are permitted to employ in pursuit of their individually chosen ends.

The character of a true or ideal law, law proper, may be further clarified by consideration of its opposite or antithesis—a true or ideal command. A law, as we have seen, is a general rule that structures the means individuals may employ to pursue their self-chosen ends. The law does not tell an individual that he must drive, where he must go, or what route he must take to his final destination. It merely informs all potential drivers, whatever their chosen route or destination, that they may not drive faster than, say, 65 mph to reach it.

The significance of such a general rule—law proper—may be illustrated by comparing two hypothetical scenarios. First, assume that an individual wants to drive to Atlanta from West Palm Beach. The general rules of the road do not mandate that he drive to Atlanta or the particular route he must take to do so. Assume that the driver in this case chooses to drive to Atlanta via the northbound interstate highway. Further imagine that, while en route, he learns of a traffic accident causing gridlock in the area through which he is about to travel. The driver, governed only by the general rules of the road, is free to use his newfound knowledge of adverse traffic conditions and make a detour, perhaps saving himself hours of idling in gridlocked traffic.

We next compare the foregoing scenario to one in which a driver operates not under the rule of law but rather its opposite—command. An ideal command, command proper, is an authoritative order, a precise and detailed directive that mandates certain specified action. Suppose that our driver did not voluntarily decide to drive from West Palm to Atlanta but was commanded to do so by some person in authority, perhaps his employer. Further suppose that the hypothetical authority not only specifies the precise destination but is also convinced he knows the best route to Atlanta. He thus stipulates in detail the route the driver must take, namely, the northbound interstate, as in the previous example. The driver obeys the command and heads north on the highway as ordered and, as before, learns of the impending gridlock. In this case, however, his newfound knowledge will prove useless. The driver was specifically ordered to drive the interstate to Atlanta. If he is to obey the command, he cannot act upon his knowledge of adverse traffic conditions and take an alternative route but instead is forced to sit for hours in traffic. His personal knowledge of the gridlock is irrelevant and wasted.

Such is an inevitable outcome of guidance by command rather than general rules of law. We have seen that law proper structures only the general means a person must employ in pursuing his particular and freely chosen ends. The first driver in our example is only obliged to obey the general rules of the road. Consequently, he is able rapidly to adapt to the changed traffic conditions, employing his newly acquired personal knowledge to avoid the gridlock. Such flexible adaptation to changing circumstances, however, is not possible for the second driver, operating under command. A command, by definition, is a specific order devised and issued by a commander. The knowledge utilized in a command is intrinsically limited to the knowledge personally possessed by the agent who formulates it. The knowledge of the person commanded, in this case, information regarding the impending gridlock, is inconsequential, to no effect. Indeed, the driver under command in our example could probably be replaced by any other capable driver without consequence. The driver, in effect, is a mere tool employed by the commander in accordance with the commander's, and only the commander's, knowledge and serving the commander's, and only the commander's, purpose. Tools are not only readily interchangeable but also unable to exercise agency or will.

The situation described is not anomalous but rather a necessary and predictable outcome of ordering human action through command and not the enforcement of law. Commands and laws are distinct *kinds* of rules, distinguished, among other attributes, by the respective knowledge utilized under their governance.[43] We have seen that an end-independent general rule, law proper, simply structures the general means that individuals may employ to realize their goals; it is silent with respect to either ends or specific means. A society wherein human activity is coordinated through law is dramatically different from a society wherein such activity is directed by command. In the former case, unlike the latter, human beings are not forced to obey detailed instructions of a commander but rather permitted to use their own knowledge to fulfill their own purposes. They are constrained only in a general way by rules that restrict, but do not specify, the means they may employ in pursuing their self-chosen goals. A society ordered by law thus encourages both the discovery and utilization of knowledge possessed by any and all members of society, knowledge, moreover, that is often fleeting and fortuitous.

It is quite otherwise in a society ordered by command. The knowledge embodied in a specific (end-dependent) command, as we have seen, is necessarily limited to the knowledge possessed by the commander. If the command is to be followed, the knowledge of the person under command is not and cannot be utilized. The commander in our example may have been convinced that he knew the best route to take from West Palm to Atlanta. Even stellar genius, however, is unable to foresee the future with certainty. The commander in our case could not possibly have gained advance knowledge of the accident that would cause the gridlock; accordingly, such vital information was not and could not have been incorporated into his command. Commands, again, can only embody the knowledge possessed by those who formulate them, and these are always human beings who are necessarily, and irremediably, ignorant of most of the fluid concrete facts and circumstances that determine the success of human action. Every human being is constrained by such epistemological limitations. No one is omniscient, and no one can consciously anticipate or take account of every contingency that may arise, even in the course of a single day. The refusal to recognize and honor such inherent limitations of the human mind caused our unfortunate driver to sit for hours gridlocked in the blazing Florida sun.

Such epistemological facts, arising from the nature of things, explain why societies ordered by law or general rules, such as traditional American society, are always and everywhere more successful than societies ordered by command. The flourishing of law-governed societies (a "government of laws") follows from the fact that the rule of law permits the potential emergence and utilization of the knowledge possessed by every member of society. Societies ordered by command, by contrast, must remain relatively primitive, insofar as the knowledge employed is restricted to the intrinsically limited knowledge possessed by those persons privileged to issue the commands (a "government of men" or "personal" government). For that reason, societies governed by the rule of law, such as traditional American society, have achieved levels of material success and civilizational development unrivaled by any society ruled by command (e.g., North Korea, Cuba, the former Soviet Union).

The complex achievements of modern American society, and modern Western society more generally, are inseparable from the historical commitment to the rule of law characteristic of such societies.[44] Such a conclusion arises from the fact that a framework of general rules, in contrast to explicit commands, is necessary to permit the emergence and social utilization of the knowledge that generated and sustains the advanced social orders of modern civilization. Moreover, only a framework of general rules permits flexible adaptation to the unanticipated circumstances of existence, a flexibility that is crucial not only to the material well-being of a people but indeed its very survival. The legal framework of a society—general rules or personal commands—has important utilitarian consequences.

The achievements of a rule-governed society, however, extend far beyond the realm of practical affairs. Of equal if not greater significance is the fact that only a society ordered by law is capable of realizing the high moral value of individual freedom. A pure command, in contrast to law, not only prevents the commanded from acting upon their own personal knowledge or pursuing their own purposes but, indeed, eliminates voluntary choice altogether. The only virtue exercised by persons under command is obedience to authority. A society ordered by command must not only remain a relatively primitive society in a material sense but also cannot know individual freedom.

Law and Legislation

We have noted the relation between the modern corruption of language and the corresponding decline of both individual freedom and the ideal of the rule of law. A "government of laws, not of men" presupposes both a conception of law as a particular kind of rule possessing specific attributes and a clear distinction between law and command. It further presupposes a distinction between law and related constructs such as legislation and policy, both of which are popularly if inaccurately conflated with "law" in contemporary American discourse.[45]

Legislation, as previously noted, comprises the rules, regulations, directives, decrees, orders, and so on enacted by a legally constituted governmental entity (typically a legislature but, increasingly, executive and judicial authorities as well). Although distinguished from law by distinct criteria (source and attributes, respectively), legislation is not, like a command, a unique kind of rule intrinsically distinct from law proper but may or may not possess the attributes of law. Legislators in many instances have the ability to consciously craft their handiwork in the form of a general rule possessing the requisite attributes of law. They may and do, however, also enact other kinds of directives that do not conform to law proper. A great part of modern legislation, confusingly termed law, is of this latter type. A helpful way to distinguish between law proper and legislation or policy is to recognize that the former, unlike the latter, is incapable of final or perfect implementation ("execution"). A true law, as we have seen, is a general standing rule, such as a standing prohibition against the deliberate killing of another human being except in self-defense. Such a law is intended to govern human action indefinitely and in a myriad of present and future cases. No matter how often a law operates to regulate or govern human action, in this case, prevents the murder of an innocent person, the law continues in full force; a standing rule can never be brought to completion.

Certain forms of legislation, as said, can possess the attributes of true law if lawmakers frame their acts as such, but modern legislation seldom meets such criteria. The Affordable Care Act of 2010, which mandates the purchase of health insurance by every American citizen, is a case in point. Such a mandate is not a law proper, not a general standing rule possessing other relevant attributes, but rather a legislative directive or policy measure. Indeed, portions of the legislation are more akin to command than law, in particular, those provisions that require fulfillment of specific concrete ends, such as mandatory purchase of both health insurance and specific coverage. In contrast to law proper, such legislative mandates are capable, in principle, of full and final execution. The executive branch of the federal government can assign the responsibility of enforcing and executing the legislation enacted by Congress to various bureaucratic agencies. Once accomplished, once every citizen has purchased the specific health insurance required, the legislative mandates will be fully implemented, brought to completion.

Law proper, in contrast to such legislation, can never be fully or finally executed in such a manner because a general standing rule is intended to govern human action in perpetuity. The Affordable Care Act is not a law so conceived. It may be legal, insofar as it was enacted by a duly authorized constitutional authority (Congress) and said by the Supreme Court to conform to the fundamental law of the U.S. Constitution, but it is not law in the traditional sense of the term. The ideal of the rule of law means far more than mere legality of governmental action. It is rather what has been called a "meta-legal" doctrine, that is, a guiding ideal that concerns not the substantive content of particular law but rather the more general question of "what the law should be."[46] The traditional answer is that law, to be authoritative and binding, should conform to certain principles and possess certain attributes, as discussed. As Hayek explains, "if a law gave the government unlimited power to act as it pleased, all its actions would be legal, but it would certainly not be under the rule of law. The rule of law, therefore, is . . . more than constitutionalism: it requires that all laws conform to certain principles."[47] Legislation, again, may or may not conform to law proper; recent health-insurance legislation, among various other acts of Congress, does not.

One of the especially troublesome consequences of the modern conflation of law and legislation is the trivialization of law and corresponding loss of respect for the rule of law. Many people recognize, however inchoately, that modern legislation seldom possesses the moral authority of law; they know that a mandate to purchase health insurance is not morally equivalent to the prohibition of wanton acts of murder. The American people have characteristically and historically displayed deep reverence for the rule of law, which long served to sustain the vitality of American constitutionalism. Such devotion must inevitably diminish as any and all acts of Congress (falsely) claim the high dignity of law. Prospects for the preservation of traditional American order, including its characteristic valorization of individual freedom, would be greatly enhanced if members of American society were again to recognize that a "government of laws" does not mean, and never has meant, a government of mere legislative enactment.

Constitutionalism and the Rule of Law

Law within Western society has traditionally been classified under two main categories—private law and public law. *Private law* involves the "rules of just conduct" that individuals are obliged to honor in their treatment of one another.[48] Examples include the prohibition of such actions as demanding a person's wallet at gunpoint, murder, theft, rape, violation of contractual obligations, and so on. The purpose of private law is to regulate relations between private individuals so that peaceful and law-abiding citizens do not suffer injustice originating in the actions of their fellow private citizens. The second class of law is traditionally called *public law*. Public law comprises the rules that regulate relations between private citizens and public officials ("government"). Its purpose is to prevent private citizens from suffering injustice that may originate in the actions of government. The fundamental public law governing American political order is the Constitution of the United States. The Constitution establishes not only the structure of the federal government but also the limits of its power, with the aim of securing the individual rights of citizens and the corporate rights of the several states against violation by the federal government. Such rights include those explicitly enumerated in the first ten amendments to the Constitution, the Bill of Rights, as well as various implicit rights held by both individuals and states. Public law also includes the numerous regulations and directives that govern the actions of public administrative bodies (the government bureaucracy) in their treatment of private citizens.

We have seen that the rule of law is the means developed within the Western tradition to protect individual freedom and other rights and that law always involves a coercive sanction of one kind or another. Such sanctions are not self-enforcing but rather administered by government. Government, as the legal enforcer of law, is the only social institution authorized, legally and morally, to employ with impunity certain forms of coercion—fines, imprisonment, lethal force, and so on—against members of society. Such authority is sometimes described as modern government's "monopoly" (exclusive authority or power) of the administration of justice. Indeed, on the traditional American view, the chief function of government is precisely to administer justice. "Justice is the end of government," remarked James Madison, and such an end is fulfilled not only by the enforcement of law but also its establishment and adjudication (charged to the executive, legislative, and judicial branches, respectively).[49] Government's role is to administer the coercive sanctions of law that secure the rights of the American people, that is, to secure justice.

The Western concept of "rights," then, is inseparable from the concept of justice, a relation especially pronounced in American political thought and extensively discussed in following chapters. For purposes of the present discussion, we simply note that a person who claims a right thereby expresses a profound sense of moral entitlement, asserting his conviction that he deserves to be treated in a certain manner by other individuals or by the government. Individual rights within the Anglo-American tradition carve out the previously mentioned private sphere—a moral and legal domain within which the individual is protected against arbitrary interference either by other individuals or government. The protection of such a private sphere, circumscribed by individual rights, has long been regarded as a primary function of government. As Thomas Jefferson eloquently summarized the American view:

> We hold these truths to be self-evident, that all men are created equal, endowed by their Creator with certain unalienable rights, that among these are life, liberty, and the pursuit of happiness; *that to secure these rights governments are instituted among men,* deriving their just powers from the consent of the governed. . . .[50] (emphasis added)

The purpose of government, says Jefferson, is to secure the unalienable rights of all men. The means by which government fulfills such an end, as we have seen, is the administration of law: "where there is no law, there is no freedom" or security for other unalienable rights. The American tradition thus conceives a triadic relationship among rights, law, and government: the goal is the protection of rights, law the means of such protection, and government the institution established to declare, adjudicate, and enforce the law that protects the rights of the people, conceived both as individuals and members of the several states. As will be discussed more fully in a following chapter, the traditional American view conceives government as the agent authorized by the people to employ the coercive sanction of law when necessary to protect individual rights. Government is authorized to employ coercion not in an arbitrary fashion, as it pleases, but for a specific and limited purpose. In terms of our previous discussion, government is authorized to employ a good or lawful form of coercion to prevent or punish bad or unlawful forms, such as an assailant demanding another's wallet at gunpoint. In the absence of such lawful coercion, the individual's rights, including the right to liberty, would be insecure. Human law, however, is neither self-enforcing, self-declaratory, nor self-adjudicating and thus government is established to perform such functions.

Our present interest concerns the significance of such a conception of government for the constitution of the free society and especially its relation to the rule of law. Government is authorized to employ coercive force to protect the rights of peaceful persons against those who would threaten or violate them. We have seen, however, that the "fire" of coercion is a double-edged sword. On the one hand, the coercive sanction of law enforced by government is necessary to protect individuals from injustice that stems from their fellow citizens; on the other, it is crucial that government employ its coercive force *only* against wrongdoers and not also against peaceful citizens. Government must not violate the very individual rights it is intended to secure. The problem is that the establishment of government simultaneously protects the rights of the people and increases potential threats to those rights. The delegation of coercive power to government means that such threats may now emanate from two potential sources—private individuals and the government itself.

Americans of the founding era were acutely aware of this problem. History and personal experience had taught them that individual rights can be threatened not only by private citizens but also by government, the organization that wields the collective coercive force of the community. Thus arose a central question of American political order—how to create a government equipped to employ the coercive force requisite to securing justice, to securing the unalienable rights of the people, but at the same time constrained to employ that force only toward that end. The answer embraced by the Americans is not surprising. The necessary constraint on the range of governmental coercion is to be achieved by the same means employed to constrain private coercion, that is, the rule of law.

The Americans did not originate the doctrine of the rule of law but were heirs to a conception rooted in antiquity, in particular, classical Greece and republican Rome.[51] More proximate sources included the celebrated Magna Carta of 1215 and the seventeenth-century formulation of the doctrine provided by Chief Justice Edward Coke. The overarching purpose of the rule of law, as we have seen, is to prevent injustice, especially the violation of individual rights. Private law aims to constrain injustice that may arise from the actions of private individuals and public law from the actions of public officials or government. On the view of the Founders, the perennial potential for both private and public injustice arises from the same source—the inherent human lust for power. The Founders' view of human nature will be discussed more fully in a subsequent chapter. For now, we simply highlight their settled conviction that the propensity to indulge the lust for power ever threatens an expansion of governmental power beyond the limits of its legitimate jurisdiction and thus toward violation of the rights of the people.

The Founders further believed that the potential for the abuse of power by government is more or less proportional to the ability of its agents to exercise "discretion," arbitrariness, or "prerogative." Their great fear was that government would employ its coercive power however, whenever, and wherever it desired, that is, in an arbitrary, willful, or ruleless manner. The remedy is to restrict the range of its discretionary authority by the establishment of fixed rules that bind the actions of government in advance and that it is obliged to follow in all cases. The remedy, in other words, is the establishment of the rule of law. As A. V. Dicey explains, the rule of law means "in the first place, the absolute supremacy or predominance of regular law as opposed to the influence of arbitrary power, and [the exclusion of] . . . arbitrariness, of prerogative, or even of wide discretionary authority on the part of government."[52] For the Americans and their Old-Whig forebears, then, the great antagonist of the rule of law is the exercise of what they variously called "arbitrary will," "arbitrary government," "discretion," or the "rule of men." As Jefferson pointedly observed, the "only greater [evil] than separation [from England is] . . .

living under a government of discretion."[53] The Americans believed that history had demonstrated time and again the evils that follow from a government that exercises wide discretionary authority. In the absence of established law that imposes prior constraints on governmental action and limits its discretionary judgment, no individual is safe from potential injustice and oppression. No individual, for instance, could be immune to the possibility of arbitrary arrest. Any person might be whisked away in the dark hours of the night on the whim of political authority, thrown into the Tower, or forced to endure the charade of a Star Chamber. Painful experience had taught the Americans and their forebears that the only security against the abuse of political power—the arbitrary exercise of will or discretion on the part of government—is the establishment of fixed rules or laws that constrain its actions in advance and limit discretion on the part of its agents.

The Magna Carta of 1215 was characteristic of such efforts. The Great Charter was thrust upon King John by medieval barons precisely to secure various legal safeguards against arbitrary exercise of political power. They demanded that rulers henceforth must agree to be bound by the terms of the Charter. King Edward I's guarantee of 1297 is representative:

> . . . [N]either We, nor our Heirs, shall procure or do anything whereby Liberties contained in this Charter shall be infringed or broken; and if anything be procured by any person contrary to the premises, it shall be had of no force nor effect. . . . And we will that if any judgments be given from henceforth, contrary to the points of the charters aforesaid by justices or by any other our ministers that hold pleas before them touching the points of the charters, they shall be undone and holden for naught (His Royal Highness).[54]

Several centuries later the banner of the rule of law was again raised in resistance to arbitrary power. The Stuart monarch James I (1566–1623) confidently proclaimed to his subjects that he was not "subject or bound" to pre-existing law but rather he himself—"the supremest thing on earth"—speaks the law. *Rex est lex loquens,* "the king is the law speaking," proclaimed he and his defenders. Such assertions by James and his heirs provoked strenuous resistance by Coke and other foes of royal absolutism and were countered by an equally confident assertion. The king was pointedly instructed that he is not in fact above the law; rather, in England, he was informed, "*Lex, Rex*" ("Law is King"), as Samuel Rutherford would later title his influential pamphlet of 1644.[55] The absolutist claims of the Stuarts were further met with the standard of Magna Carta. "Magna Carta," retorted Coke, "is such a Fellow, that he will have no Sovereign"; within the political order of a free people *lex, rex,* law is king.[56] Indeed, the leading idea underlying the Anglo-American conception of the rule of law defended by Coke and fellow travelers had been expressed as early as the thirteenth century. The king, declared the medieval jurist Bracton (1210–1268), most assuredly is not above the law but, on the contrary, "under God and under the law": "The king must not be under man but under God and under the law, because the law makes the king. . . . [F]or there is no *rex* where will rules rather than *lex*."[57] The King does not "make" or "speak" the law but rather is himself "made" by the law and, moreover, subject to a higher and ultimate law that derives not from man but from God. As Hayek explains,

> This medieval view, which is profoundly important as background for modern developments, though completely accepted perhaps only during the early Middle Ages, was that "the state cannot itself create or make law, and, of course, as little abolish or violate law, because this would mean to abolish justice itself, it would be absurd, a sin, a rebellion against God who alone creates law." For centuries it was recognized doctrine that kings or any other human authority could only declare or find the existing law, or modify abuses that had crept in, and not create law.[58]

Later conflicts in England, especially during the tumultuous seventeenth century, led to ever greater clarification of the meaning of the rule of law. The Petition of Grievances of 1610 sent by Parliament to James I declared: "There is no[thing] which [we] account . . . more dear and precious than this, to be guided and governed by the certain rule of law, . . . and not by any uncertain and arbitrary form of government . . . not in accordance with received general laws."[59] The Petition of Right of 1628, written primarily by Coke and signed by the king and Parliament, established further limits on monarchical power by means of the rule of law. It guaranteed, for instance, that no taxes can be imposed on the people unless levied by Parliament, that martial law cannot be declared in time of peace, and that prisoners have the right under the common law to challenge the lawfulness of their detention through the writ of habeus corpus.[60] Subsequent conflict between Crown (Cavaliers) and Parliament (Roundheads) led to civil war (1642–1651); the trial and execution of Charles I; the establishment of the Commonwealth of England and then the Protectorate under Oliver Cromwell (1649–1660); the restoration of the Stuart monarchy in 1660; and, ultimately, the so-called Glorious Revolution of 1688, which established in England the principle of limited constitutional monarchy. William of Orange and his wife Mary were raised to the throne on the express condition of their agreement to be bound by the laws established in Parliament.

Although such limits on royal power were supported by both Tories (supporters of the Crown) and the opposition Whigs (Parliamentarians who took the lead in resisting royal absolutism), the Glorious or Bloodless Revolution of 1688 represented the triumph of Whig ideals. Locke was a leading player in the constitutional drama of the era, returning to England from exile in Holland in the company of William's wife Mary.

Scholars once believed that Locke wrote his celebrated *Second Treatise of Government* (1689) to justify the Glorious Revolution, although such is no longer the accepted view.[61] What is clear, however, is that the *Second Treatise* is an embodiment of the Whig ideals that animated not only the English conflict of the seventeenth century but also the later American War of Independence. Old Whigs such as Locke and Americans of the founding era were united by a common passion—the hatred of arbitrary power—and the prevention of arbitrary action by government ever remained the guiding aim of their political practice. Locke eloquently summarized both the Whig goal and the means of its realization in his classic definition of freedom-under-law:

> Freedom is . . . to have a standing rule to live by, common to every one of that society, . . . a liberty to follow [one's] own will in all things, where that rule prescribes not; and not to be subject to the inconstant, uncertain, arbitrary will of another man. . . . [W]hoever has the legislative or supreme power of any commonwealth is bound to govern by established standing laws promulgated and known to the people and not by extemporary decrees. . . . [Even the legislature has no] absolute arbitrary power . . . but is bound to dispense justice . . . [and the] supreme executor of the law . . . has no will, no power, but that of the law. . . . [The] ultimate aim is to . . . limit the power and moderate the dominion of every part and member of that society.[62]

Although the translation of Whig ideals into law and public policy was inevitably a slow and imperfect process, central Whig principles were widely embraced not only in England but also in the American colonies. Indeed, Whig conceptions of liberty and law came to define the traditional American ideal of freedom-under-law. We have seen that liberty, to the Whig mind, had a precise and definite meaning—freedom from arbitrary coercion, whether emanating from Crown, Parliament, or the people. Such freedom was to be secured by strict adherence to the rule of law, that is, to "something permanent, uniform, and universal [and] . . . not a transient sudden order from a superior or concerning a particular person."[63] The Constitution of the Commonwealth of Massachusetts (1780) explicitly affirmed the goal of the Old Whigs—the establishment of a "government of laws, and not of men."[64]

A "government of laws, not of men," such as that constructed by the American Founders, is one that forbids persons from ruling over other persons. A free society is governed not by personal rulers but rather impersonal law. Impersonal and sovereign law, as discussed, comprises both private law, governing relations between private persons, and public law. Public law governs not only relations between private persons and government but further aims to govern the government itself, that is, provide a set of rules and norms that constrain and regulate the actions of government officials. No public official is entitled to do as he pleases or even wield wide discretionary authority; all members of government are rather bound by and required to follow previously established law. When taking the oath of office, American officeholders do not swear fealty to a personal superior, as in feudal or fascist societies. They rather promise to protect and defend the impersonal rule of law, that is, the U.S. Constitution, the fundamental public law that limits and binds the power of the federal government over private citizens as well as the several states. By such means—the rule of law—the Founders sought to secure justice, to secure the unalienable rights of the individual, including the right to freedom, threatened as they may be by both private persons and government itself.

The Anglo-American conception of the rule of law, as previously mentioned, is best understood as a "meta-legal" doctrine or ideal, concerned not with the substance of particular laws but rather the general nature and purpose of law itself—"what the law should be." It is an ideal in the sense of a guiding principle, a standard toward which to aspire. Its realization or efficacy ultimately depends upon the extent to which it is supported by public opinion, which means that such an ideal may never be perfectly achieved in practice. Nevertheless, its fundamental constitutional purpose is clear—to prevent arbitrary government, the exercise of personal will or discretion on the part of government officials, by requiring that governmental coercion only be employed in the manner prescribed by established law. Such a requirement means that the American people may only legitimately be subjected to coercion by government in the enforcement of a known general rule that possesses the attributes previously discussed. It further means that the range of legitimate government action is bounded by the fundamental law of the Constitution. Both requirements establish known limits to the coercive action of government by preventing the exercise of discretion and arbitrary will. The restrictions entailed by the rule of law so conceived jointly circumscribe a sphere within which the individual may act without the expectation of coercive interference by government.

We have seen, moreover, that a second and related function of the rule of law, in both its private and public dimensions, is to enhance the *certainty* of human affairs. Law in this respect has been described as a kind of man-made relation of "cause and effect."[65] The existence of announced general rules permits individuals to know in advance certain consequences of their choices and to plan their actions accordingly. Criminal law such as the prohibition of murder, for instance, signals a kind of causal relation to all concerned—a person who murders another person (cause) will lose either his liberty or his life (effect). Such a law establishes a causal nexus (murder-punishment) that people can rely upon as they go about their affairs and which enhances their ability to predict the behavior of other members of society. Its existence means that people can engage in their daily activities more or less secure in the expectation that they probably will not be murdered. All forms of law, private and public, enhance such security of expectation.

To further illustrate the manner in which law serves such a purpose, consider the enactment of legislation that establishes the personal income tax rate at, for example, 30 percent. Such legislation permits individuals to know in advance and with certainty how much of their income, present and future, will remain under their personal control. It thus allows them to plan their personal economic activities with a greater measure of confidence than would be possible in the absence of a fixed tax code. If government could simply tax people at whatever rate it deems best at the moment, through ad hoc legislation or fiat, individuals would have no way of knowing the percentage of income they would be permitted to keep in the future. Such uncertainty would hinder every person's efforts rationally to plan his activities. Decisions regarding investment, savings, expenditure, hiring, as well as one's personal employment efforts, necessarily involve an anticipation of future income. In the absence of a known and fixed income-tax rate, the future would be even more uncertain than in the normal course of events. The rule of law assists human beings in the realization of their goals by establishing a greater measure of certainty in human affairs than is possible in its absence.

Hayek sums up the two related aspects of the rule of law—prevention of arbitrary government and enhanced security of expectation—as follows:

> Nothing distinguishes more clearly conditions in a free country from those in a country under arbitrary government than the observance in the former of the great principles known as the Rule of Law. Stripped of all technicalities, this means that government in all its actions is bound by rules fixed and announced beforehand—rules which make it possible to foresee with fair certainty how the authority will use its coercive powers in given circumstances and to plan one's individual affairs on the basis of this knowledge. Though this ideal can never be perfectly achieved, since legislators as well as those to whom the administration of the law is entrusted are fallible men, the essential point, that the discretion left to the executive organs wielding coercive power should be reduced as much as possible, is clear enough. While every law restricts individual freedom to some extent by altering the means which people may use in the pursuit of their aims, under the Rule of Law the government is prevented from stultifying individual efforts by ad hoc action. Within the known rules of the game the individual is free to pursue his personal ends and desires, certain that the powers of government will not be used deliberately to frustrate his efforts.[66]

A "government of laws, not of men"—a government that honors the rule of law—must be sharply distinguished not only from "personal government" but also a "government of legislation" or one that that merely honors proper legal form. As we have seen, both the general doctrine of the rule of law and the particular meaning of law embodied in traditional American constitutionalism implicitly distinguish law proper not only from command but also legislation, policy, and mere legality. Not every legal measure emanating from government, whether a formal legislative body such as Congress, the office of the modern presidency and its numerous bureaucratic agencies, or a hyper-politicized Supreme Court, bears the moral status of law.

NOTES

1. Edward T. Cook, *The Life of John Ruskin* (London: George Allen and Company, Ltd., 1911), 10.

2. John Locke, *Second Treatise of Government*, ed, C. B. Macpherson (Indianapolis: Hackett Publishing Inc., 1980 [1690]), subtitled *An Essay Concerning the True Origin, Extent and End of Civil Government*, 17. This is the second of "Two Treatises of Government," the first consisting of Locke's response to Robert Filmer, who argued on behalf of the Divine Right theory of monarchy and thus absolute government. Hereinafter cited as *Second Treatise*.

3. A modern paraphrase of Confucius (551 B.C.–479 B.C.), *Analects*, tr. Arthur Waley (New York: Vintage, 1989), XIII, 3, 171–2. Apparently the Chinese language has no explicit word for "freedom" or "liberty" and thus the passage in question has also been translated as "if the language is incorrect . . . the people will have nowhere to put hand and foot."

4. The earliest known appearance of the word "freedom" or "liberty" (*amagi*) appears as cuneiform script on a clay document written about 2300 B.C. in the Sumerian city-state of Lagash.

5. Benjamin Constant, "The Liberty of Ancients Compared with that of Moderns." Speech delivered to his fellow citizens in 1816. *Constant, Political Writings*, ed Biancamaria Fontana (Cambridge: Cambridge University Press, 1988). Hereinafter cited as "Liberty of Ancients."

6. Sometimes described as "civic republicanism" or "neo-Roman" liberty. See Quentin Skinner, *Liberty Before Liberalism* (Cambridge: Cambridge University Press, 1988).

7. "Beyond question it is a happier thing to be the slave of a man than of a lust; for even this very lust of ruling, to mention no others, lays waste men's hearts with the most ruthless dominion." Augustine, *City of God*, trans. G. Walsh, D. Zema, G. Monahan, D. Honan, ed. and intro, Vernon J. Bourke (New York: Image Books, 1958), Book XIX: 15, 461–62). Hereinafter cited as *City of God*. Paul addresses spiritual slavery in Romans 7:15, 19, 23, and elsewhere.

8. Winfred P. Lehmann, *A Gothic Etymological Dictionary* (Leiden, Netherlands: Brill Publishers, 1986).

9. William of Ockham, cited in Takashi Shogimen, *Ockham and Political Discourse in the Late Middle Ages* (Cambridge: Cambridge University Press, 2010), 249.

10. Luther, to take one well-known example, adamantly insisted that since the Fall man's will is necessarily a slave to sin (Martin Luther, "On the Bondage of the Will," 1525). In 1851, St. Philaret of Moscow counselled that "true freedom is the active ability of a man who is not enslaved to sin . . . to choose the better in the light of God's truth, and to bring it into actuality with the help of the gracious power of God." (Sermon on the Birthday of Emperor Nicholas I, 1851)

11. F. A. Hayek, *The Road to Serfdom*, ed and intro, Bruce Caldwell (Chicago: University of Chicago Press, 2007), 77–78. Hereinafter cited as *Road to Serfdom*. Hayek (1899–1992) is among the preeminent economists, social theorists, and political philos-

ophers of the twentieth century. He was awarded the Nobel prize in economics, which he shared with Gunnar Myrdal, in 1974.

12. "I have but one lamp by which my feet are guided, and that is the lamp of experience. I know no way of judging of the future but by the past." Patrick Henry, Speech at the Second Virginia Convention at St. John's Church in Richmond, Virginia (March 23, 1775). n1.

13. Edmund Burke, *Appeal from the New to the Old Whigs* in *The Works of the Right Honorable Edmund Burke*, 7th ed., (Boston: Little, Brown, and Company, 1881), Vol. IV: 188.

14. Emphasis added. Locke, *Second Treatise*, 32.

15. "Rightful liberty is unobstructed action according to our will within limits drawn around us by the equal rights of others. I do not add 'within the limits of the law' because law is often but the tyrant's will, and always so when it violates the rights of the individual." Thomas Jefferson, Letter to Isaac H. Tiffany, April 4, 1819. Founders Online, National Archives, last modified Dec. 6, 2016.

16. Hayek, *Road to Serfdom*, 77.

17. Justice Clarence Thomas, dissenting opinion, *Obergefell v. Hodges* (June 2015), 4.

18. Magna Carta, Ch. 39, in A. E. Dick Howard, *Magna Carta: Text and Commentary* (Charlottesville: University of Virginia Press, 1964), 43.

19. Edward Coke, Sec1 Blackstone 123. Second Part of the *Institutes of the Laws of England* (1797), 45.

20. Ibid, 125. William Blackstone (July 10, 1723–February 14, 1780), English jurist, judge, and Tory politician.

21. Thomas, dissenting, *Obergefell v. Hodges*, 4.

22. The historic relation between voluntariness and free will is pointedly indicated by the German word for "voluntary"—*freiwillig*.

23. Constant, "Liberty of Ancients."

24. Thomas, *Obergefell*, 7.

25. Ludwig von Mises, *Human Action* (Auburn: Ludwig von Mises Institute, 2010).

26. F. A. Hayek, *The Constitution of Liberty* (Chicago: University of Chicago Press, 1960), 20–21. Hereinafter cited as *Constitution*. Accordingly, Hayek sometimes defines freedom as "the ability to use [one's] own intelligence or knowledge . . . to follow one's own aims and beliefs."

27. Coercion can be exercised by one person or several persons jointly. The crucial point is that the coercer or coercers must be *persons*, human agents with minds and wills. A gang of persons, several robbers, for instance, can jointly press guns against an individual's head, thereby exercising coercive power over him.

28. ". . . [F]reedom refers solely to a relation of men to other men, and the only infringement on it is coercion by men." Hayek, *Constitution*, 12.

29. In the present case, we are assuming that Mother is deliberately making such a threat in order to coerce her son. It is possible that a different Mother in a different situation may make the same statement, but in a simply declarative sense, that is, with no deliberate intent to coerce.

30. "The price of liberty," counseled the Framers, "is eternal vigilance." Variously attributed to Patrick Henry, Thomas Jefferson, and others.

31. Hayek, *Constitution*, 163.

32. Mortimer Adler, *The Idea of Freedom: A Dialectical Examination of the Conceptions of Freedom* (New York: Doubleday, 1958).

33. *Bellum omnium contra omnes*. Thomas Hobbes, *Leviathan*, ed, John Gaskin (Oxford: Oxford University Press, 1996), 84. Hereinafter cited as *Leviathan*.

34. Locke, *Second Treatise*, 32.

35. The so-called Sugary Drinks Portion Cap Rule, enacted in 2013. In 2014, the New York Court of Appeals, the state's highest court, overturned the regulation, arguing that the New York City Board of Health exceeded the scope of its regulatory authority in adopting such a rule.

36. The "Patient Protection and Affordable Care Act" passed by Congress and signed into law by President Obama on Mar. 23, 2013.

37. The "Energy Independence and Security Act" of 2007 called for gradual phase-out of bulbs that did not meet efficiency standards established by the legislation, which included most incandescent bulbs. The legislation was blocked by Congress in 2014.

38. John Adams, "Novanglus Papers," no. 7, in *The Works of John Adams*, ed. Charles Francis Adams, vol. 4 (Boston: Charles Little & Brown, 1851), 106. Adams published articles in 1774 in the *Boston Gazette* using the pseudonym Novanglus. He there credited James Harrington with expressing the leading idea. Harrington described government as the empire of laws and not of men in his 1656 work, *The Commonwealth of Oceana*, 35. The phrase gained wider currency when Adams used it in the Massachusetts Constitution, Bill of Rights, article 30, *Works*, Vol. 4: 230.

39. F. A. Hayek, *Law, Legislation, and Liberty*, in three volumes (Chicago: University of Chicago Press, 1973–79).

40. Hayek, *Constitution*, 164. Law may further be categorized as customary, statutory, or constitutional law. Many aspects of Western law are offshoots of custom, which had the force of law throughout the centuries preceding the modern era. Both customary law such as common law and judge-made law contributed to the protection of freedom in Western society, but it is not clear that such would be sufficient to sustain the free society under contemporary circumstances. In any event, the American Founders were convinced that statutory and constitutional law were also essential toward that end, hence the valorization of the ideal of the rule of law and demand for a written constitution.

41. Locke, *Second Treatise*, 32.

42. Hayek, *Road to Serfdom*, 117.

43. Hayek, *Rules and Order*, 96–143; *Constitution*, 148–61.

44. Indeed Hayek argues that civilization itself may be defined in terms of knowledge: "civilization begins when the individual in the pursuit of his ends can make use of more knowledge than he has himself acquired . . . profiting from knowledge he does not himself possess." *Constitution*, 22.

45. See Bruno Leoni, *Freedom and the Law* (Indianapolis: Liberty Fund, 1991).

46. Hayek, *Constitution*, 205–6.

47. Hayek, ibid., 205.

48. F. A. Hayek, *The Mirage of Social Justice*, vol. 2, *Law, Legislation, and Liberty*, (Chicago: University of Chicago Press. 1976), 34. Hereinafter cited as *Mirage*.

49. "Justice is the end of government. It is the end of civil society. It ever has been and ever will be pursued until it be obtained, or until liberty be lost in the pursuit." James Madison, *Federalist* No. 51, in Garry Wills, ed., *The Federalist Papers by Alexander Hamilton, James Madison and John Jay* (New York: Bantam Books, 1982), 265. Hereinafter cited as *Federalist Papers*.

50. Declaration of Independence. Jefferson's language in the Declaration is indebted in part to George Mason. In the "Fairfax Country Resolves" of 1774 Mason wrote: "all men are by nature equally free and independent, and have certain inherent rights. . . Namely the enjoyment of life and liberty, with the means of acquiring and possessing property, and pursuing and maintaining happiness and safety."

51. Hayek, *Constitution*, 162–75.

52. A. V. Dicey, *Introduction to the Study of the Law of the Constitution*, 8th ed. (London: Macmillan and Co., 1915), 198.

53. Thomas Jefferson to William Gordon (1826) in *The Writings of Thomas Jefferson*, eds, Lipscomb and Bergh (Monticello: The Thomas Jefferson Memorial Association of the United States, 1904), 10:358.

54. Magna Carta, 1297.

55. Samuel Rutherford, *Lex, Rex or, The Law and the Prince* (Berryville, VA: Hess Publications, 1998). Rutherford was a Scottish Presbyterian minister.

56. Sir Edward Coke, debate in the House of Commons regarding the House of Lords' Amendment to the Petition of Right of 1628 (May 17, 1628).

57. "The king has no equal within his realm. Subjects cannot be the equals of the ruler, because he would thereby lose his rule, since equal can have no authority over equal, not *a fortiori* a superior, because he would then be subject to those subjected to him. The king must not be under man but under God and under the law, because the law makes the king, . . . for there is no rex where will rules rather than lex." Henry of Bracton, cited in W. Holdsworth, ed, *A History of English Law,* (London: Methuen & Co. Ltd., 1903), Vol. 2:33.

58. Hayek, *Constitution*, 163.

59. Great Britain, Public Record Office, Calendar of State Papers, Domestic Series, July 8, 1610.

60. The Petition of Right of 1628 is a major English constitutional document that sets out specific liberties of the subject that the king is prohibited from infringing. It was produced by the English Parliament in the controversy that ultimately led to the English Civil War, passed by Parliament in May 1628 and given the royal assent by Charles I in June of that year.

61. See, for instance, Peter Laslett, "The English Revolution and Locke's 'Two Treatises of Government'," *Cambridge Historical Journal* 12 (1956), 41, and Richard Ashcraft, *Revolutionary Politics and Locke's Two Treatises of Government* (Princeton: Princeton University Press, 1986), 545–55.

62. Locke, *Second Treatise*, 17, 68, 71, 111.

63. Blackstone's *Commentaries*, cited in Hayek, *Constitution*, 173.

64. John Adams, as previously noted, attributed such a conception to James Harrington. Hayek traces its ultimate origin to Aristotle: "There is clear evidence that the modern use of the phrase 'government by laws and not by men' derives directly from Aristotle. Thomas Hobbes believed that it was 'just another error of Aristotle's politics that in a well-ordered commonwealth not men should govern but the law', whereupon James Harrington retorted that 'the art whereby a civil society is instituted and preserved upon the foundations of common rights and interest . . . [is], to follow Aristotle and Livy, the empire of laws not of men'." Hayek, *Constitution*, 166.

65. Ibid., 153.

66. Hayek, *Road to Serfdom*, 112–13.

TWO

Freedom and Rights

[Every individual possesses]. . . rights antecedent to all earthly governments; rights that cannot be repealed or restrained by human laws; right[s] derived from the Great Legislator of the Universe. —John Adams[1]

Among the natural rights of the colonists are these: first, a right to life; secondly, to liberty; thirdly to property; together with the right to support and defend them in the best manner they can. —Sam Adams[2]

Since well before 1787, liberty has been understood as freedom from government action, not entitlement to government benefits. —Justice Clarence Thomas[3]

Both freedom and law are, of course, intimately related to another concept central to Anglo-American political and legal discourse—the concept of rights. Indeed we have seen the difficulty of discussing American political values such as freedom and justice without recurrence to the idea of rights. The time-honored association of freedom and rights in the American experience even leads to attempts to define freedom in terms of rights—to be free, it is often said, is to have a right to worship as one chooses, a right to speak freely, a right to publish one's opinions, and so on. While this is true, such statements fail to capture the essential attributes of either freedom or rights more generally. The traditional American conception of freedom has been analyzed in the preceding chapter. A similarly careful analysis must be applied to the related concept of rights. Such scrutiny is particularly important at the present juncture of American history. The meaning of the term rights has undergone significant transformation over the course of modern history, and contemporary discourse increasingly employs the term in a sense alien to the American moral and political heritage. The preservation or revitalization of that heritage thus requires a recovery not only of the traditional meanings of freedom and law but also the traditional American meaning of a right.

The American Founders emphatically spoke the language of rights. The Declaration of Independence forthrightly proclaims that all men are "endowed by their Creator with certain unalienable rights," which include the celebrated trilogy, "life, liberty, and the pursuit of happiness."[4] The Bill of Rights further specifies the treatment to which Americans are entitled by law and justice. Such rights as free exercise of religion, freedom of speech, freedom of press, and so forth have been deeply assimilated by American consciousness and, throughout most of American history, taken more or less for granted.[5] Increasingly, however, the language of rights in American society assumes various meanings greatly at odds with that embodied in its founding documents. It is not uncommon, for instance, to hear claims of a "right" to health care, education, welfare, "affordable housing," "a living wage," and on. The rights of homosexuals were said to be violated by prohibition of same-sex marriage. The human rights of illegal immigrants are said to be violated by attempts to enforce immigration laws, as are the alleged rights of nonsmokers to live in a smoke-free environment. The list of such contemporary rights-claims could be extended almost indefinitely. Indeed, many if not most political demands in contemporary American society are expressed in the language of rights, a phenomenon that Mary Ann Glendon has described as the American penchant for "rights talk."[6] It is not difficult to understand the popularity of such "talk"—to claim a right is to make a strong moral claim with tremendous resonance in American political culture. Such popularity, however, often means that the term is employed carelessly and also for effect, leading, among other consequences, to trivialization of the concept of a right. The transformation of the *meaning* of American rights in the popular mind is even more problematic. The problem is that false interpretation of a right may lead to destruction of the authentic rights traditionally guaranteed to the American people.

The English word right stems from the German word for justice, *Recht*, indicating that a right is something to which a person is entitled by justice (Latin *jus*—law or right), that is, something he deserves in a profound moral sense. A person who claims a right is claiming moral entitlement to a certain kind of treatment by other persons. Thus, every right-claim necessarily imposes a corresponding or correlative moral obligation on another person or persons, namely, the obligation to treat the right-claimant in the way demanded. For that reason, the concept of a right, like the related concept of justice, is only meaningful within human society. Robinson Crusoe has many concerns, but the status of his rights is not among them. Any right claim he might make, any claim to deserve a particular kind of treatment by other persons, must be met with stony silence. Alone on his island, there are no other human beings to bear the moral obligation of honoring his right. The question of rights—how other persons should treat him or how he should treat other persons—simply does not arise.

American political ideals are saturated with, one might almost say defined by, the moral concept of rights. American resistance to perceived British tyranny of the eighteenth century was grounded in the very concept of rights, leading the colonists and revolutionaries to clarify ever more precisely their understanding of rights in general and the traditional concept of "natural rights" in particular. The philosophical defense of armed resistance to British rule mounted by the Americans evolved over the course of conflict with the mother country. The colonists launched such a defense by asserting against the British a traditional view of rights. The actions of Crown and Parliament, they insisted, violated the historical or "prescriptive . . . rights and liberties of Englishmen," the hard-won legal protections achieved over centuries of experience in the struggle for liberty and justice and to which the colonists, as British subjects, claimed entitlement.[7] For reasons that will be discussed in a following chapter, the English denigrated and dismissed such initial American rights-claims. One fortunate if unintended consequence of the British position was that it more or less forced the Americans onto higher moral ground. More particularly, they found it necessary to make their stand for liberty and justice not on the basis of inherited English rights and liberties but rather on the basis of natural rights derived from a source beyond government or human agency. As John Adams expressed the consensus of the era, each individual possesses ". . . rights antecedent to all earthly governments; rights that cannot be repealed or restrained by human laws; right[s] derived from the Great Legislator of the Universe."[8] The American people must be forever grateful for English recalcitrance. The rejection of the colonists' claim to prescriptive rights led the founding generation to formulate a moral defense of their rights unrivaled in history and valid for eternity. Indeed the body of literature produced by their efforts is arguably the greatest of the many American contributions to free government.

The colonists' defense of their rights against the British government led, in particular, to the express formulation of what can only be regarded as the first principle of American political order: the conviction that every human being, simply by virtue of his status as a human being, is morally entitled to be treated in a certain manner. More formally stated, every human being possesses certain natural rights, certain moral claims against other human beings, including human beings organized as government. The Declaration of Independence famously identifies such rights as the unalienable rights to life, liberty, and the pursuit of happiness. It further identifies the source of such rights—the "Creator." On the American view, rights are not entitlements or privileges granted by human authority but rather inherent to human nature, originating in a source beyond human will and history, and existing prior to the establishment of government. In the language of formal rights theory, individual rights are "subjective" rights, inhering in the human subject, the human person. Such a conception of rights is implicit in both American founding principles and the institutional structures erected on their basis, a topic extensively explored in the following chapter.

Rights, on the traditional American view, are simultaneously characterized by several distinct dimensions. First, we have seen that rights are conceived as *natural*, a constituent of human nature, itself regarded as beyond the reach of man. Second, they are regarded as *unalienable*. The term is of legal origin, derived from the traditional legal distinction between alienable and unalienable property. Alienable property refers to possessions that a person can make "alien" or "other," that is, property whose title may be transferred to another person by sale or otherwise; such action alienates the original owner's property. Unalienable property, by contrast, cannot be sold or transferred or made the possession of another person. Natural rights, according to the Americans, fall into the latter category. Natural rights cannot be sold, transferred, rejected, given away or somehow made the possession of another—they are unalienable because they are constituent of human nature. A human being cannot dispossess or alienate his natural rights even if he should so desire. Such a conception of natural rights constitutes the firmest imaginable foundation for a right. Rights are not given by man and thus cannot be taken away by man. They cannot be disentangled from human nature, from what a person *is*; to be a human being is to possess natural rights or inherent moral entitlement to certain kinds of treatment. American law has long recognized and honored this profound American conviction. No court in the land, for instance, will honor a contract by which a person attempts to sell himself into slavery. Such an agreement cannot be permitted even if a person should so despise his right to liberty as to voluntarily seek his own enslavement. His free choice in this matter cannot be honored because he is a human being and thus possesses an unalienable right to liberty. Such a right cannot be separated from his personhood even if he imagines he would prefer the status of a slave.

A third defining attribute of the natural and unalienable rights proclaimed in American founding documents is their status as *individual* rights. All human beings share a common human nature, but every person is nevertheless regarded as an individual and as individually endowed with certain rights. The American tradition does not generally recognize any system of so-called collective rights, that is, rights that belong to an individual by virtue of his membership in a particular group (ethnic, religious, economic, professional, and so on) or "group" rights (rights possessed by a group qua group and not by its members severally). The modern conceptions of collective or group rights must be sharply distinguished from the corporate rights possessed by the several states that constitute the American federal union and discussed more fully in a later chapter. Excluding such corporate rights, the only group membership that is relevant to American constitutional rights is the universal "group" of human beings, each member of which possesses identical rights ("All men are created equal, and endowed by their Creator with certain unalienable rights"). Belief in the universality of human nature underlies the American commitment to both *universal* rights and *isonomia* or equality under law: all persons are to be universally governed by identical general rules because all persons possess equal substantive worth, the intrinsic worth of a human being as such. Such ideals were not invented by the American Founders. Jefferson and others consummately summarized the longstanding biblical convictions of a universal human nature and spiritual equality of all human beings before God.

The concept of rights is of course related not only to justice but also to government. Such is distinctly the case with respect to traditional American government, whose overarching purpose is precisely to protect the natural and unalienable rights of the individual. It does so, as we have seen, by enforcing and adhering to the rule of law, administering the private law that aims to prevent the violation of individual rights by private persons and confining its own exercise of coercive power within established constitutional boundaries. The historical record on this subject is rich and clear. Not only does the Declaration affirm the individual's unalienable rights to life, liberty, and pursuit of happiness but also pointedly asserts government's responsibility for securing such rights (" . . . to secure such rights governments are instituted among men . . ."). The Bill of Rights asserts certain individual rights against the "general" or federal government established by the U.S. Constitution and enumerates specific restrictions on its authority intended to protect both individual and corporate rights against potential abuse of political power by the federal government. The powers reserved to the several states by the Tenth Amendment are further to be employed toward the protection of individual rights. The rights-bearers, in this case, the individuals organized within their respective states, demand certain kinds of treatment from, and impose corresponding moral duties on, the federal government. The Bill of Rights instructs the federal government that certain kinds of actions toward the citizens of the states, and toward the states themselves, will not be permitted. Each of the first ten amendments imposes limits on the potential action of the federal government, and the rights therein claimed generate corresponding moral and legal obligations on the part of that government to honor the specified limits. Additional constitutional safeguards against the violation of individual and corporate rights, including the all-important principles of federalism and separation of powers, will be discussed in following chapters.

KINDS OF RIGHTS

Negative Rights and Negative Liberty

We have seen that the rights proclaimed in American founding documents are multidimensional, simultaneously unalienable, natural, universal, and individual. They are further distinguished by yet another defining attribute—their so-called *negativity*. The concept of negative values was previously encountered in the description of traditional American liberty as "negative liberty." Liberty of course is regarded as a foundational right in American political culture, one that belongs to a general class or kind of right conventionally, and correspondingly, termed "negative rights." Negative in this context does not imply dour pessimism but rather points to the fact that such rights, including the right to liberty, are secured by the *absence* of certain conditions. We have seen that every right imposes a corresponding moral obligation on other persons. In the case of negative rights, the moral obligation so generated involves the duty to *refrain* from certain actions; one individual's negative right is secured not by the positive action of another person or persons but rather their (negative) self-restraint.

A few concrete examples will illustrate the meaning of negative rights and the dynamic involved in their protection. The American Declaration states that every person is endowed by the Creator with unalienable rights to life, liberty, and the pursuit of happiness, all of which are conceived as negative rights. What does it mean to possess an unalienable (negative) "right to life" and what does its security entail in practice? The universal right to life means, first and foremost, that every human being is morally entitled, has a right, to exist, to live, to be. A person's right to exist is not the gift of government or any human being but inherent in his very nature, his human nature. The next consideration is the kind of moral obligation the possession of such a right imposes on other human beings. The corresponding duty entailed by an individual's right to life is a negative obligation: all other persons are morally and legally obligated not to violate the life of the individual right-bearer, in other words and more bluntly, not to kill him. To do so would be a moral violation of the first order. The individual's unalienable right to life, then, imposes a specific moral obligation on all other persons—to refrain from murder or any action that destroys the existence of the right-bearer. An individual's right to life is secure if, and only if, all other persons exercise such self-restraint. The obligation to refrain from murder is of course engendered not only by a constitutionally guaranteed right to life but also a foundational moral injunction of Judeo-Christian civilization—"thou shalt not kill." Indeed the individual's right to life is so crucial to human flourishing that it has always and everywhere been acknowledged, explicitly or implicitly, and, moreover, enforced by human authority, whether as custom in earlier stages of social development or as formal legal protection embodied in positive laws that forbid the murder of an innocent person.

All of the unalienable rights proclaimed by the American Founders are negative rights in the sense described. The unalienable right to liberty, like the right to life, is secured not by positive action of any kind but rather the absence of certain conditions. A universal right to liberty means that each individual is morally entitled to carry out his existence in the manner that he himself voluntarily chooses and this requires protection against arbitrary coercion by another person or persons. Liberty requires the absence of coercion; thus the right to liberty is secured by the absence of coercion. The right to liberty, like every right, imposes a corresponding moral obligation on other persons. In the case of liberty, the specific moral obligation so imposed is the duty to refrain from exerting or threatening coercive force in pursuit of one's goals. One person, for instance, may desire to obtain another person's wallet. The owner of the wallet, however, like every individual, possesses a right to liberty. This means that the person who desires the wallet is forbidden to employ coercion in reaching his goal. He must restrain himself from demanding the owner's wallet at gunpoint or otherwise exerting coercive force against the owner. He must do so because such coercive action would violate the owner's unalienable and natural right to liberty (as well as his right to property). He will have to find another way to realize his purpose, perhaps offering to purchase the wallet or engage in some other form of voluntary exchange. The right to liberty, like every unalienable and natural right, is universal (possessed by "all men"); every person possesses an equal right to liberty. This means that every person is morally entitled to make his own decisions, pursue his own values and purposes, without arbitrary threats or intimidation or coercive pressure from others. It further means that every person bears a corresponding moral obligation toward every other human being—the obligation to refrain from exercising (arbitrary) coercive force against them.

The identical analysis applies to the individual right to property, another traditional negative right that imposes a corresponding negative moral obligation on all other persons. The specific moral obligation generated by the individual's right to property is the duty to refrain from taking the individual's property without his consent. The security of one individual's right to property does not require any positive action on the part of others; no one is obligated to give or transfer property to the right-bearer. The moral obligation correlative to a right to property is, again, a negative obligation that imposes the duty of self-restraint. An individual's right to property is secure so long as all other persons refrain from employing coercion or force to gain control of his possessions. No one is permitted to obtain another person's wallet by pointing a gun to his head but must rather obtain the owner's voluntary consent. The American Founders regarded the right to property, like the rights to life and liberty, as a legal and constitutional right but it too derives in the West from fundamental Judeo-Christian moral precepts, in this case, the injunction against theft, "thou shalt not steal." The moral prohibition of theft implicit in the right to property, like the moral prohibition of murder implicit in the right to life, has been regarded as so essential to human flourishing that it too has been enforced by human authority in almost every society known to man.[9]

Several of the individual rights enumerated in the Bill of Rights—specific rights asserted against the federal government—are also negative in the sense described. The First Amendment is representative: *Congress shall make no law respecting an establishment of religion, or prohibiting the free exercise thereof; or abridging the freedom of speech, or of the press; or the right of the people peaceably to assemble, and to petition the Government for a redress of grievances.* Every right guaranteed by the First Amendment is a negative right, secured by the absence of certain actions on the part of the federal government and, moreover, imposing a corresponding moral obligation on its agents. More particularly, the First Amendment obliges the federal government to refrain from enacting any law concerning the establishment of religion or prohibiting its free exercise; to refrain from prohibiting free speech, a free press, peaceful assembly, and petitioning for a redress of grievances. The federal government is prohibited from any and all action in the specified areas. The enumerated rights of the Bill of Rights, as well as the natural rights of the Declaration, thus circumscribe the aforementioned private sphere wherein the individual is assured a range of action free from interference with his voluntary choices by the federal government. The Tenth Amendment establishes similar limits to federal authority with respect to the several state governments. American constitutional rights, then, impose a moral and legal obligation on the federal government to refrain from interfering with individual and state belief and practice in all specified areas. The Bill of Rights implicitly acknowledges that every individual is morally entitled to a domain of noninterference, that is, every individual has a right to freedom, and that every state is similarly entitled, that is, possesses a right of corporate liberty.

The negative rights championed by the American Founders, as we have seen, are also universal rights; every person, simply by virtue of being a person, possesses such rights. The universality of subjective individual rights is fundamental to the traditional American sense of justice, summarized in its ideal of equality under law. Every person is assumed to be of equal worth and thus every person is to be judged by the same rules. There is to be one law for both the rich and powerful and the poor and powerless. There is to be one law for both African Americans and Italian Americans. There is to be one law for both elected officials and private citizens; the president and the garbage collector are to be judged by the same rules. Everyone is under the rule of law, and "Justice is blind." The ideal of equal treatment under the law, like the concept of the rule of law more generally, did not originate with the American founding but is rather of ancient lineage. As previously noted, the early Greeks coined the term *isonomia* for the ideal that the Anglo-American tradition would later uphold as equality under law.

It should also be emphasized that the regime of rights traditionally embraced within American constitutional order, embedded explicitly and implicitly in its founding documents and ideals, is both internally consistent and realizable in practice. Individual rights, as we have seen, are regarded as natural, unalienable, individual, negative, and universal. They are natural and unalienable because they are inherent to human nature and universal because human nature is universal. The universality of rights is among the firmest of American convictions: "all men are created equal . . . and endowed by their Creator with certain unalienable rights." Each and every individual bears identical rights and thus identical moral obligations. Traditional American rights, moreover, are not only universal but, equally important, also *universalizable*. That is, in principle, each individual is able to enjoy the protection of natural and constitutional rights without conflicting with the equal and simultaneous enjoyment of such rights by every other person in society. One individual's rights are not gained at the expense of another person's rights.

The internal harmony and universalizability of the traditional American constellation of rights derives from the fact that such rights are negative rights. We have seen that an individual's negative rights are secure so long as other persons honor their moral and legal obligation to refrain from certain actions. The security of an individual's negative rights does not require other persons to undertake positive action of any kind but only to exercise self-restraint. Every individual can thus simultaneously enjoy equal rights to life, to liberty, and to property; all that is required is that other persons refrain from murder, coercion, and theft. Although such a perfect observance of rights is improbable, given the imperfection of human beings, it is possible in principle. There is no inherent contradiction or conflict between or among traditional and universal American rights but rather an internal harmony that minimizes potential for social conflict. Every person can rest more or less secure in the enjoyment of his rights insofar as coercive laws exist to provide penalties and disincentives for those tempted to cross moral boundaries and violate the rights of others. A regime of negative rights thus tends to secure not only life, liberty, and property but also peace.

Positive Rights and Positive Liberty

The harmony and security of a system of justice based on negative rights may be more clearly perceived by considering the alternative kind of rights increasingly asserted in American society—alleged "rights" to health care, education, welfare, and other so-called entitlements. Such claims belong to a kind and class of right conventionally designated "positive" rights, highlighting the sharp distinction between such claims and the negative rights presupposed by traditional American political thought. As we shall see, the two kinds of rights have little in common beyond the mutual assertion of moral entitlement. The concept of positive rights derives from an ideology alien to traditional American values and convictions—the ideology of socialism. Positive rights are a hallmark, not of a free society, but rather collectivist and totalitarian political regimes of all stripes, socialist, communist, fascist, or some variant thereof. The 1936 Constitution of the Union of Soviet Socialist Republics (USSR), for instance, guaranteed a wide range of positive rights to all Soviet citizens: a guaranteed right to employment; the right to maintenance in old age, sickness, or loss of capacity to work; the right to education; the right to pre-maternity and maternity leave with full pay; and so on. Its 1977 Constitution expanded positive rights to include the right to health protection, ensured by "free" medical care; rights to housing; the right to "enjoy cultural benefits" such as libraries, and so on. The UN Charter of Rights of 1948 also asserts numerous positive rights that should be guaranteed to every person in the world: "Everyone has the right to a standard of living adequate for the health and well-being of himself and of his family, including food, clothing, housing and medical care and necessary social services, and the right to security in the event of unemployment, sickness, disability, widowhood, old age or other lack of livelihood in circumstances beyond his control."[10] The Charter makes no mention of who is to bear the moral obligation of providing the positive goods and services necessary to fulfill such world-wide universal rights. The positive rights of the 1972 Constitution of North Korea include "free" medical care; the right to education; and even the "right to relaxation," to be ensured by "accommodation at health resorts and holiday homes at State expense." The positive rights guaranteed by the 1992 Constitution of Cuba include medical care for the sick, food, clothing, schooling for children, as well as "a comfortable place to live."

The concept of negative rights, as we have seen, is correlative to a particular concept of liberty—negative liberty. Negative liberty is regarded as a moral entitlement, symbolized by the term "right" and secured by the absence of certain actions on the part of other persons. The concept of positive rights is similarly correlative to a concept of liberty—so-called positive liberty. Positive in this regard does not mean cheerful or optimistic but rather signifies the requirement of *presence* or *provision*. In contrast to the requirement of absence bound up with the concept of negative liberty, positive liberty is secured if and only if certain conditions are present. In other words, the achievement of positive liberty typically requires the actual provision of one thing or another, typically material goods and/or services of some kind. Positive liberty, as we recall, is generally defined as the power or ability to realize one's goals or fulfill one's potential. Proponents of positive liberty so conceived maintain that a person is unfree if confronted by various obstacles that prevent the achievement of his aims or actualization of his potential abilities, including and especially obstacles posed by lack of requisite material resources. The ability to realize positive freedom—to realize one's goals and potential—is said to require possession of a certain minimum of positive goods, such as income, food, health care, housing, education, and so on. On such a view, a person who does not possess such material necessities cannot be free. The unalienable right to liberty is thus said to imply a corollary right to be provided with the material goods requisite to the exercise of (positive) freedom. We have seen that every right-claim by its nature imposes a corresponding moral obligation on some other person or persons. In the case of positive rights, every right-claimant implicitly asserts that some other person or persons bear the moral obligation to provide him with the good or service claimed as a right (health care, housing, college tuition, and so on). The provision of the goods and services requisite to the achievement of positive freedom is said to be more than a matter of charity; such provision is said to be a matter of justice, that is, a positive right.

The conception of positive rights and liberty stands in stark opposition to the traditional American conception of negative rights and liberty. The moral obligations generated by a system of negative rights, as we have seen, are invariably negative obligations—to refrain from certain actions. The moral obligations generated by a system of positive rights and liberty, by contrast, are invariably positive obligations—to provide another person with certain material resources. The assertion of positive rights thus means that some persons—those who bear the right—must in justice be provided with particular tangible goods by other persons—those who bear the duty to provide them. The moral claims and obligations embodied in the two systems of rights and liberties could not be more distinct. There is a vast difference between the moral claim to a private sphere of noninterference and the moral claim of entitlement to certain positive goods. There is a vast difference between the moral obligation to refrain from action (do not steal) and the moral obligation to do something for another person, in this case, actually provide him with material possessions or wealth.

Of particular concern is the fact that the two types of rights, negative and positive, are inherently in conflict and cannot simultaneously be fulfilled in a free society as traditionally conceived in the American experience, that is, a society committed to the universal protection of certain negative rights. The attempt to do so must inevitably generate not only social conflict but outright injustice. We have seen that the system of negative rights and liberty established by the Founders is inherently harmonious and practicable, capable in principle of serving equal justice and the peaceful co-existence of all members of society. Every person can enjoy the security of his rights so long as all others refrain from certain actions that would violate the bearer's rights. Such harmony and security, however, are undermined by the assertion of positive rights. The problem is that positive rights are not universalizable in a society that also recognizes traditional negative rights. A regime of positive rights can only be implemented in a socialized or collectivized society that does not enjoy the protection of such traditional American rights as life, liberty, and property. Widespread demand for positive rights necessarily eviscerates the Founders' system of negative rights, a process which in fact has been underway for a considerable period in the United States. Members of American society must ultimately choose between the two conceptions of liberty and rights because they involve inherently incompatible values incapable of simultaneous realization.

A concrete example may illuminate the difficulties involved in the attempt to incorporate positive rights into the traditional American constitutional framework. Consider the case of an individual who claims a right to the provision of health-care services. Perhaps he justifies his claim by appealing to his unalienable right to life; his moral entitlement to exist, he argues, cannot be secured without good health and this requires access to medical care. He thus claims such medical services by right, something to which he is morally entitled by law and justice. Medical care, of course, requires provision of a complex array of goods and services: specialized knowledge; surgical skills; diagnostic equipment and tests; medicine; hospital beds; immunizations; bandages; and so on. The individual's claimed right to health care can only be fulfilled if some other person or persons actually provide him with such material and intellectual resources. We have repeatedly emphasized that every right necessarily imposes a corresponding moral obligation on some other person or persons. In the case under discussion, the person claiming a right to health care is thereby claiming, explicitly or implicitly, that some other person or persons bear a moral duty to provide him with the concrete goods and services comprised by health care.

Such a rights claim thus raises a crucial moral question—*who* bears the moral obligation to supply him with such goods and services? Who bears the moral obligation to diagnose his illness and provide him with necessary treatment? Who bears the moral obligation to provide him with medicine and surgery, a hospital bed, and so on? It is obvious that such health-care resources are not available from nature's bounty, free for the taking, but rather must be brought into existence. Someone must first produce the medical goods and services demanded as a right and this entails cost that someone must pay. Who bears the moral obligation to pay such cost, that is, employ his own resources to produce them and, further, provide them to the right-claimant who asserts entitlement? There is a finite set of possible duty-bearers: either one other person bears the moral obligation to provide the health care; several persons; certain groups of persons; all other persons in a particular society (such as the United States or Mexico); or all other persons in the world (the "global" community). A final putative possibility is that "government" or perhaps "society" bears the moral obligation to fulfill the claimant's supposed right to health care. There are no other conceivable entities capable of bearing moral obligation or paying the costs involved in providing health care.

Having identified the possible bearers of such moral obligation, the next task is to determine which of them should be charged with the legal duty of providing health-care resources to the right-bearer and explain the moral grounds of that obligation. The resolution of such issues is far from self-evident. It is not self-evident why one person—the bearer of the right—should be morally entitled to the material resources of another person or persons. It is not self-evident why one person or group should bear a moral duty to provide another person or group with the concrete positive goods that constitute health care. The moral issues involved in the assertion of positive rights are further complicated by the fact that American society proclaims that "all men are created equal." Such a belief, as we have seen, leads to the American conviction that rights are, and should be, universal and individual. American constitutionalism, as we recall, historically rejects the concept of collective or group rights (members of certain groups have rights denied to those outside the group) and rather affirms a profound commitment to equality under law. The traditional American ideal is that of equal and universal rights, simultaneously possessed by each and every individual. Accordingly, if one person possesses a right to health care, then every person possesses a right to health care.

The American commitment to universal rights, however, cannot be honored in a regime of positive rights. The attempt to fulfill positive rights in American society must rather divide its members into two distinct and antagonistic moral and legal classes—those who bear the positive right and those who bear the moral obligation to secure it. Such an outcome, as previously observed, can lead only to social discord and, worse yet, injustice.

To perceive the problem more clearly, we return to the situation under discussion: the individual claiming a right to health care. Such a claim, as we have seen, immediately raises the question of *who* bears the moral obligation to provide the health care so demanded. The task is to determine which of the possible duty-bearers should be charged with the duty of providing the requisite medical resources. The first possibility, a single bearer of the obligation, can be readily dismissed. No one has yet suggested that one individual member of American society is solely responsible for providing health care to another individual or group. The second possibility—some select group of persons bears the obligation to provide medical resources to those claiming a right to health care—requires more careful analysis.

For purposes of illustration, imagine a hypothetical situation in which Congress enacts legislation entitling all persons whose annual income is less than a million dollars to health care. All persons whose annual income is greater than a million dollars ("the rich") are assigned the legal obligation to pay the costs of the new entitlement (the requisite funds are acquired by raising federal taxes on the latter group). Perhaps such legislation is justified on the grounds that "the rich" possess significantly greater resources than the majority of citizens and thus have greater "ability to pay" or that they bear a moral responsibility to "give back" to the society that enabled the accumulation of their wealth. Whatever the justification, such legislation creates two distinct classes in society—those who receive health-care benefits and those who must pay for them, those who bear the right and those who bear the duty. The two groups are governed by different set of rules: one group receives benefits without cost (a right) and the second bears costs without benefits (an obligation). Such hypothetical legislation would directly violate various foundational moral principles intrinsic to the traditional American sense of justice. Traditional justice, as we have seen, is informed by convictions that "all men are created equal" and "Justice is blind," convictions inseparable from the principles of universal individual rights and equal treatment under law. All persons, rich and poor, high and low, possess identical rights and are to be governed by identical laws. Legislation that establishes rights for a select group of persons (those with income less than a million dollars) relegates those who are obliged to secure such rights (those with income over a million dollars) to an inferior moral and legal status. The latter group bears no right to health care but only the obligation to pay for the former's health care. On the traditional American view, such legislation would be blatantly unjust.

Suppose, then, that Congress avoids such a situation by enacting legislation that establishes a positive right to health care not only for those who fall below a certain level of income but every American citizen. Congress grants, by legislative enactment, a universal "right" to health care; every American is said to be morally and legally entitled to the provision of medical resources. Every American citizen is thereby entitled to stretch out an empty hand, so to speak, demanding resources from someone else—from some other American citizen(s), all of whom, however, are simultaneously displaying the same posture. A universal right to health care means that every American citizen simultaneously claims moral entitlement to provision of medical resources by some other person or persons. Accordingly, someone, some person or some group, must bear the correlative moral obligation to provide every American citizen with such resources. If every member of American society, however, claims a positive right to medical resources, then no one remains standing to bear the corresponding obligation to provide them. Every American citizen cannot possibly receive medical resources at the expense of someone else because some American citizens must actually provide and pay for such resources. Everyone cannot live at everyone else's expense; someone must actually bear the expense.

Such a problem arises in American society as a result of its particular constitutional values and structure, including its traditional commitment to limited government, universal negative rights, and a conception of justice that demands equality under law. Such constitutional principles preclude the possibility of securing universal positive rights to health care or anything else. The impossibility of securing such rights within the framework of American founding principles is obscured by the careless and misleading language often employed in public discussion about positive rights. One typically hears the kind of vague generalities previously mentioned—that "government" or "society" bears the moral obligation to fulfill positive rights to health care, housing, and so on. Such assertions, however, evince either intellectual or moral confusion or a misconception of the nature and structure of American constitutional order (or both). The conception of universal positive rights fulfilled by government or society is only meaningful within regimes of an entirely different character—collectivized societies with a high degree of economic centralization—whose ideology, as mentioned, is in fact the source of the modern conception of positive rights. Such a conception is inapplicable to traditional American society, historically characterized by limited government, the rule of law, negative rights to life, liberty, and property, a market economy, and a particular view of justice.

The irreconcilability of a regime of universal positive rights with American constitutional order may be perceived more clearly by engaging in several thought experiments. First, let us assume that "society" is to bear the moral obligation of securing the right to health care for every American citizen. What could this mean? A moment's reflection reveals that there exists no entity called society capable of bearing the moral obligation to provide Americans with health care or, indeed, of bearing any sort of moral obligation whatsoever. An entity capable of bearing obligation or duty must be a conscious, thinking, willing, intentional being. An entity incapable of intention, thought, or action, such as "American society" or any conceivable society, does not and cannot bear moral agency. American society is not a conscious intentional being but rather an abstract term conventionally employed to refer to the more than three hundred million human beings united by a common American identity. A search for "society" will never yield an encounter with a discrete entity called "society" but only with individual persons who constitute that society. The term society is merely a general name, a nominal abstraction that does not and cannot possess the requisites of moral agency. These can only be possessed by actual persons—conscious human beings capable of acting, morally or immorally.

A claim that society must provide medical resources to the American people evidences at best intellectual confusion and at worst deliberate subterfuge. It is as meaningless as the notion that similarly nominal abstractions such as trees, animals, or humanity—none of which are thinking, willing beings capable of moral agency—bear an obligation to provide positive goods to human beings. A right of any kind, negative or positive, is a claim of moral entitlement to certain treatment by another human being. A positive right, such as a right to health care, can only be fulfilled by requiring some actual person or persons to bear the moral obligation of providing relevant resources to the right-claimant. An entity bearing a moral obligation to provide another person with material resources must be an entity capable of engaging in human action and of bearing moral responsibility, that is, a human person.

Let us next consider whether there exists an entity called "government" capable of bearing the moral obligation to secure a universal right to health care, that is, provide medical resources to every American citizen, resources claimed as a requirement of morality, law, and justice. The general nature and purpose of government as conceived in the American tradition will be extensively explored in the following chapter. With respect to the present analysis, the concept of government may be regarded as the abstract term applied to a set of legally established public institutions and officials who wield a certain kind of power or authority in society. "Government," in other words, is no more a thinking, willing, acting being than the similarly nominal term society. A search for the entity "government" would yield the same results as the search for "society." In both cases one would find only particular human beings and never a concrete entity named government or society, which are merely nominal symbols that assist the organization of thought. Clarity of thought in political and moral theory, as in every realm of human inquiry, involves the recognition that only individual human beings think and act and thus bear moral agency. With respect to the present discussion, intellectual precision involves the attempt in every instance to trace the actions of "government" to the actions of the particular individuals or policymakers responsible for particular governmental decisions and policy.[11] "Government" could only be held morally responsible for securing a right to health care if one intends by such a statement to charge particular persons acting within or through governmental institutions with the moral responsibility to provide such resources. Those who claim that government is obligated to fulfill a right to health care generally do not mean to suggest that the president or their congressional representatives or the justices of the U.S. Supreme Court are personally responsible for providing them with medical resources.

Beyond the recognition of the merely nominal character of the term government lies the further complication that traditional American political order is characterized by limited government, the rule of law, and a regime of negative rights and liberty. Such facts have decisive bearing on the issue of whether government can be charged with the moral obligation to fulfill positive rights. Government in traditional American society can never bear such an obligation not only because the abstract term government is incapable of moral agency but for the additional reason that American government does not autonomously possess the material resources necessary to fulfill such an obligation. The essential point with respect to the issue of positive rights is that the vast bulk of the resources employed by the American government must first be acquired from the American people. Government has few resources of its own, few independent means of supporting its activities. A government that assumes the obligation to provide people with health care cannot simply snap its figurative fingers and command medical resources to fall from the sky. Any resources it spends for health care, or any other purpose, must first be obtained, directly or indirectly, from American taxpayers through taxation, borrowing, or money creation. American government has little if any involvement in the autonomous production of goods and services, whether sold on the market or politically distributed to American citizens. It is thus largely confined to the redistribution of resources brought into existence by American workers and producers. The *redistribution of wealth*, that is, the legal transfer of resources from one person or group to another person or group via the political process, is in fact one of the major activities of contemporary American government, especially the federal government. It typically accomplishes such redistribution not by the literal extraction of material goods and services from particular citizens but rather by taxation. Government agencies then transfer the resources so obtained from politically selected producers to politically selected beneficiaries, in the form of direct cash transfers, subsidies, loans, material goods and services such as housing and health care, and similar vehicles.

To recapitulate the argument thus far: government in American society can never bear the moral obligation to secure a positive right such as health care for two reasons. First, the abstract term government does not and cannot possess moral agency and thus cannot bear moral obligation; second, the American government does not possess sufficient material resources of its own by which to meet such an obligation, even if somehow assigned. The limited government established by the Framers' Constitution possesses few resources apart from those acquired from the citizens in one fashion or another. Thus, the American government could only secure a right to health care by obtaining material resources from some persons and transferring them to other persons, that is, engaging in a politics of wealth redistribution. We again note that such a politics establishes two classes of citizens—those who receive the material entitlements and those who must pay for them—which, as we have seen, violates the traditional American commitment to equality under law. Traditional American government cannot fulfill a universal right to positive goods and services of any kind. All goods and services have a cost. American government does not and cannot autonomously fund the costs of health care or any positive good or service but must rather obtain the necessary resources from some segment of the American populace. Some American citizens must actually pay for the goods and services needed to fulfill a positive right such as health care, and such persons, not "government," bear the cost of providing medical benefits to the right-bearers. For that reason, a positive right can never be a universal right; *every* American cannot be morally entitled to a positive good provided by others. Some persons may obtain material benefits by means of political redistribution but other persons must pay their cost. "There is no such thing as a free lunch" or "free" health care.[12]

A society that engages in a politics of wealth redistribution is one in which political authority decides whose resources are to be taken and who is privileged to receive them, that is, who benefits and who bears the cost. Such political determination of material resources inevitably generates social conflict. Certain individuals or groups are selected as the fortunate bearers of positive rights, entitled to demand goods and services that others are forced by law to provide. Yet other individuals or groups are selected as those who must bear the duty and cost of providing such resources. The individuals comprised by either class are determined by political power. The result is the emergence of two antagonistic groups in American society—the net tax beneficiaries, those who receive more in government benefits than they pay in taxes, and the net taxpayers, those who pay more in taxes than they receive in government benefits. The first group is constituted in part by American citizens who claim positive rights ("entitlements") that legally transfer to them the resources or property of other American citizens. The second group includes those who are held legally responsible for providing the first group with particular resources. The attempt to graft a regime of positive rights onto the American constitutional framework necessarily leads to a politics of redistribution, a politics which tends to lead toward social conflict. Net taxpayers and net tax beneficiaries are pitted one against the other as persons and groups attempt to secure positive rights or entitlements for themselves or their group at the expense of other persons or groups. There are winners and losers in such a system, a fertile breeding ground of resentment not to say injustice.

The morality of a regime of positive rights, then, ultimately hinges on the morality of the political redistribution of wealth, the ethics of redistribution. The central point of the present analysis is that a regime of universal positive rights secured by government cannot be realized in the kind of political order established by the U.S. Constitution. Beyond a defendant's right to public counsel in a court of law, the Constitution makes no mention of positive rights, of moral entitlements to particular concrete goods or services, whether provided by government or private citizens.[13] It establishes instead a "charter" of negative rights and liberties inherently capable of universalization and actualization.[14] Every individual, as we have seen, can enjoy an equal right to life, liberty, and property for the simple reason that other people are not required to undertake positive action to fulfill such rights but only refrain from action that would violate them. Such is well within the moral grasp of most persons. The situation is very different in a regime of positive rights. Every individual cannot enjoy an equal right to health care—to the provision by some other person(s) of "free" medical resources—for the simple reason that some of them must be required to provide such resources. An individual cannot be morally entitled to receive free of charge and simultaneously compelled to pay. Moreover, as previously observed, it is one thing to bear the obligation to refrain from stealing, quite another to bear the obligation to transfer one's personal material resources to another.

The moral problem in this regard stems from the previously mentioned fact that positive and negative rights are inherently in conflict and incapable of simultaneous realization. The case under discussion well illustrates the problem: fulfillment of one person's positive right to health care may well entail the violation of another person's negative rights to liberty and property. Such a potential may be brought to light by reconsidering our earlier example, the hypothetical legislation that secured a universal right to health care for all Americans. We previously considered scenarios in which one person or a select group of persons is charged with the obligation to bear the requisite costs of fulfilling the newly enacted right to health care. We now consider a final possibility—the legislation charges *every* American citizen with such an obligation. Congress, in other words, mandates that every member of American society will simultaneously be entitled to medical care and required to pay taxes to fund it. We have seen that fulfillment of positive rights in a free society requires the transfer of resources from one person (the producer) to another (the beneficiary) by the legal redistribution of wealth. In the case of universal taxation to fund a universal right to health care, every American citizen is simultaneously regarded as both producer and beneficiary.

At first glance, such a solution seems to solve the moral problem raised by selective taxation of certain groups to fund the entitlement, in particular, the violation of equal treatment under law. Everyone is entitled to health care and everyone is required to pay for it. The achievement of such a happy outcome, however, is highly improbable. The American tradition has insisted from the outset that the legitimacy of governmental activity, as Jefferson restated the long-standing conviction, depends upon "consent of the governed."[15] The resources of every individual are protected by the traditional right to private property. Such a right means that other persons, including those organized as government, must refrain from taking the individual's property without his consent. The legitimacy or justice of legislated universal health care thus depends upon the consent of those persons taxed to fund it, in the case under discussion, every American citizen. Justice requires that every American citizen consent to be taxed for the purpose of securing health care for every member of society.

We have seen that fulfillment of a positive right necessarily entails the transfer of resources, by the coercive force of law, from producers to beneficiaries, and this remains true even if such roles are confounded within the individual. While everyone is subject to the identical tax (assuming for purposes of illustration that all persons are taxed equally), the benefits provided will not be equally distributed. Persons with significant health problems will undoubtedly receive greater benefits than healthier persons, which means that the resources of healthier taxpayers will be redistributed to unhealthier members of society. For such reason, and others, it is more than possible that some persons subject to the universal tax do not want to be taxed for the purpose of providing universal health care, even if they themselves are legally entitled to receive such care. Some individuals may consent to be taxed to fund the health-care entitlement, but it is fair to assume that others may not; they may prefer to use their limited personal resources for other purposes. Indeed, if every person consented to the redistribution of wealth in this fashion, there would be no need to pay for anyone's health care by means of taxation. Nothing prevents individuals from voluntarily transferring their personal resources, in friendship or charity, to those in need. In any event, it is difficult to believe that *every* person taxed to fulfill a legislated universal right to health care will consent to such taxation. The property of all those opposed to the policy will nevertheless be taken, without their consent, which is only to say that their individual right to property will be violated.

It may be objected that the relevant consent to the particular form of wealth redistribution here described is in fact conveyed by prior general or implied consent to the U.S. Constitution itself. Such general consent, it might be argued, implies consent to the particular consequences or outcomes of constitutional procedures, in this case, the legislative mandate that redistributes wealth from the relatively more healthy to the relatively less healthy. Such a view, however, ignores the limits to legitimate governmental power implicit in the American conception of social contract, which will be fully examined in the following chapter. As we shall see, on its terms, the legitimate jurisdiction of government is intrinsically limited by the purpose for which it is established, namely, security of the natural rights of each and every person, including the right to property. No one may consent to the violation of his own or another's natural rights because such rights are unalienable and their protection the very reason government is instituted in the first place.

In the absence of unanimous consent, then, a politics of redistribution necessarily violates not only the traditional principle of consent of the governed and the individual right to private property but also the traditional ethical injunction against stealing (taking a person's property without his consent). There is no way around such a consequence except in the improbable event that *every* taxpayer voluntarily agrees to pay taxes to fulfill a universal positive right to health care (or any substantive positive right). Stealing is stealing whether conducted by persons in their role as private citizens or by their political representatives in Congress. Because no one possesses the moral right to steal, no one, individually or collectively, can delegate such a right to political authority (one cannot give away more power than one inherently possesses, to paraphrase John Locke). Involuntary wealth redistribution enacted by a representative legislature cannot and does not overcome the moral difficulties involved in such action. The unavoidable conclusion is that a moral and political order that respects the inherent and unalienable (negative) right to property of each and every individual cannot also and simultaneously fulfill positive rights. A regime of positive rights can only be established in a society in which private property is severely circumscribed or eliminated.

We conclude the discussion by again emphasizing that the United States Constitution makes no provision for positive rights beyond a defendant's putative right to legal counsel in a court of law. The assertion of positive rights, on the other hand, is universal in the constitutions of socialist, communist, and other collectivized societies. This is related to the unique economic structure of such societies, namely, a structure defined by extensive governmental ownership or control of social resources. In a society wherein government owns or controls most if not all resources, it makes sense, at least in principle, that government should bear the moral obligation to provide the people with certain positive or material goods and services. Such a conception, however, is irreconcilable with a free society as historically conceived within the American experience. Traditional American society is characterized, not by governmental ownership or control of resources but rather private ownership and direction of material resources, which, indeed, is the linchpin not only of its capitalist economic order but way of life more generally. The concept of positive rights is antithetical to traditional American order in all its myriad dimensions, political, legal, economic, and moral. The hallmark of the constitution of liberty crafted by the American Framers is the security of negative individual rights, including the natural and unalienable right to private property.

NOTES

1. John Adams, *Dissertation on the Canon and Feudal Law,* 1765. https://founders.archives.gov/documents/Adams/06-01-02-0052-0007.

2. Samuel Adams, *The Rights of the Colonists,* 1772.

3. Clarence Thomas, *Obergefell v. Hodge* 576 U.S.: 2015.

4. The Declaration of Independence was written primarily by Jefferson but revised in part by the five-member committee of the Continental Congress, including Jefferson, Roger Sherman of Connecticut; Benjamin Franklin of Pennsylvania; Robert R. Livingston of New York, and John Adams of Massachusetts. Jefferson's original draft, which included the Lockean rights of life, liberty, and property, was revised to read "life, liberty, and the pursuit of happiness," no doubt in sensitivity to the prevailing and contentious issue of slavery. Slaves were regarded by their owners as property.

5. Even such foundational First Amendment rights as free exercise of religion and freedom of speech, however, are under stress in contemporary American society.

6. Mary Ann Glendon, *Rights Talk: The Impoverishment of Political Discourse* (New York: The Free Press, 1991).

7. Edmund Burke employed the term "prescriptive" rights in pointed distinction to rights that resulted from intellectual speculation and construction, as he believed was typical of the French revolutionaries of his era. George Mason, among many others, referred to such inherited or prescriptive rights as the "liberty and privileges of Englishmen," cited in John Chester Miller, *Origins of the American Revolution,* 2nd ed., (Stanford: Stanford University Press, 1959), 168. William Blackstone, as noted, described them as "the absolute rights of every Englishman."

8. John Adams, "A Dissertation on the Canon and the Feudal Law" (*Boston Gazette,* August 12 and October 21, 1765).

9. Ancient Sparta may be an exception to this generalization. The Spartans encouraged stealing, regarding it as a useful skill for military purposes. Punishment was administered not for stealing but getting caught engaging in that activity. According to Thomas Aquinas, the Germanic tribes in the times of Caesar also condoned theft.

10. "The Universal Declaration of Human Rights," adopted by the United Nations General Assembly on Dec. 10, 1948.

11. A methodology of the social sciences generally termed "methodological individualism." See F. A. Hayek, *The Counterrevolution of Science: Studies on the Abuse of Reason* (New York: The Free Press, 1955), 36–43.

12. The phrase has been in currency since the 1930s and 1940s, but its first appearance has not been conclusively identified. The "free lunch" in the saying refers to the nineteenth-century practice of offering a "free lunch" in certain American bars and saloons, aiming of course to entice drinking customers. The phrase was popularized by its use in both Robert Heinlein's 1966 novel *The Moon is a Harsh Mistress* and as a title for a 1975 book by free-market economist Milton Friedman.

13. Certain scholars, however, dispute the modern Court's reading of the Sixth Amendment as equivalent to a positive right. It has been argued, on the contrary, that the original meaning of the Amendment simply prohibited the federal government from interfering in the relation between lawyer and defendant. I am grateful to Dr. James Todd for this observation.

14. Howard Diaz, *A Charter of Negative Liberties: Defining the Bill of Rights and Other Commentary* (Bloomington, IN: Westbow Press, 2012).

15. ". . . to secure such rights, Governments are instituted among Men, deriving their just powers from the consent of the governed." U.S. Declaration of Independence.

THREE

The Nature and Purpose of Government: A Lockean View

We hold these truths to be self-evident . . . that all men are created equal and endowed by their Creator with certain unalienable rights. . . . To secure such rights, governments are instituted among men. —U.S. Declaration of Independence[1]

The concept of freedom is invariably associated with the concept of government in the American mind. Such spontaneous association is eminently justified. Freedom and government are inextricably if indirectly linked in the Anglo-American tradition, a linkage forged by the correlative concept of the rule of law. The Anglo-American conceptions of freedom and the rule of law were examined in a preceding chapter. The next task is to examine the traditional American view of the nature and purpose of government, including its relation to freedom and to law.

American political thought of the founding era did not emerge in a vacuum but is rather a unique variant of a long-standing tradition of political reflection within Western civilization. The American colonists inherited a well-developed corpus of political thought formed by the contributions of various influential thinkers over the centuries and conventionally described as the "liberal tradition." Such a designation will surely give pause to many American readers. "Liberalism" in contemporary American society is widely and correctly understood to involve extensive governmental direction, if not outright control, of social affairs. Such contemporary usage of the term, however, is radically at odds with the traditional meaning of liberalism over the centuries. The liberal tradition, as its name suggests (from Latin *liber*, "free"), is historically characterized, not by valorization of "Big Government" but, on the contrary, individual liberty and its corollary, limited government. Liberalism is yet another term associated with the Western political heritage whose meaning has dramatically changed over the past century, and the word must be used with care. In order to distinguish contemporary American liberalism from historical liberalism, scholars thus refer to the former as *modern liberalism* and the latter, traditional liberalism, as *classical liberalism*. American political thought of the founding era is a development of the liberal tradition in its classical sense—the tradition of limited government in service of individual freedom and related values.

Among the various thinkers who informed the development of the liberal tradition, one of the most important for American belief and practice is the seventeenth-century Whig theorist, John Locke, previously encountered in the examination of the meaning of freedom. Locke himself stood in the stream of tradition, inheriting many of the conceptions that he in turn transmitted to Americans of a later generation. Locke, however, also made significant original contributions to the development of the liberal tradition, including and especially a more precise clarification of both the purpose of government and the nature of political obligation. The theoretical framework he formulated would have immense appeal to the American colonists, informing both their efforts of resistance to British rule and, later, constitutional construction in the newly independent states. Lockean political thought, as well as the historical context within which it emerged, are essential background to the American elaboration of his insights. America no more emerged from the clouds than did Locke.

THE PROTESTANT REFORMATION

Locke's particular conception of government, while ultimately rooted in millennia of historical development, was forged in the crucible of conflict set in motion by the Protestant Reformation of 1517. Martin Luther was a religious and not a political reformer. Nevertheless, the inevitably intimate relation between religion and politics ensured that the conflict with Rome would not be confined to strictly religious or spiritual concerns. Luther's challenge to Papal authority would engender tremendous, if unintended, political consequences throughout Europe and beyond. The post-Reformation contest between Catholicism and Protestantism led to an extended period of bloody conflict in Western Europe, a series of religious and political wars that lasted well into the seventeenth century. Passions of the era fueled an extreme religious intolerance of which all sides were guilty: Catholics slaughtered Protestants and Protestants slaughtered Catholics.[2] Strictly religious motives of parties to the conflict, however, are not easily disentangled from political motives, including the desire of certain rulers and groups to extend their political power. What is clear, however, is that religious conflict conjoined with political conflict in a lethal mix that would permanently shatter the unity of Christendom—the traditional term for Euro-Christian or Western civilization—and bring about the emergence of novel religious and political arrangements that definitively shaped the development of modern Western society.

The enormity of the political consequences wrought by the Reformation, and their relevance for Anglo-American developments, is best perceived in light of the inherited politico-religious conceptions and practices prevailing in sixteenth-century Europe. Prior to the 1517 Reformation, Europe was unified by a more or less universal commitment to the Christian faith, institutionally represented by the Roman Catholic Church under government of the Papacy. There was, so to speak, only one flavor of Christianity—if one was Christian, one was Catholic. Of particular significance for post-Reformation developments, Christendom was characterized by a unique understanding of the proper relation between religion and government, between the spiritual realm of God (represented by the Church) and the temporal realm of Caesar (represented by secular government). Every Christian, in principle, was bound to a dual allegiance, to "Church" and "State," each legitimate within its respective sphere of jurisdiction.

From the late Middle Ages onward, however, the Church extended its authority well beyond its traditional spiritual sphere, acquiring significant political and temporal power. Indeed, by certain measures, the Roman Church of the era was scarcely distinguishable from a secular state ruled by a secular monarch. The Church had its own law (canon law) and jurisdiction (ecclesiastical courts), its own governmental bureaucracy (the Curia), as well as widespread powers of taxation. Over time, popes and other important church officials assumed the role of worldly power-players, often ruling more as temporal monarchs than spiritual leaders. Religious reformers such as Luther were appalled at the spiritual corruption inseparable from such developments. Various attempts had been made in previous centuries to reform and purify the Church, to restore it to its authentic spiritual mission, but with little significant effect.

Luther's reform, by contrast, took fire, in part due to the support of various secular rulers in Germany and elsewhere who chafed under Roman authority and the restrictions it placed on their power. Certain German princes and their subjects, for instance, resented the taxes they were forced to pay directly to Rome. They wished, on the contrary, to employ such resources for the local benefit of the German people and not for purposes established by a remote central government in Rome. Such rulers threw their weight behind Luther and facilitated the eventual triumph of his cause. Moreover, Luther's challenge to the established Roman Church inspired other reformers, most notably Huldrych Zwingli and John Calvin, to mount similar protests, and the reform impulse spread widely throughout Europe. The ensuing century, as mentioned, witnessed several series of persecution, resistance, and armed conflict between Catholic and Protestant forces in various European nations. Such events ultimately led to the establishment of Protestantism as the official religion in England, Scotland, the Netherlands, Scandinavia, and various cantons and principalities in Switzerland and Germany. Other nations, including France, Italy, Belgium, Spain, Austria, Ireland, and Poland, remained loyal to Catholic Rome.

The Reformation thus resulted in a decline in the power of the Roman Church. Successful religious reform, however, was achieved only at high cost, both in terms of violence and political order more generally. Among other major consequences, the weakening of Roman authority was accompanied by a dramatic if unanticipated rise in power among secular rulers in both reformed and unreformed nations. The traditional Christian distinction between the "spiritual" and "temporal" realms of society, in the language of medieval jurists, had made it difficult for secular rulers within Christendom to demand either the total allegiance of their subjects or the right to exercise unlimited control over society. Political power was limited, in principle, by the two-pronged obligation of all Christian rulers—to render to God what belonged to God and to confine their actions within the bounds of His higher moral law. Such limits were enforced, however imperfectly, by the countervailing power of the Roman Church, which claimed and exercised authority and jurisdiction of its own.

Feudalism, the characteristic political-economic organization of the Middle Ages, further reinforced the prevailing Christian conception of limits to secular power. Particularly important in this regard was the Christian-feudal conception of political allegiance as deriving from a quasi-contractual relation between rulers and ruled, a relation intrinsically characterized by conditionality and contingency. Such a conception, like that of the higher moral law, controverts the very idea of absolute government—a government entitled to unconditional allegiance and obedience. The feudal origins of modern social-contract political theory will be discussed more fully in a following section. The present discussion aims to highlight the inherently limited power and jurisdiction of secular government in pre-Reformation Europe and, moreover, the existence of an independent authority, the Roman Papacy, willing and able to enforce such limits. The medieval notion of two distinct dimensions of social order, spiritual and temporal, thus prevented, in principle, a concentration of power in one center or the other, Church or State. If James Madison is correct—if the "accumulation of all powers . . . in the same hands . . . may justly be pronounced the very definition of tyranny"—then the dispersal of power characteristic of pre-Reformation Europe well served the growth of freedom.[3]

The Reformation, however, would inadvertently raise various obstacles to such growth by eliminating one of the chief historical checks to the concentration of political power in the West, namely, secular subjection to the authority of an autonomous Church. Secular rulers who joined forces with religious reformers freed themselves from subjection to Rome's canon law, system of taxation, and moral authority. In some instances, such rulers also seized the (considerable) property of the Church and asserted the right to control religion within their borders. The break with Rome enabled monarchs in reformed nations to consolidate substantial new powers within their governments.

The Age of Absolutism was upon Europe. Secular governments throughout Europe asserted newfound power and recognized few limits to their authority. Such post-Reformation developments were reinforced by the revival of classical culture in the Renaissance era, including ancient Roman conceptions of law and secular power. Various monarchs of the era claimed absolute power to rule as they saw fit, asserting the right to unconditional obedience from their subjects. Such power was at times justified on the grounds of the *Lex Regia* of imperial Roman law, the supposed right of the Roman people to confer authority on the emperor. Champions of monarchical power also invoked the maxim of Roman civil law "what pleases the prince has the force of law" and reinvigorated the doctrine of the "Divine Right of Kings."[4] Monarchs claimed or were said to have been appointed to their positions by God himself; to challenge their authority was thus to challenge God himself.[5]

England is a case in point. Few monarchs asserted their divine right to rule more vigorously than King James I (1566–1625). Not only did James regard himself as appointed to the royal position by God, and thus above criticism, but also identified kingly with divine attributes. In a speech addressed to Parliament on March 21, 1609, he explained that

> The state of monarchy is the supremest [*sic*] thing upon earth. . . . Kings are justly called Gods, for that they exercise a manner or resemblance of divine power upon earth. For if you will consider the attributes to [*sic*] God, you shall see how they agree in the person of a king. God has power to create, or destroy, make, or unmake at his pleasure, to give life, or send death, to judge all, and to be judged nor accountable to none: to raise low things, and to make high things low at his pleasure, and to God are both soul and body due. And the like power have Kings; they make and unmake their subjects: they have power of raising, and casting down: of life, and of death: judges over all their subjects, and in all causes, and yet accountable to none but God only. . . . I conclude then this point touching the power of kings, with this axiom of divinity, that as to dispute what God may do, is blasphemy . . . so is it sedition in subjects, to dispute what a king may do in the height of his power.[6]

The Stuart monarchs, beginning with James I, repeatedly made such bold claims to absolute power and authority. "*Rex est lex loquens*" ("the king is the law speaking") the royalists declared; the will of the king, they proclaimed, is the ultimate determinant of law, superior to the common law, Courts, or Parliament. The will of James I included his desire to enforce religious conformity. The English Reformation of the sixteenth century not only divorced England from the Roman Church but also led to the official establishment of an English national church, the Church of England. Such an establishment of religion significantly enlarged the realm of the king, who now ruled jointly as head of both the secular government and the national church. The king, in other words, came to unite in his person the previously dual powers of church and state. Accordingly, the Stuart monarch claimed the right, as did many other rulers of the period, to control the religion of his subjects, in his case, to force conformity to the newly established Church of England.

James's assertion of absolute, unconditional, power was not confined to religion but extended to other important matters such as trade and commerce. Such monarchical claims to absolute sovereignty did not go unchallenged but were vigorously resisted by both Parliament and the Courts, leading, among other consequences, to Coke's articulation of the modern concept of the rule of law, as noted in a previous chapter. The arbitrary exercise of monarchical power also led to the emigration of religious dissenters suffering under James's efforts to enforce religious conformity, some of whom are of course known to American history as the Puritans. James's son, Charles I (1600–1649), continued the policies of his father, intensifying conflict to the point of civil war and beheading of the king. The ensuing dictatorship of Oliver Cromwell and the Roundheads ultimately led to restoration of the Stuart monarchy in the person of Charles II (1630–1685) in 1660. Religious and political conflict in seventeenth-century England only came to a final resolution, however, with the Glorious Revolution of 1688, which, as we recall, culminated in the ascent of William and Mary to the throne as constitutional monarchs bound under law established by Parliament.

The intense political and religious struggle within seventeenth-century England is inseparable from early American history. It of course led to the exodus of religious dissenters seeking refuge from political oppression in the wilds of America. As important, however, the fundamental issue—the rise of political absolutism—provoked an outpouring of political literature that would provide inspiration and sustenance to a later generation of Americans suffering, as they believed, under similar political oppression. Among such works, few were more influential than Locke's celebrated *Second Treatise of Government*. His treatise, motivated by the constitutional crisis of his era, would provide American colonists with a moral and philosophical foundation upon which to stake their own claims of rightful resistance to British tyranny. The political order they ultimately established is scarcely comprehensible apart from certain Lockean presuppositions.

THE SOCIAL CONTRACT

The most significant aspect of the English struggle of the seventeenth century with respect to American developments involves the issue of political obligation. The English crisis, as discussed, was provoked by the rise of political absolutism in post-Reformation Europe. The central question that exercised Locke and other opponents of royal sovereignty is whether rulers are morally entitled to absolute or unconditional obedience on the part of their subjects, as the Stuarts demanded. The question, in other words, is whether the ruled ever possess the moral right to resist the demands or commands of political authority. Locke's answer, elaborated in the *Second Treatise,* would not only profoundly shape the minds of the American colonists but become ever more relevant as they found themselves struggling with the very same question in the following century.

American government is widely associated with the concept of "social contract" or "compact." Government is conceived as arising from voluntary agreement among various parties who willingly establish formal political institutions and, in so doing, acquire and assume certain mutual and reciprocal rights and obligations. The Americans did not originate such a conception. Social contract symbolism is rather of ancient lineage, first appearing in the political writings of the ancient Greeks, significantly developing during the Christian-feudal period, and rising to heightened prominence in the early-modern era. Indeed social contract symbolism is widely associated with early-modern political thought, receiving its most influential formulations in the writings of Thomas Hobbes (1651–1679), Locke, and the later French thinker Jean-Jacques Rousseau (1712–1788). The three major social-contract theorists are united not only by their common concerns—to identify the purpose of government in general and the nature of political obligation in particular—but also by common methodology and symbolism. The present chapter will examine the views of Hobbes and Locke, which are of special relevance to the American experience. Rousseau profoundly influenced modern political developments, particularly in Continental Europe and nations influenced by Continental thought. His work, however, had little relevance to our central concern—American political thought of the founding era—and the discussion will thus be confined to his English predecessors.

The Nature of Contractual Agreement

An examination of the Hobbesian and Lockean versions of the social contract begins with an examination of the general meaning of "contract." A contract is a particular kind of legal agreement between two or more parties specifying rights and obligations voluntarily acquired and assumed by the contracting parties. Contractual rights and obligations are typically qualified by the elements of reciprocity and conditionality, as readily illustrated by common contractual agreements such as leasing an apartment or automobile.[7] Consider the case of a person who enters into a contract to lease an apartment. The written agreement is, of course, voluntarily signed by all contracting parties, in this case, the renter and the owner (lessee and lessor), who thereby establish mutual and reciprocal legal commitments. More particularly, the renter, the lessee, commits to pay a specified sum of money for the use of a specified apartment for a specified period of time. The owner, the lessor, commits to provide the lessee with a specified apartment for a specified sum of money for a specified period of time. All relevant specifications are enumerated in the contract itself. As a consequence of signing the lease, both parties acquire certain rights and assume certain obligations. The lessee acquires the right to live in the specified apartment for a specified period of time; and the lessor acquires the right to receive the specified amount of money from the lessor. The lessee assumes the obligation to pay the lessor the specified amount of money, and the lessor assumes the obligation to provide the lessee with the specified apartment.

The next issue concerns the nature of the mutual rights and obligations acquired and assumed by the contracting parties. There are two possibilities in this regard: rights and obligations may be either *absolute* or *conditional*. An absolute right or obligation is one that binds regardless of any and all circumstances or considerations. The exercise of an absolute right or fulfillment of an absolute obligation does not depend on any conceivable conditions or contingencies. Nothing can interfere with the exercise of an absolute right or abrogate the duty of fulfilling an absolute obligation. Such rights and obligations are unconditional, that is, they are absolute.

The rights and obligations normally acquired as a result of contractual agreement are emphatically not of this nature but exemplify, on the contrary, the second, and opposing, possibility—conditionality. Contractual rights and obligations are generally conditional rights and obligations. The renter in our example does not acquire a right to live in the apartment under any and all circumstances nor does he assume an obligation to pay the agreed-upon rent under any and all circumstances. The owner, correspondingly, does not acquire a right to receive the agreed-upon rent under any and all circumstance nor does she assume the obligation to provide the specified apartment under any and all circumstances. The rights and obligations acquired and assumed by parties entering into contractual agreement are conditional, that is, contingent or dependent upon the existence of certain circumstances or conditions.

In the case under discussion, the renter's right to occupy the apartment specified in the lease is contingent upon fulfillment of his contractual obligation to pay the specified monthly rent. The owner's right to receive a certain sum of money each month is contingent upon fulfillment of her contractual obligation, namely, to provide the renter with the apartment specified in the lease. The contractual obligations assumed by both parties are also conditional or contingent. The renter's obligation to pay the rent depends upon whether the owner has fulfilled her contractual obligation, that is, actually provided the renter with the specified apartment. In the same manner, the owner's obligation to provide the renter with the specified apartment is contingent upon whether the renter has fulfilled his contractual obligation, that is, actually paid the specified rent. The rights and obligations acquired by the contracting parties are conditional rights and obligations; their binding quality is contingent upon the actions of the respective parties. A renter who does not pay his rent dissolves the owner's moral and legal obligation to provide him with the apartment. An owner who fails to provide the renter with the specified apartment absolves the renter from his moral and legal obligation to pay the rent. Every court in the land adjudicates contract law in this manner. Finally, the rights and obligations acquired and assumed by means of contractual agreement are not only conditional but also reciprocal, that is, mutually obligatory and mutually binding on all parties. The rights and obligations of the renter presuppose corresponding rights and obligations on the part of the owner; the owner's rights and obligations presuppose corresponding rights and obligations on the part of the renter.

Having examined the general nature of a contract—a voluntary agreement between two or more parties that establishes conditional and reciprocal rights and obligations—the next task is to apply the concept of contract to the social institution called "government."

The Hobbesian Social Contract

Early-modern social contract theory, as we have seen, was inspired by the rise of political absolutism in the wake of the Protestant Reformation and during the Renaissance. Hobbes and Locke offered rival responses to the great question of the day: What is the nature of political obligation? Must the people obey government absolutely, as the Stuarts and other monarchs of the era claimed, or is the duty to obey contingent upon circumstances of one kind or another? Is political obligation absolute or conditional? Hobbes will defend the monarchical claim to absolute sovereignty; Locke will repudiate political absolutism in no uncertain terms.

We begin with an examination of the Hobbesian version of the social contract, which was published several decades prior to Locke's and is essential background to the latter's interpretation. In 1651, toward the end of the English Civil War, Hobbes published his political masterwork, *Leviathan or The Matter, Forme and Power of a Common Wealth Ecclesiasticall and Civil*, wherein he champions the legitimacy and necessity of political absolutism. He develops his argument by employing certain traditional symbols characteristic of modern social-contract theory, in particular, the so-called *state of nature* and *law of nature*. The state of nature is a conventional term employed by Western thinkers to represent the pre-political condition of mankind, that is, the state of human society thought to exist prior to the formal establishment of government. The symbol of the law of nature classically refers to objective, binding, and universal rules of moral conduct deduced by reason and independent of human preference. Such moral values and rules are held to be both inherent to human nature and universally recognizable as such by virtue of the universal human capacity for reason.

Hobbes, like other social-contract theorists, addresses the issue of political obligation by inviting his readers to consider the nature of human existence in a society without established governmental institutions. The picture of the state of nature he develops has achieved nothing less than classic status in Western political thought. According to Hobbes, society without government is a sad, sorry, and dangerous place, utterly devoid of law, order, morality, and justice. Every individual in the state of nature is rather driven by unbridled lust for power after power, by the passion to fulfill his massive and inordinate desires, and do so, if need be, at the expense of every other individual. The complete absence of law, order, and morality eliminates the fundamental requisite of civilized life, namely, basic security of person and property. Existence in the state of nature thus precludes the possibility of civilizational development, of the cultivation of the arts and sciences, trade and commerce. The chaos of anarchy reduces if not eliminates the possibility of satisfying even basic requirements of social existence, let alone achieving its graces and luxuries. In Hobbes's famous description, life in the state of nature is reduced to a perpetual "war of all against all," an existence that is "solitary, nasty, brutish, and short."[8] We previously mentioned Thucydides' earlier depiction of the Hobbesian conception—a state of existence wherein "the strong do what they can and the weak suffer what they must"—a social state in which might makes right.[9]

The transition from such barbarism and anarchy to civilized society, Hobbes maintains, is only made possible by voluntary establishment of absolute government, one that brooks no resistance and whose laws are unconditionally binding on each and every member of society. Law is as crucial to civilization as government, but, according to Hobbes, law does not and cannot exist apart from established government. Government makes the law and also enforces it, meting out punishment to lawbreakers; for Hobbes as for Augustine, government is the executioner who wields the sword of force against evildoers. Contrary to Augustine, however, Hobbes regards secular government as both maker and enforcer of law, that is, as the *ultimate* source of social order. The Hobbesian view assumes or implies that the sole motivation capable of restraining violent and predatory behavior is the threat of human punishment. Government's role is precisely to pose such a threat by administering the coercive force of law.

As the sole and indispensable source of law and order, government, the "Sovereign," is thus entitled to demand absolute obedience to its rules and commands from every member of society. There can be no possibility of a right to resist lawful governmental authority or indeed to claim any rights against Leviathan, the "mortal god." The assertion of rights—of moral entitlement to certain treatment—against an absolute sovereign would undermine its authority. It would weaken the sense of obligation to obey the exclusive source of law and order, which in turn would lead back to the anarchy of the state of nature. Hobbes thus insists that no challenge or resistance to lawful government is permissible, under any circumstances. The obligation to obey the Sovereign must be regarded as absolute.

Hobbes's solution to the purported anarchic barbarism of the state of nature, then, is the establishment of government, an absolute Sovereign, by voluntary agreement among the subjects, that is, by a social contract. The vast majority of people, he suggests, will undoubtedly prefer the security of person and property provided by the sovereign government over the violent chaos of the state of nature. The terms of the Hobbesian social contract involve several key elements. First, each individual in the state of nature agrees to an equal and universal abdication of his "rights." Second, the individuals mutually agree to establish a Sovereign whose task henceforth is to make and enforce the law in the interest of securing peace and order. As Hobbes put it,

> The commonwealth is instituted when all agree in the following manner: I authorise and give up my right of governing myself to this man, or to this assembly of men, on this condition; that thou give up, thy right to him, and authorise all his actions in like manner. This done, the multitude so united in one person, is called, a COMMONWEALTH . . . This is the generation of the great LEVIATHAN, or rather, to speak more reverently, of that mortal god, to which we own under the immortal God, our peace and defense.[10]

Each person agrees to relinquish his individual right to self-government so long as everyone else does the same. The rights of the individuals are then transferred, so to speak, to the newly created Sovereign, however institutionally organized, which is then entitled to rule as it sees fit, having been "authorised" to do so by the terms of the social contract. Having authorized all future actions of the Sovereign by agreeing to the initial contract, all persons henceforth are forbidden to criticize let alone actively resist the absolute Sovereign. The Hobbesian social contract is further characterized by the peculiar fact that the Sovereign it establishes is not itself party to the contract. The only parties to the Hobbesian contract are the individuals who agree among themselves to establish the Sovereign in the first place. The government thus established, the "mortal god," is not party to the contract but rather the creation thereof, which means that the Sovereign is not bound by contractual obligations to the people but permitted to do as it pleases. Such a feature is considered essential to realization of the Sovereign's purpose—securing peace and order by lawful suppression of wrongdoers.

We note in this context that Hobbes, while a champion of absolute government, is not an advocate of unlimited or *totalitarian* government. The two concepts—absolutism and totalitarianism—are often conflated in the popular mind, but there is a clear distinction between them. A totalitarian government is one that claims the moral right to control every aspect of human existence; it claims the right of total control over society and acknowledges no pre-existing moral limits to its power or authority. A totalitarian government, in other words, is an unlimited government. An absolute government, by contrast, is one that demands unconditional obedience to its laws and decrees; it acknowledges no right of resistance to law or government on the part of the people. This is Hobbes's preferred system. He is not an advocate of totalitarian rule but rather conceives the range of governmental authority in a more or less traditional—limited—sense. Hobbes, like Augustine and various medieval thinkers, tended to regard government as "defender of the peace," its role more or less limited to suppression of evildoers bent on harming peaceful and innocent persons.[11]

Seventeenth-century English society was rooted in such traditional political conceptions. Its problem was not the problem of modern and postmodern society—the rise of totalitarian or unlimited government. Hobbes does not chiefly address the *extent* of political authority, the issue of limited versus unlimited government, but rather the nature of political obligation, a different, if related, issue. Indeed one suspects that Hobbes and his contemporaries gave precious little thought to the modern phenomenon of totalitarianism. The laws to be established and enforced by the Hobbesian Sovereign do not aim to govern every aspect of human existence but rather resemble traditional Judeo-Christian moral injunctions against violation of other persons (thou shalt not kill, steal, lie, and so on). Hobbes did advocate governmental control of religion, precisely as demanded by the Stuart monarchs and other rulers of the period, but he was not an apologist for unlimited or totalitarian government. He was an absolutist who nevertheless envisioned limited government along lines more or less traditional for his time.

Hobbes's vision of human nature and his corollary argument for absolute government possess a certain plausibility and even seem to be confirmed by historical experience. Consider, for instance, the catastrophic event of Hurricane Katrina, which devastated New Orleans in 2005. For a short period, certain parts of the city came to resemble a Hobbesian state of nature—a state of society with no operative institutions of formal government. Everyone recalls the chaos that prevailed in the initial days following landfall. The city of New Orleans, including the local government, was brought to its knees. Police and other officials responsible for administration of justice fled the city, as did many ordinary citizens. The world witnessed a breakdown of law and order that were not restored for days or even weeks. The nation was horrified by incomprehensible images of hoodlums attempting to shoot down helicopters rescuing stranded children from local hospitals. Looting and other forms of lawlessness were common. Similar scenes emerged in the immediate aftermath of the American invasion of Baghdad in 2003. The Iraqi government was toppled, and certain quarters of the city seemed to return to a Hobbesian state of nature. The world watched as museum treasures were looted, property violated, and a general sense of lawlessness spread throughout the city. Hobbes would not be surprised. Anarchic violence in the absence of government, such as that which erupted in New Orleans and Baghdad, is precisely what a Hobbesian would expect. Hobbes seems vindicated.

Such a conclusion, however, may be based more on appearance than reality; the events described do not necessarily support the view that absolute government is essential for civilization. The main problem with the Hobbesian argument arises from its excessive generalization. Hobbes identifies an undeniable propensity of certain individuals—the propensity to engage in lawless behavior absent a threat of human punishment (government)—and assumes that all or most people do or will behave in such a manner under similar conditions. Experience, however, shows that this is far from true; the threat of human punishment is not the only reason human beings refrain from violating their fellows. Not everyone resorts to predatory behavior the moment such a threat is removed, the moment government is incapacitated, as is also and clearly confirmed by experience in New Orleans and Baghdad. Most people during those chaotic days and weeks were not molesting other persons or violating their property but no doubt hiding in fear, hoping for imminent rescue by local authority. Only a relatively small number of people grasped the opportunity created by the disastrous circumstances to engage in violent and lawless behavior. Hobbes's vision of human nature does contain a partial truth—some people will indulge a lust for power and violence in the absence of the threat of human punishment. There will always be a certain segment of the populace that recognizes no moral law but the law of the club. History, however, the record of human experience, shows that most people, most of the time, do not behave in such a manner, a fact undoubtedly related to the influence of moral, religious, and other cultural norms. In any event, it seems fair to conclude that Hobbes erred in erecting his entire political edifice on the propensities and behavior of the few and discounting the role of religion and culture in shaping human behavior. Such a conclusion is not proven but strongly supported, at least for American patriots, by the additional fact that both Locke and the Americans would roundly and unequivocally reject Hobbes's argument. If Locke and the Americans are right, then Hobbes is wrong.

The Lockean Social Contract

Locke, in dramatic contrast to Hobbes, rejects the concept of absolute sovereignty root and branch and vigorously defends the right of resistance to political authority. His most important writing on this topic is the previously mentioned *Second Treatise of Government*. Significant excerpts of the work were widely circulated in the American colonies in the decades leading up to the War of Independence, chiefly through a series of pamphlets known as *Cato's Letters* (1720–1723), estimated to have been found in at least 50 percent of colonial homes.[12] Over time, the ideas and arguments articulated in the *Second Treatise* would saturate American consciousness. Lockean concepts and ideals found expression not only in political polemic of the revolutionary period but also official documents of the era, for instance, the constitutions of the newly independent states and the American Declaration of Independence. An examination of Locke's *Treatise* thus provides important insight into the convictions that impelled the American colonists to take their improbable stand against the most powerful government of the era.

Locke, like Hobbes, is a social-contract theorist, and he too develops the argument of the *Second Treatise* by employing the symbolism characteristic of that tradition, the state of nature and law of nature. He begins the *Treatise* with a forthright statement of its purpose—to examine the validity of claims of political absolutism. Locke, like Hobbes, approaches this issue by imaginatively reconstructing the process by which formal institutions of government might have come into existence. Such "conjectural history," he suggests, should shed light on the purpose of government, which in turn should shed light on the main subject of interest—the nature of political obligation.[13] Thus Locke, like Hobbes, invites the reader to imagine a state of society in which formal institutions of government have not yet been established, the pre-political state of nature. Hobbes's portrayal of the state of nature—the amoral, lawless, and anarchic "war of all against all"—led, as we have seen, to an ardent defense of absolute government. Locke's vision of the state of nature is entirely different and will lead to an entirely different conclusion.

The starkly opposing conclusions reached by Hobbes and Locke concerning the nature of political obligation—the kind of obligation government can rightfully demand from individual members of society—follow from their fundamentally opposing conceptions of human nature and social existence. Locke follows Aristotle and Aquinas in regarding man, by nature, as a political and social animal; Hobbes embraces the opposing view of the ancient Cynics and also Rousseau, who regarded man as a fundamentally solitary being.[14] Hobbes was widely believed to be an atheist. Locke, the son of a Puritan dissenter, held a more or less conventional Christian view of human beings, that is, creatures made in the image of God, endowed with reason and free will. As he says in the *Second Treatise*, "For God having given man an understanding to direct his actions, has allowed him a freedom of will, and liberty of acting. . . ."[15] According to Locke, freedom and rationality are inherent to human nature; human beings, he maintains, "are born free, as [they] are born rational." Human nature is further characterized by attributes of universality and equality. The state of nature, Locke says, is not only a state of "perfect freedom" but also radical and universal equality, one in which "all the power and jurisdiction is reciprocal."[16] Locke emphatically denies that God divinely appointed one person or group to rule over other persons.[17] Indeed, he denies that God intended any person or persons to rule over any other person, however such rule is achieved or sanctioned. All human beings are rather God's "property," put on this earth to go about his business and not that willed by other human beings:

> For men being all the workmanship of one Omnipotent, and infinitely wise maker; all the servants of one Sovereign Master, sent into the world by his order and about his business; they are his property, whose workmanship they are, made to last during his, not one another's pleasure. And being furnished with like faculties, sharing all in one community of Nature, there cannot be supposed any such subordination among us, that may authorize us to destroy one another, as if we were made for one another's uses.[18]

Locke suggests that "all men are created equal," a substantive equality of value that derives from the universal spiritual equality of man, the equality of man before God. Human beings belong not to other human beings but rather to God and to themselves (the right of self-possession). There is no question of a "divine right" to rule, as asserted by Stuart and other monarchs of the period. Locke contends, on the contrary, that the legitimacy of political rule invariably requires consent of the governed: "[m]en being . . . by Nature, all free, equal and independent, no one can be . . . subjected to the political power of another, without his own consent."[19]

Such presuppositions and convictions led Locke to develop an image of the state of nature dramatically at odds with that of Hobbes. The Lockean state of nature is not a Hobbesian "war of all against all" but rather a relatively benign society inhabited by free, rational, equal human beings, each of whom is born to fulfill a divinely established purpose. Nor is the state of nature, as Hobbes claims, an anarchic state of license, devoid of law and morality. According to Locke, pre-political society is governed, on the contrary, by a moral law, a universal law that exists prior to, and independent of, established institutions of government, namely, the law of nature. The "state of Nature," he emphatically declares, "has a law of nature to govern it," a moral law that every human being can recognize and acknowledge.[20] Such a capacity follows from the fact that all human beings possess reason, the faculty that enables every person to apprehend the moral order inherent to existence. Every rational creature not only recognizes the existence of a given moral order but also possesses knowledge of its substance:

> [Since] every one . . . is bound to preserve himself, and not to quit his station willfully [because this would be to violate God's property] so by the like reason when his own preservation comes not in competition, ought he, as much as he can, to preserve the rest of mankind, and may not unless it be to do justice on an offender, take away, or impair the life, or what tends to the preservation of the life, liberty, health, limb or goods of another.[21]

Such, according to Locke, is more or less the first principle of the law of nature, governing in the state of nature as in every state of human society. Every person knows that he himself does not want other persons to harm his life, liberty, health, or property. Thus every person knows that other human beings, who share the same human nature, also do not want to be harmed in their lives, liberty, health, or property. All men possess reason and thus all men recognize the moral obligation to do unto others as they themselves would be done by. Locke, unlike Hobbes, does not regard the establishment of law, and thus order, as dependent on prior establishment of formal human government. Rather, on his view, the converse is true: the establishment of government is dependent on pre-established law, the moral law: the "state of Nature [already] has a law to govern it."

Locke did not originate the concept of the moral law of nature but inherited it from a well-developed Western tradition of moral and political discourse. The symbol of the law of nature was first advanced by the ancient Greeks, impressively elaborated by the Roman Stoics (most notably the Roman orator Cicero [106–43 B.C.]), and later incorporated into the Christian tradition as the "unwritten" law embedded in the heart of man and similar constructs.[22] During the Middle Ages Thomas Aquinas (1225–1274), the "Angelic Doctor," provided Christian civilization with a philosophical elaboration of the natural law that remains a characteristic element of Roman Catholic teaching to the present day. Locke's particular formulation of the law of nature, then, carried forward a long-standing tradition that ascribes an intrinsic moral dimension to human nature. All human beings, regardless of culture, religious belief, biology, or any other circumstances, are thought to possess an inherent ability to distinguish between right and wrong. All human beings possess the rational capacity to recognize the bounds of moral action one toward another. Every human being knows that he is not to violate another person; every human being knows, as Locke says, that he is obliged, "as much as he can, to preserve the rest of mankind."[23] Moreover, Locke further maintains, human freedom itself is dependent upon man's rational ability to apprehend the law of nature: "The freedom . . . of man and liberty of acting according to his own will, is grounded on his having reason, which is able to instruct him in that law he is to govern himself by, and make him know how far he is left to the freedom of his own will."[24]

The Lockean state of nature, then, is as different from the Hobbesian variant as the different conceptions of human nature and social existence presupposed by the two thinkers. The rational and orderly state of pre-political society conceived by Locke knows nothing of Hobbesian anarchy and lawlessness. Every person is endowed with reason and thus the capacity to recognize the given moral law, established by an authority superior to human preference or will. Every person knows that life is to be preserved, that people are not to harm one another without just cause. All human beings exercise their freedom on the basis of perfect spiritual equality; no person is inherently entitled to exercise dominion over another. Locke further assumes the spiritual significance of every individual, each of whom is charged with fulfilling the purpose for which God created him. The Lockean state of nature is a lawful spiritual community rooted in the brotherhood of man, conceived as common children of one divine Father and equally subject to His law.

"Inconveniences" of the State of Nature

Locke's benign portrayal of pre-political society raises an interesting question: why would human beings choose to leave the state of nature and agree to live under established government (a state that Locke terms "civil" or "political" society")? What would motivate them to relinquish a state of perfect freedom and equality, inhabited by rational persons who recognize the moral law? The answer to this question is all-important, not only for the cogency of Locke's account but also the achievement of his overarching goal—to identify the nature of political obligation. A discovery of the purpose for which men compact to form government, he suggests, will shed significant light on the moral duty owed to that government by members of society.[25] Locke's careful analysis of such issues led him to develop a view of political order that shaped not only American founding principles and practice but also modern Western order to the present day.

We have seen that existence in the Lockean state of nature is relatively congenial and even pleasant, certainly in contrast to the Hobbesian conception. Nevertheless, Locke says, certain "inconveniences" arise within the state of nature that inevitably detract from its more desirable aspects. Such inconveniences lead men to conclude that the conditions of existence could be even further improved by voluntary establishment of certain formal institutions of government. More particularly, the three "inconveniences" identified by Locke are remedied by establishment of the three branches of government characteristic of modern Anglo-American political order.

The first inconvenience, Locke says, arises from the moral law, the law of nature that governs the state of nature and whose general principle (life is to be preserved, so far as possible) is recognized by every human being. The problem posed by the law of nature involves the application of that general principle to particular situations and circumstances. The precise entailments of the moral law are not always obvious or clear. The law of nature establishes only general principles of morality, not a detailed code of law, and thus does not provide unequivocal guidance in each and every particular instance. Persons of equally good faith may disagree on the requirements of the general moral law in particular situations. An example relevant to contemporary society is the present controversy over the death penalty. The morality of capital punishment is not self-evident to all members of American society; valid moral arguments can be, and have been, made on both sides of the issue. We have seen, however, that one of the essential requirements of law is certainty. Vague and shifting rules cannot provide stable guidance for human action and inevitably lead to confusion or even chaos and injustice. To remedy the inconvenience arising from the generality of the law of nature, Locke recommends the voluntary establishment of an organization whose specific task is to declare the law, to clarify precisely the individual's rights and responsibilities under the law and the penalties attached to its violation. Such an organization is, of course, represented by the "legislative" branch of government (from the Latin, *leges*—enactments of a constitutional authority such as Congress or Parliament). The "want of a known, certain, established law" in the state of nature, as Locke put it, is to be remedied by the creation of the first of the three traditional branches of government, the legislature.

The second inconvenience of the state of nature arises from the irremediable problem of human partiality. Western law has long upheld the common-sense principle that no person is permitted to be a judge in his own case. No party to a legal or moral conflict is capable of the impartiality requisite to justice. Every person involved in such conflict believes, on the contrary, that right and justice lie on his side. In the state of nature, as in every human society, conflict between persons, conflict that may simply arise from the circumstances of human existence, inevitably raises its head. Suppose, for instance, two individuals who live side-by-side in the state of nature, their adjoining properties separated by a small stream. Further suppose that both individuals are sincerely convinced that the stream belongs to their respective properties. Both parties cannot be right, yet both believe they are right and their individual claims just. (Even in the case where legislation relevant to the conflict might exist, the two parties may disagree on its meaning or interpretation.) Who is to decide which party actually holds the legitimate claim in law and justice? In the state of nature, there is no established institution that may be called upon to resolve the conflict in an impartial manner, that is, impartially interpret and adjudicate the law. Locke proposes a remedy. All members of society would be better off, he suggests, if they agree to create a second organization and assign to it the specific task of adjudication. What is needed is a disinterested third party, an impartial agent who can examine conflicting claims in light of the facts and the law and decide which party actually holds a valid claim to justice. Such of course is the traditional role of the judge. The remedy for human partiality (as well as conflicting interpretation of law) in the state of nature, then, is the creation of the second traditional branch of government, the judiciary.

The third and final inconvenience of the state of nature is of special importance for Locke's theory of government. The state of nature, as we have seen, is governed by law—the law of nature, rules of right and wrong valid for all times and all places, moral rules that exist prior to the establishment of government and that can be recognized through the human capacity of reason. The other side of the law of nature, as conceived by Locke, is the corresponding conception of "natural rights," previously encountered in our discussion of freedom. Natural rights, as we recall, are moral entitlements inherent to human nature and thus existing prior to and independent of government and social arrangements. According to Locke, each individual possesses specific natural rights—the celebrated trilogy of "life, liberty, and property" that would become central to the moral and political worldview of the American colonists, revolutionaries, and Founders.

The possession by every individual of natural rights has profound implications for social life in both the state of nature and civil society. We first examine its significance for the state of nature. Every person, says Locke, has a natural right to life, to liberty, and to property, all of which, like traditional American rights, are negative rights. We have previously discussed the practical entailments of negative rights—one person's rights are secure if and only if all other persons refrain from actions that violate the possessor's rights. In the case of the natural right to life, this means that the individual's right is secure so long as others refrain from killing him or otherwise endangering his life. A right to life can only be meaningful or secure, however, if its bearer also possesses the right to defend himself against those who would unjustly destroy his existence. Thus, according to Locke, the natural right to life implies the existence of a corollary right—the right to defend one's life against unjust violation, that is, the right of self-defense. "Self defence," he clearly states, "is a part of the law of nature."[26]

The individual's possession of a right of self-defense, however, raises a great inconvenience in the state of nature. Suppose a solitary individual walking along a deserted road is suddenly confronted by another person, strong and powerful, who leaps upon him with the clear intent to kill. According to Locke, the victim possesses a natural right to defend himself against such an aggressor. The moral law is unequivocally on his side, and he would be justified in killing the aggressor if that should be necessary to preserve his own life. It is possible, however, that the innocent person cannot exercise his natural right of self-defense because he is physically unable to do so; perhaps he is substantially weaker than the attacker and thus incapable of overcoming his aggression. Under such circumstances, the victim may meet his Maker in clear conscience, knowing that he himself has committed no violation, but his existence has nevertheless been destroyed. Transcendent justice is all-important but the right to live on this earth is also important. The victim's natural right to exist has been invalidated merely by his relative physical disadvantage. This is wrong; it is unjust. The potential to experience similar injustice, moreover, exists for many individuals in the state of nature. All relatively weaker persons will be unable physically to defend themselves against relatively stronger predators; the right to life of such persons will be as insecure as the victim under discussion. Many individuals will thus have an interest in remedying this particular inconvenience. Locke again suggests a solution.

The individual's natural rights to life, liberty, and property, as we recall, are correlative to the law of nature. A person who unjustly destroys the life of an innocent person has violated the fundamental moral law—life is to be preserved so far as possible. In the state of nature, however, there is no established government and thus no organized agent responsible for enforcing the moral law. Not only the right but also the responsibility to enforce the law remains in the possession of each individual. Each individual, as Locke puts it, personally possesses the right to "execute" the law of nature, that is, administer justice to those who violate it. In the case under discussion, as we have seen, the individual unjustly attacked may enforce his right to life even to the extent of killing his attacker, if such is necessary to preserve his own life. In the absence of formal governmental institutions, responsibility for enforcing the law necessarily falls upon the individual right-bearer.

That said, however, there is an alternative open to those individuals who do not possess sufficient physical strength to serve as effective enforcers of their rights: such individuals may *delegate* or transfer their natural right to execute the law of nature to another party. Because each individual possesses a natural right to self-defense, each individual may legitimately delegate that right to another agent acting on his behalf, perhaps a person he considers more capable of enforcing it. An elderly grandmother, for instance, might choose to delegate her right of self-defense to her adult grandson, who is probably physically stronger than she. If she chooses such an option, and if the grandson agrees to her request, she herself would not personally have to tackle an aggressor who threatens her life. Her grandson could engage in such action as her authorized delegate or agent, securing his grandmother's right to life by disarming or even killing the predator. Such action on his part would be perfectly legitimate. The grandson is the grandmother's delegated agent or trustee, whom she has specifically authorized to exercise her natural right of self-defense on her behalf. The grandson's (delegated) right to use force against a predator derives from his grandmother's right to use force against a predator.[27] Indeed, it might be said that the two apparent rights are, in reality, one and the same—the grandmother's natural right of self-defense.

We are now prepared to examine Locke's proposed solution to the third and final inconvenience of the state of nature. Most individuals, he suggests, would be better off, that is, have greater security for their natural rights, if they agree to the following condition. Each individual voluntarily delegates or transfers his natural right of self-defense to a common agent created by mutual agreement among all parties to the compact. Such an agent will thus embody collectively the natural right of self-defense possessed by each individual participant in the compact. Henceforth, in the event an individual's right to life (or liberty or property) is threatened by an aggressor, he or she will no longer bear the personal responsibility of executing the law, that is, personally overcoming the assailant. Instead, each individual can now call upon the communal agent of defensive coercive force, whose task is precisely to execute the law on behalf of each individual, just as the grandson enforced the law on behalf of his grandmother. The organized agent's (delegated) right to use force against predators derives from the contracting individuals' natural right to use force against predators. Again, the two apparent rights—of the delegator and the delegatee—are, in reality, one and the same right—the natural right of self-defense possessed by every individual. Each individual delegates that right to the collective agent in order to provide greater security for his natural rights than is possible in the state of nature, where he and every other individual must personally enforce the law.

The organized embodiment of the collective defensive force of the community is, of course, represented by the third traditional branch of government, the executive branch—the executive agencies responsible for "law enforcement." Simply put, and in contemporary language, a person whose life is threatened by a predator is not personally required to forcibly defend his life but can instead call "911." The police, the organized collective force of the community, stand ready to assist him, in this case, to protect his right to life. The police are morally authorized to use coercive force against aggressors because every individual is morally authorized to use such force; the police, as said, are simply exercising the individual's natural right of self-defense on his behalf. The right of the police to use force against aggressors, like the right of the grandson in our example, is not an inherent but rather delegated right that derives from the individual's natural right of self-defense. The police, like the grandson, simply enforce the individual rights of self-defense delegated or entrusted to them by the individual members of the community. They execute the law of nature on the individual's behalf, as he has authorized by agreeing to the terms of the social compact. The organized agent of law enforcement, the executive branch of government, thus arises as a remedy for the third and final inconvenience of the state of nature: the insecurity of rights engendered by the individual's responsibility to execute the law of nature on his own behalf. The executive's purpose and responsibility is to enforce the law as the delegated agent of the individual parties to the compact and do so, moreover, in the interest of securing their natural rights.

In sum, the three inconveniences of the state of nature—lack of a known, settled, established law; lack of an impartial adjudicator of the law; and lack of individual ability to enforce or execute the law—are remedied by the voluntary establishment of three organizations traditionally regarded as the three branches of government—the legislature, judiciary, and executive. The purpose of such organizations, the reason for their creation, is clear and unequivocal—to better secure the natural rights to life, liberty, and property possessed by each individual but rendered insecure by the intrinsic inconveniences of the state of nature. The law of nature, as we have seen, establishes and secures correlative individual natural rights; tripartite government is instituted to ensure the more effective administration of the law that secures such rights. On the Lockean view, government is thus conceived as a utilitarian organization voluntarily established by the people to serve their purpose, namely, greater security of their natural rights, and to do so by articulating (legislature), adjudicating (judiciary), and enforcing (executive) the law that protects such rights. Its authority derives solely from its creator. Government has no life or force or authorization apart from that delegated or entrusted to it by the people, for a specific purpose, through voluntary agreement or consent. That purpose is clear, defined, and limited—to secure the individual's natural rights to life, liberty, and property by securing the rule of law.

As Locke himself summarizes the leading idea, "the great and chief end . . . of men's uniting into commonwealths, and putting themselves under government, is the preservation of their property."[28] His use of the word "property" in this context has led various commentators to accuse Locke of championing a materialistic if not vulgar conception of government, one whose main purpose is to protect the mere accumulation of material wealth. Such, however, is not Locke's meaning. Locke employs the term "property" in a broad sense that comprises, as he says, "life, liberty, and estate."[29] Locke's "estate" is equivalent to the contemporary conception of material property or possession. Contemporary usage, however, does not generally regard an individual's "property" as including his life and liberty, as does Locke. In so doing, he speaks the language of an older tradition. The word "property" derives from the Latin word *proper* (self). "Property" thus refers to all that rightly belongs to a self, a person, and this, for Locke, includes not only his material possessions or estate but also his life and his liberty. Locke, as we recall, regards every individual as ultimately the "property" of God. The practical effect of such a belief, Locke suggests, is the individual's rightful claim to "self-possession" within historical existence: no person belongs to another person but rather each person owns himself.[30] Such personal ownership includes his very being or existence, his very life, as well as the exercise of his liberty. Such qualities inhere in the self proper, belong to the individual self by nature, and thus, along with material possessions or estate, constitute "property" in the wide or traditional sense of the term.

To recapitulate Locke's argument thus far: Human beings in the state of nature, born free, rational, equal, and independent, possess certain natural rights, to life, liberty, and property. They are governed in pre-political society by a moral law—eternal and objective principles of right and wrong, which human beings recognize by means of the universal capacity to reason. No human being has been granted authority or power to govern other human beings. In the state of nature, however, the individuals' natural rights are somewhat insecure, for various reasons. First, there can be ambiguity with respect to the requirements of the moral law in particular situations; second, there is no disinterested judge to determine the locus of justice when conflict arises; and third, mere physical weakness can prevent certain persons from executing the moral law against those who violate their natural rights. These three inconveniences render the individuals' natural rights insecure. Such insecurity can be remedied by a voluntary compact of the people that establishes three utilitarian organizations, a legislature, a judiciary, and an executive, whose responsibilities, respectively, are to declare, adjudicate, and enforce the law. The purpose of establishing the three branches of government is clear and unequivocal—to secure or protect the natural rights of the individual. Such is precisely why individuals compact to form a government, why they agree to leave the state of nature and enter the state of civil or political society. The purpose of government, as Locke says, is the preservation of "property," that which properly belongs to the individual self, namely, life, liberty, and estate.

Terms of the Lockean Contract

Lockean government, like Hobbesian government, arises from social compact or contract, a voluntary agreement comprising the elements of conditionality and reciprocity characteristic of contractual relation as such. The terms of their respective contracts, however, are as different as their respective depictions of human nature and the state of nature. We have discussed the terms of the Hobbesian contract. The next task is to specify more precisely the explicit and implicit terms of the Lockean counterpart.

The parties to the Lockean contract include, on the one hand, those individuals in the state of nature who believe the formal establishment of government will strengthen the security of their rights and, on the other, "government."[31] Every contract, as we have seen, establishes reciprocal rights and obligations for the contracting parties. In the case of the Lockean contract, individuals acquire the right to expect government to employ its coercive power in defense of their natural rights to life, liberty, and property. Government, for its part, acquires the moral and legal right to employ coercive force against those who would violate such rights. The contract also establishes corresponding obligations for both contracting parties. The people have established the government for their purposes and are thus obliged to do what is necessary to enable the government to fulfill those purposes. Such obligation involves the duty to pay taxes to support the government which, as a creature of the people, clearly has no independent means of financing its activities. The people also obligate themselves to obey the laws that the government administers on their behalf, in the interest of protecting their natural rights. Government acquires the corresponding right to expect both payment of taxes in support of its activities and obedience to the laws it administers.

The corresponding contractual obligation assumed by government is to fulfill the purpose for which it was established, namely, protection of the natural rights of the contracting individuals. It is obliged to legislate with the aim of securing the legitimate rights of the individual against violation; to adjudicate the laws thereby established with the aim of securing the legitimate rights of the individual; and to execute the laws for the same purpose. Such is government's contractual responsibility, as the people's delegated agent charged with that specific duty. Government, Locke says, is the "trustee" established by the social contract.[32] Its moral and legal obligation, like that of any contractual trustee, is to protect the interests and welfare of the "trustor," in this case, the individual participants in the compact. Government is a fiduciary entity, bound by the obligation of faith to fulfill the purpose for which it was established—the protection of the property (life, liberty, and estate) of each and every individual.

The contractual rights and obligations acquired and assumed by both parties are conditional rights and obligations, contingent upon the actions of the other contracting party. The government's right to collect taxes and enforce obedience to the laws is not absolute but dependent upon whether it actually fulfills its end of the contract, whether it actually aims to secure the individual rights of the people. Government's obligation—to legislate, adjudicate, and enforce the law that secures individual rights—is similarly conditional. It is contingent upon whether the citizens fulfill their contractual obligations, in particular, pay the taxes necessary to fund the operations of the government. Obviously, government cannot be obliged to fulfill its contractual obligations without resources provided by the people.

The moral and legal obligations assumed by the people—to pay taxes and obey the law—are similarly contingent, that is, dependent upon whether government fulfills its contractual obligation to protect the individuals' natural rights. Their situation is identical to the case of the person who contracts to lease an apartment. As we have seen, the lessee is obliged to pay the specified rent if and only if the lessor fulfills her end of the contract, that is, actually provides the renter with the apartment specified in the contract. In the case of the Lockean contract, the people are obliged to obey and support the government if and only if government fulfills its end of the contract, that is, if and only if it uses its delegated authority and acquired resources to actually secure their rights.

The social contract so conceived imposes intrinsic constitutional limits on the power and authority of government. More specifically, it generates what may be called the Lockean Principle: *government is inherently limited by the ends for which it is created*. Such a principle is implicit in the metaphor of "compact" or "contract" and presupposed by Locke's discussion of the scope of the legislative power formed by the social compact. The fulfillment of government's legitimate legislative purpose, he suggests, will often involve the conventional method of decision-making known as representative majority rule. Everyone realizes the improbability of achieving unanimity with respect to the vast majority of legislative proposals. In agreeing to the social compact, then, the people implicitly agree to be bound by the decisions of the majority in both the original establishment of government and subsequent enactment of law.

Locke, however, contrary to a common misperception, is not an advocate of pure or majoritarian democracy. Although he recognizes the necessity of majority decision-making in certain circumstances, his commendation of majority rule is implicitly qualified by the Lockean Principle as stated. Majority rule is an indispensable tool of representative government but such a decision process raises an obvious danger: the subjugation of the minority by the sheer numerical superiority of the majority. The people presupposed by Locke's account of the rise of government would never agree to a social contract that established unlimited majority rule. Every person readily understands that he may find himself in a minority position at one time or another and that a regime of straightforward majority rule would continually place not only the minority's but any individual's rights at the mercy of the majority. The very purpose of establishing government in the first place is to better secure the natural rights of each and every individual. Pure or majoritarian democracy would provide even less security for natural rights than the state of nature, where the minority and the individual at least possess the right to execute the moral law on their own behalf.

Locke, then, does not advocate unqualified rule by the majority. Majority rule is to prevail but only within the legitimate sphere of legislative competence. Such competence is narrowly bounded by the terms of the social compact, limited to the establishment and administration of law that secures the natural rights of the individual. Law or legislation that ranges beyond that purpose or, worse yet, contradicts it, is beyond the legitimate scope of legislative authority, whether sanctioned by majority approval or not. Moreover, Locke, as we have seen, does not conceive law, law proper, as the product of majority decision. The law that government is established to secure ultimately derives not from man, individually or collectively, but rather from a source beyond human opinion or will. The law of nature embodies timeless moral principles that are independent of human preference, majority or minority. Lockean government, as we recall, does not construct the law from whole cloth but merely declares, adjudicates, and enforces an objective moral law that preexists the institution of government. The law of nature so conceived establishes further intrinsic limits on legislative power, majoritarian or not.

Lockean government is emphatically not a majoritarian democracy in which a numerical majority prevails in every instance. As will be discussed more fully in the following chapter, it is rather a *constitutional* or *liberal* democracy in which majority decisions are bounded by law, both man-made constitutional law and the given law of nature. Majoritarian opinion is to prevail in certain instances, but only within the limited and defined sphere of legitimate governmental authority and only in accord with the higher moral law, the law of nature. Majority decisions are to prevail, moreover, if and only if they further the fundamental purpose of government, the protection of individual natural rights. The legitimate action of government, like the action of any contractually designated trustee, is limited to the purpose for which it is created. A trustee, such as Lockean government, cannot enlarge its power and authority by its own will but is bound, explicitly and implicitly, by the terms of the contract from which its authority derives.

The Right of Resistance

The overarching purpose of Locke's treatises on government, as we have seen, is to answer the burning question of his era—whether the obligation to obey government is absolute, binding on the people in every instance, or conditional, contingent or dependent upon circumstances of one kind or another. Having mentally reconstructed the rise of government and thereby identified the purpose for which it was established, the answer to the question of political obligation, Locke believes, is clear: the obligation borne by the people toward government is unequivocally conditional. Accordingly, he concludes, the people do indeed possess the moral right to resist government under certain circumstances.

We have seen that the obligations voluntarily assumed by those individuals who agree to the Lockean compact consist of the duties to pay requisite taxes and obey the law. Such contractual obligations are conditional. The people are morally bound to pay taxes and obey the law if and only if government fulfills its corresponding contractual obligation, that is, if and only if it actually secures the natural rights of the individuals. A government that fails to secure such rights behaves like a landlord who fails to provide a tenant with the apartment specified in his lease, a failure that releases the tenant from his obligation to pay the rent. The tenant's situation is, of course, analogous to the situation of an individual living under a Lockean government that fails to secure his rights or, worse yet, itself violates his rights. Such failure on the part of government absolves the individual's obligations toward that government, both the payment of taxes and obedience to its laws. The social contract, like the leasing contract, becomes null and void. Thus the people not only have the right but indeed the "duty," as Jefferson says in the Declaration of Independence, to resist a government that fails to honor its fiduciary obligation to secure their individual rights.

Locke is adamant on this point. The *Second Treatise* explicitly discusses various possible situations that can lead to the "dissolution of government." Among such possibilities is the case in which government "act[s] contrary to [its] trust."

> The reason why men enter into society, is the preservation of their property; and the end why they choose and authorize a legislative, is, that there may be laws made, and rules set as guards and fences to the properties of all the members of the society, to limit the power, and moderate the dominion of every part and member of the society. . . . [W]henever the legislators endeavour to take away, and destroy the property of the people, or to reduce them to slavery under arbitrary power, they put themselves into a state of war with the people, who are thereupon absolved from any further obedience, and are left to the common refuge, which God has provided for all men, against force and violence [i.e., resistance, rebellion, revolt]. Whensoever therefore the legislative shall transgress this fundamental rule of society; and . . . endeavour to grasp themselves . . . an absolute power over the lives, liberties, and estates of the people; by this breach of trust they forfeit the power, the people had put into their hands, for quite contrary ends, and it devolves to the people, who have a right to resume their original liberty, and, by the establishment of a new legislative (such as they shall think fit) provide for their own safety and security, which is the end for which they are in society.[33]

Locke's argument should sound familiar to American ears: the argument of the *Second Treatise* is essentially the argument employed by

Americans of the revolutionary period to justify their resistance to the British government. Indeed, Jefferson's eloquent and immortal restatement of the Lockean view is nothing less than the centerpiece of the American Declaration of Independence:

> We hold these truths to be self-evident, that all men are created equal, endowed by their Creator with certain unalienable rights; that among these are life, liberty, and the pursuit of happiness; that to secure these rights, governments are instituted among men, deriving their just powers from the consent of the governed; that whenever a government becomes destructive of these ends, it is the right of the people to alter or abolish it, and to institute new government, laying its foundation on such principles and organizing its powers in such form as to them shall seem most likely to effect their safety and happiness. (Declaration of Independence)

Although the Lockean and American formulations of social contract are justly celebrated for the cogency and elegance of their construction, neither Locke nor the Americans can claim originality of conception. Nor did such modern thinkers invent the right of resistance to unjust or tyrannical government. The Anglo-American social contract and correlative right of resistance are rather rooted in feudal or medieval constructs inherited by the political tradition that significantly informed the views of both Locke and the Americans. Compare the language of Manegold of Lautenbach, the eleventh-century writer who was among the first to employ the language of compact to justify resistance to arbitrary power:

> Just as the royal dignity and power surpasses all earthly powers, so too the man appointed to exercise it should not be base and infamous but should excel others in wisdom, justice and piety as he does in place and dignity. It is necessary, therefore, that the one who is to have charge of all and govern all should display greater virtue than others and should be careful to exercise the power committed to him with a fine balance of equity; for the people do not exalt him above themselves so as to concede to him an unlimited power of tyrannizing over them, but rather to defend them against the tyranny and wickedness of others. However, *when he who is chosen to repress evil-doers and defend the just begins to cherish evil in himself, to oppress good men, to exercise over his subjects the cruel tyranny that he ought to ward off from them, is it not clear that he deservedly falls from the dignity conceded to him and that the people are free from his lordship and from subjection to him since it is evident that he first broke the compact by virtue of which he was appointed. Nor can anyone justly or reasonably accuse the people of perfidy when it is evident that he first broke faith with them....*
>
> . . . Since then no one can make himself an emperor or king, the people raise some man above themselves for these reasons, to rule and govern them by virtue of his just authority, to apportion to each his own, to

> protect the good, to repress the wicked and to deal out justice to all. *If, however, he breaks the compact by which he was elected and ruins and confounds what he was established to order correctly, reason justly considers that he has absolved the people from their duty of submission to him since he himself first broke the bond of mutual fidelity by which he was bound to them and they to him.*[34] [emphasis added]

Locke and Jefferson are scarcely distinguishable from Manegold. The similarity of perspective is not coincidental. The Anglo-American thinkers built on a political tradition significantly informed by Christian-feudal conceptions, including the contractual nature of the relation between rulers and ruled. Manegold, Locke, and the Americans all regard government as a fiduciary agent, a trustee, bound to fulfill its contractual obligations to the people. All agree that a government that fails to do so breaks trust with the people. All agree that such breach of trust on the part of government releases the people from any prior obligations to that government.

Locke and the Americans share various other noteworthy perspectives, including their mutual indifference to Hobbes's chief concern: resistance to government will engender social upheaval, anarchy, and chaos. The Lockean view dismisses such a concern. It rather envisions political resistance with equanimity because, unlike its Hobbesian counterpart, it recognizes a clear distinction between "government" and "society." As Locke said, "He that will with any clearness speak of the dissolution of government, ought, in the first place to distinguish between the dissolution of the society and the dissolution of the government."[35] Thomas Paine's celebrated remark in *Common Sense* is based on the same distinction: "society in every state is a blessing, but Government, even in its best state, is but a necessary evil; in its worst state, an intolerable one."[36] Such views were a commonplace of the revolutionary and founding era.

Defenders of political absolutism and other forms of tyranny, however, were (and are) prone to conflate political order with social order more generally, thereby implying that the dissolution of government necessarily entails the catastrophic dissolution of society itself. Hobbes, again, is characteristic. Although neither Hobbes nor Locke conceive established government as coeval with society, Hobbes conceives government as the exclusive author and enforcer of law and thus the exclusive agent of social order. Locke, by contrast, regards the law of nature as the source of order; the moral law is prior to government and thus society, an orderly community of human beings, is also prior to government. Government, on such a view, is the creator of neither society nor law but rather their creature. Human community, for Locke, is crafted not by mundane political forces but rather, ultimately, by spiritual forces ("we are God's property"). Government is coextensive with neither society nor law but rather a circumscribed entity established by the people, operating within an overarching and pre-existing social order and entrusted with securing a pre-existing order of law.

For such reasons, neither Locke nor the Americans greatly apprehend the consequences of resisting arbitrary government, even to the point of revolution. All that happens in such an event is the dissolution of government and the return of the people, as Locke says, to community within the state of nature. The people are free, so to speak, to try again, that is, establish another governmental organization better designed to secure the safety of their rights. Society and law do not collapse upon dissolution of government but continue to operate in precisely the same manner as in the original state of nature. Not only is American political writing of the revolutionary era replete with passages that reiterate such a view but it is also explicit and implicit in the Declaration of Independence.[37]

> . . . [W]henever any Form of Government becomes destructive of these ends [securing the unalienable rights of the people] it is the Right of the People to alter or to abolish it, and to institute new Government, laying its foundation on such principles and organizing its powers in such form, as to them shall seem most likely to effect their Safety and Happiness. Prudence, indeed, will dictate that Governments long established should not be changed for light and transient causes; and accordingly all experience hath shewn [*sic*] that mankind are more disposed to suffer, while evils are sufferable than to right themselves by abolishing the forms to which they are accustomed. But when a long train of abuses and usurpations, pursuing invariably the same Object evinces a design to reduce them under absolute Despotism, it is their right, it is their duty, to throw off such Government, and to provide new Guards for their future security.[38]

CIVIL SOCIETY AND THE NATURE OF GOVERNMENT

The Lockean distinction between government and society is central to traditional American political thought. It is particularly important for understanding not only the purpose and role of government within American society but also the nature of the institutions collectively categorized as "government." The nature of an entity in this context refers to its defining attributes, the qualities that make an entity what it is, in distinction to other entities. Identifying the nature of government thus involves specification of the unique attributes that differentiate government from every other institution or entity in society. Such a differentiation implicitly informs not only the narrow field of American political thought but also the wider academic discipline of "political science." If government were not distinct from other social institutions, its study could simply be subsumed under a more general field such as history, sociology, or cultural studies. Government, however, is defined by certain unique attributes that require a unique classification and specialized field of study.

An examination of the social institution conventionally termed government requires a preliminary discussion of the general meaning of "social institution." Scholars typically employ the term to refer to a social practice (custom or habit) that has developed over time from an informal and perhaps transitory or sporadic practice to a more structured and enduring feature of society. Educational institutions represent a classic example of a social institution so conceived. In every society, however primitive or sophisticated, parents and other adults have taken care to transmit knowledge of one kind or another to the rising generation. In the early stages of cultural development such transmission of knowledge is usually accomplished informally, irregularly, and perhaps even without deliberate intent. During the course of social and cultural development, however, the transmission of knowledge from generation to generation moves beyond such informal processes and becomes formalized in educational "institutions" (schools, colleges, and so on). Religious institutions possess the same character. People in every society known to history have generally worshiped a deity of one form or another. In early stages of human society, such religious practice is typically customary, informal, and relatively unorganized. Over the course of cultural development, however, such informal religious practices become institutionalized as, for instance, an organized church, synagogue, or mosque. Trade and economic activity provide yet another example of a customary practice that may develop into a social institution. Human beings have always engaged in economic activity, however informally and sporadically. Over the course of social development, however, customary economic practices may develop into formal institutional structures within a society. The organized economic institutions of modern capitalist society, such as governmental provision of a common currency, stock exchanges, banks, and so forth, emerged in precisely such a manner, evolving from informal practice to social institution. Government and law represent further examples of formal social institutions. Authoritative persons (rulers, judges) and informal or customary rules of conduct (law) have existed in every society known to man, but such practices are formalized in relatively stable governmental and legal institutions only over time and in line with cultural development.

A social institution may be further described as an abstract or general structure that persists within a society over time despite the continually changing composition of its individual participants. Particular individuals come and go while the institution itself endures as an identifiable entity or kind of entity. Consider, for example, a typical educational institution such as an established college or university. Assume that the university has recently hired a new faculty member. In most instances, the university will have existed long before the new professor accepts the position and, moreover, is expected to continue in existence after the professor retires, quits, or dies. Similarly, the university probably existed long before matriculation of the present student body and, if successful, will continue to exist as a recognizable entity long after all current students have graduated. Over time, the present faculty and student body will be replaced by other particular faculty members and students, yet, despite such a complete change of personnel, the institution itself endures. Other social institutions have the same character. Religious institutions such as the Church of England, economic institutions such as Microsoft or McDonald's, and governmental institutions such as the Supreme Court of the United States are social structures that persist over time despite the fact that the particular individuals associated with them are continually in flux. The institution of the Supreme Court existed long before the birth of the particular justices who presently serve on the Court and is expected to endure long beyond their tenure.

Every society, then, may be analyzed in terms of its institutional structure so conceived. Such an analysis is particularly helpful for the purpose of the present discussion—to identify the defining attributes of government and differentiate it from other kinds of social institutions. Our particular interest is, of course, American society and the discussion will be confined to its particular institutional structure.

Every member of American society participates in various social institutions throughout the course of life and, indeed, throughout the course of a single day. The first and primary social institution encountered by human beings is the family, an identifiable abstract structure that has existed in every society known to man. The institution of the family persists over time despite the fact that particular families come and go, as do particular individuals within a particular family. The "family" endures as a recognizable social entity even while particular participants are born and pass away. Similarly, many Americans are members of a particular church, a religious institution that probably existed before they themselves joined their church and is expected to continue in existence if and when they themselves are no longer members of the congregation. Most people attend schools at some point in their lives—formal educational institutions ranging from pre-school to post-graduate facilities—schools that existed prior to their enrollment and that are expected to continue in existence when they depart. Most Americans work for a living, that is, participate in business or economic institutions on an ongoing basis, whether as employees or owners of a business enterprise. In the case of those who choose to work for existing institutions, the place of employment (Microsoft or McDonald's) has usually been established long before present employees joined its workforce and, if successful, is expected to exist long after present employees have retired, died, or taken other employment. Entrepreneurs and the self-employed also participate in economic institutions. The abstract structure of a "Mom-and-Pop" grocery store, for instance, is a recognizable social institution that endures over time despite the fact that particular owners of local grocery stores come and go. Other kinds of social institutions in which many people participate on an ongoing basis include non-profit entities and clubs of various kinds—animal-welfare organizations such as the SPCA; the Red Cross; stamp-collectors' clubs; amateur sports teams; political parties; and so on. All such organizations are institutions in the sense that they possess an abstract and identifiable structure that persists over time despite the fact that the particular individuals participating in their respective activities are continually in flux. The Red Cross existed long before most of its present employees were born and is expected to exist long after the present generation has departed this world. The daily activity of most Americans, then, involves participation in numerous social institutions of one kind of another—family, workplace, church, school, and other organizations in which they pursue personal interests with like-minded individuals.

A discussion of social institutions and social structure may seem far removed from the topic of freedom central to this work. Such issues, on the contrary, are intimately related not only to traditional American political principles but also, and in particular, to the issue of freedom in American society. Such linkage is forged by the common attribute shared among the various social institutions that structure typical American experience—family, churches, schools, business enterprises, clubs, and so on—namely, participation in all such institutions is *voluntary*. In a free society such as traditional American society, individuals possess the right to freely choose the institutions with which they associate. No one is forced to work for a particular employer. No one is forced to attend a particular church. No one is forced to attend a particular school (excluding public or government schools, which, as we shall see, fall into a distinct category). No one is forced to do business with a particular firm. No one is forced to join a particular social club or donate to a particular charitable organization. Individuals are free to participate or not, as they think fit. That is only to say that the defining moral attribute of the myriad social institutions that characterize American society—the attribute that establishes institutions as diverse as church, school, business firms, clubs, and so on as members of a unique class—is precisely their common attribute of voluntariness or freedom.

For this reason the social sector carved out by the principle of voluntariness is traditionally if unoriginally designated as the sector of "voluntary association."[39] The attribute of voluntariness, as we have seen, is precisely the defining attribute of traditional American freedom. Individual freedom, along with life and property, are conceived as rights that circumscribe a private sphere wherein the individual may act without fear of arbitrary coercion, that is, voluntarily. Accordingly, the sector of voluntary association is also conventionally designated as the "private sector" of society. The institution of the family is not, strictly speaking, a voluntary association; individuals are born into a particular family without their consent or choice.[40] To account for this fact of life, the biologically based family is usually termed a "natural association."

The sphere of society comprised of the natural and voluntary associations so conceived, eminently characteristic of traditional American society, is formally designated by the term "civil society."[41] Civil society refers to the voluntary or private sphere wherein most daily activities take place in a free society. The designation "private" highlights not only the expectation of noninterference associated with individual rights to life, liberty, and property but also a second defining attribute of civil society. In addition to the moral element of voluntariness, civil society is further distinguished by the characteristic means by which its institutions are funded. The sole source of income or revenue for the associations of civil society—families, churches, schools, business enterprises, clubs, and so on—is the voluntary contributions made by those persons who choose to participate in them. Particular churches are funded by the voluntary contributions of members of their congregations. The family is funded by the income earned by the family's breadwinners. McDonald's is funded by the voluntary purchases of customers who consume its products. Private universities are funded by the students who choose to attend them. The costs of operating the institutions of civil society—the "private sector"—are borne by those persons who directly and voluntarily participate in them. "Private" in this regard refers to the fact that no "public" or governmental funds (e.g., taxes) are used to support the institutions of civil society; they are all, by definition, privately funded.

To this point, the examination of the institutional structure of American society has been limited to the arena of typical daily experience—the natural and voluntary associations of civil society. The sphere of civil society, however, does not encompass the whole of the institutional structure of modern society. There is another distinct class of institutions that form a second sector of society—the so-called public or governmental sector. Governmental institutions are of course a constituent of society as a whole, but they are sufficiently distinct from those that comprise the voluntary or private sector as to form a unique class. We have seen that the defining moral attribute of the institutions of the private sector is their common attribute of voluntariness. Persons who have reached legal maturity are free to participate or not in the institutions of civil society, as they choose. Such, however, is clearly not the case with respect to the institutions of government. Government or the public sector, like the private sector, comprises a myriad of institutions united by two defining attributes, one moral and one practical. The defining moral attribute of the institutions of government, in contrast to the institutions of civil society, is precisely the absence of voluntariness, that is, the omnipresence of coercion, force, or compulsion. The defining practical attribute of governmental institutions, in contrast to the private funding characteristic of civil society, is "public" funding of their operations, that is, taxation and similar methods of obtaining revenue.

The private sector, the voluntary sector, is distinguished by the preclusion of coercion from its sphere—no business, church, or club is permitted to force people to participate in its activities. Individuals are free to enter and exit such institutions at will. The institutions of government, by contrast, possess the legal right to employ coercive force toward achievement of their ends. All government institutions employ the force of law, which, as we have seen, is always backed by a coercive sanction of one form or another. The defining moral attribute of the various institutions that constitute government, then, is the unique legal authority to employ coercion toward realization of their goals. The defining practical attribute of government, the public sector, is the unique means employed to fund its activities and operations—taxation. "Public" in this regard is, of course, the counterpart of "private"; both terms refer to the means of funding the respective activities of the two sectors. The private sector, as discussed, is supported by the voluntary contributions of those persons who choose to participate in the various associations of civil society. The public sector, by contrast, is supported by public funds, the most important source of which is taxes. Taxes are not voluntary contributions but rather payments mandated by the coercive sanction of law. Moreover, unlike the one-to-one correspondence between payment rendered and service received typical of private-sector transactions, there is generally little if any direct correspondence between taxes paid and governmental benefits received. The chief point, however, is that government is distinct from all other institutions in society because only government is permitted the legal use of coercive force. A law enforced by government is not a suggestion but a rule to which a coercive penalty is attached. Only the institutions of government are permitted to employ coercive force with impunity, which places such institutions in a class of their own. As civil society is defined by the moral attribute of voluntariness, so government is defined by the moral attribute of coercion.

Society as a whole, then, consists of two institutional sectors, private and public, voluntary and coercive, civil society and government. American society is, of course, a finite entity, which necessarily generates an inverse relation between the two sectors: the larger the private or voluntary sector, the smaller the public or coercive sector, and, conversely, the smaller the private sector, the larger the public or governmental sector. An ideal or pure communist society, defined by exclusive government ownership and control of all social resources, utterly eliminates the private or voluntary sector; every institution—churches, schools, businesses, and so on—belongs within the governmental, public, or coercive sphere. The opposite extreme, ideal or pure anarchy, defined by the complete absence of government, utterly eliminates the public or coercive sphere; every institution belongs within the voluntary or private sphere. Both pure communism and pure anarchy are best regarded as "ideal types" chiefly useful for purposes of theoretical clarity and explication; few if any actual societies have realized either conception in practice. Communism and anarchy should be regarded as two extremes of a continuum along which most actual societies fall. Most societies have been, and are, characterized by some mixture of private and public sectors. As a general rule, the larger the private or voluntary sector, the more free a society; the larger the public or coercive sector, the less free a society. Such a recognition underlies the apprehension of "Big Government" characteristic of American popular culture.

The political order established by the American Founders, like every form of government, falls along a continuum between the extremes of pure communism and pure anarchy. A pure communist society is one without opportunity for voluntary action, that is, without freedom. A pure anarchic society, by contrast, characterized by the perfect absence of coercion, is a society of perfect freedom. Neither such option relates to the vision or goals of the American Founders. They rejected not only the destruction of freedom inherent in totalitarian rule but also the license of anarchy. The American ideal, as previously discussed, is neither perfect slavery nor perfect freedom but rather liberty-under-law. The Americans aimed to establish conditions that maximize opportunities for voluntary action, and such conditions, as we have seen, necessarily involve the ongoing exercise of coercion. Perfect freedom—the perfect absence of coercion—is neither possible nor desirable, if only because the coercive sanction of law must be employed against criminals and predators who threaten the freedom and other rights of innocent citizens.

A society that aspires to freedom-under-law, as we recall, fights fire with fire. On the traditional American view, government is the agency established by social compact for the purpose of employing the fire of lawful coercion against those persons who would employ the fire of unlawful or arbitrary coercion against their fellow men, thereby violating their natural rights. We have further seen that government's moral authority to employ such defensive coercive force derives from its status as delegated agent (trustee) of the individual's right to self-defense, that is, the individual's moral entitlement to employ coercive force in defense of his natural rights. By agreeing to the social compact, individuals morally authorize government to employ coercive force on their behalf, more particularly, toward protection of their rights. Government is the delegated agent of coercion, in an older language, the wielder of the sword, the hangman and executioner.[42] Coercive power, as Madison and others well understood, is of its essence.

The advocacy of governmental action of any kind is thus always and simultaneously advocacy of the use of coercion. It is to suggest that the activity in question properly belongs not to the sphere of voluntary activity, the private sphere of freedom, but rather the sphere of coercion or compulsion, the public sector. There may be good reason for such advocacy: who among us would not demand the employment of intense coercive force if such would prevent the rape of a child? We have seen, however, that coercion is a tool or strategy that can be employed for both moral and immoral purposes. Coercive power, as Madison warned, "lodged as it must be in human hands, will ever be liable to abuse."[43] Thus, counsels the American tradition, the people must exert "eternal vigilance" against the possibility, and even probability, of the abuse of power by government, a vigilance long acknowledged to be "the price of liberty." It should not be forgotten that advocacy of governmental action is always advocacy of coercion, that is, advocacy of the curtailment of freedom. As such, the question of government's legitimate sphere of activity raises serious moral concerns that deserve equally serious consideration.

NOTES

1. John Grafton, ed, *U.S. Declaration of Independence and Other Great Documents of American History*, 1775–1865 (Mineola, NY: Dover, 2000).
2. And, it has been said, those who tried to remain neutral were mowed down by both sides. I here paraphrase David Walsh, professor of politics, The Catholic University of America.
3. James Madison, *Federalist* No. 47, *Federalist Papers*, 244.
4. *Quod principi placuit legis habet vigore*—Ulpian.
5. "Let every soul be subject unto the higher powers. For there is no power but of God: the powers that be are ordained of God" (Romans 13:1).
6. James I. Speech to Parliament, March 21, 1609, *Historic Speeches* (London: Penguin Books, 2013 reissue).
7. The law in certain instances does recognize the concept of an absolute contract, defined as one wherein "every covenant is independent and the breach of one does not relieve the obligation of another. In a conditional contract, the covenants are dependent upon each other and the breach of one is a release of the binding force of all dependent covenants." State of Georgia Law Code § 13-1-7 (2015).
8. Hobbes, *Leviathan*, 84.
9. Thucydides, "Melian Dialogue," in *On Justice, Power and Human Nature: Selections from the History of the Peloponnesian War* (Indianapolis: Hackett Publishing, 1993). Hereinafter cited as *Justice, Power, and Human Nature.*
10. Hobbes, *Leviathan*, 114.
11. Marsilius of Padua, trans. Alan Gewirth, *Defensor Pacis* (New York: Columbia University Press, 2001).
12. Written by Thomas Gordon and John Trenchard. The *Letters*, rather than the *Second Treatise* itself, proved to be the most popular source for political ideas in the colonial period. Ronald Hamowy, ed., *Cato's Letters* (Indianapolis: Liberty Fund, 1995), four volumes.
13. The phrase is associated with Scottish moral philosophers of the eighteenth century. See F. A. Hayek, *The Fatal Conceit: The Errors of Socialism*, Appendix A, "'Natural' v. 'Artificial'," ed, W. W. Bartley III (Chicago: University of Chicago Press, 1988), 145. Hereinafter cited as *Fatal Conceit.*
14. ". . . [H]e who is unable to live in society, or who has no need because he is sufficient for himself, must be either a beast or a god: he is no part of a state. A social

instinct is implanted in all men by nature. . . . [Man] is by nature a political animal. And he who by nature and not by mere accident is without a state, is either a bad man or above humanity." Aristotle, *The Politics*, vol. 1, trans. Benjamin Jowett, in *Introduction to Aristotle*, ed. Richard McKeon (New York: McGraw-Hill, 1947), 557, 556.

15. "For God having given man an understanding to direct his actions, has allowed him a freedom of will, and liberty of acting, as properly belonging thereunto, within the bounds of that law he is under." Locke, *Second Treatise*, 32–33.

16. Ibid., 8.

17. See John Locke, *The First Treatise of Government* in Peter Laslett, ed., *Two Treatises of Government* (Cambridge: Cambridge University Press, 1988).

18. Locke, *Second Treatise*, 9.

19. Ibid., 52.

20. Ibid., 9.

21. Ibid.

22. ". . . Which shew the work of the law written in their hearts." (Romans 2:14); "For when the Gentiles, which have not the law, do by nature the things contained in the law, these, having not the law, are a law unto themselves" (Romans 2:15).

23. Locke, *Second Treatise*, 9.

24. Ibid., 35.

25. See Donald S. Lutz, *The Origins of American Constitutionalism* (Baton Rouge: Louisiana State University Press, 1988), for a discussion of the distinction between "compact" and "contract" in early Anglo-American thought.

26. "Self defence is a part of the law of nature; nor can it be denied the community, even against the king himself." *Second Treatise*, 118.

27. The grandson is merely exercising his grandmother's natural right to use such force, which she has voluntarily delegated or transferred to him.

28. Locke, *Second Treatise*, 66.

29. Ibid., 46.

30. Ibid., 19.

31. "Men being, . . . by nature all free, equal, and independent, no one can be put out of his (her) estate and subject to the political power of another without his (her) own consent, which is done by agreeing with other men (women), to join and unite into a community for their comfortable, safe, and peaceable living, one amongst another, in a secure enjoyment of their properties, and a greater security against any, that are not of it." Locke, *Second Treatise*, 52.

32. Ibid., 112.

33. Locke, *Second Treatise*, 111.

34. *Manegold of Lautenbach* (1080–85), ed. K. Francke, MGH *Libelli de Lite*, I (Hanover, 1892), 325, 358, 365, 391–92. Cited in Brian Tierney, *The Crisis of Church and State* 1050–1300 (Toronto: University of Toronto Press, 1988), 79–80. Hereinafter cited as *Crisis of Church and State*.

Whensoever . . . the legislative . . . endeavor to grasp themselves, or put into the hands of any other an absolute power over the lives, liberties, and estates of the people; by this breach of trust they forfeit the power, the people had put into their hands, for quite contrary ends, and it devolves to the people, who have a right to resume their original liberty, and, by the establishment of a new legislative (such as they shall think fit) provide for their own safety and security, which is the end for which they are in society. . . . (Second Treatise, 111)

. . . [T]o secure these rights, governments are instituted among men. . . . [W]henever a government becomes destructive of these ends, it is the right of the people to alter or abolish it, and to institute new government, laying its foundation on such principles and organizing its powers in such form as to them shall seem most likely to effect their safety and happiness. . . . (Declaration of Independence)

35. Locke, *Second Treatise*, 107.

36. Thomas Paine, *Common Sense: and Related Writings,* in Philip B. Kurland and Ralph Lerner, eds., *The Founders' Constitution* (Indianapolis: Liberty Fund [reprint University of Chicago Press], 1987), Vol. I:103. Hereinafter cited as *Founders' Constitution.*

37. The concept is also explicit in several of the state constitutions written in the aftermath of the colonies' break with England, e.g., Virginia; Pennsylvania; Massachusetts; Vermont.

38. Compare Locke's formulation in the *Second Treatise*: "But if a long train of abuses, prevarications, and artifices, all tending the same way, make the design visible to the people, and they cannot but feel, what they lie under, and see, whither they are going; it is not to be wondered, that they should then rouse themselves, and endeavour to put the rule into such hands, which may secure to them the ends for which government was at first erected." (113)

39. Alexis de Tocqueville, *Democracy in America* (Indianapolis: Liberty Fund, 2015).

40. That aside, however, it is clear that persons who continue in relation with their biological families beyond the age of majority do so voluntarily. Children who choose not to associate with their families beyond that age are not forced by law to do so.

41. Not to be confused with the Lockean concept of "civil society," the term employed by Locke as a synonym for what he also calls "political society," that is, a society whose members have compacted to establish formal political or governmental institutions.

42. "Government is not reason, it is not eloquence, it is force; like fire, a troublesome servant and a fearful master. Never for a moment should it be left to irresponsible action." Variously attributed to George Washington and others. Scholars disagree on whether the conventional attribution of the phrase to Washington is legitimate or apocryphal.

43. "The essence of Government is power; and power, lodged as it must be in human hands, will ever be liable to abuse." James Madison, speech in the Virginia constitutional convention, December 2, 1829, *The Writings of James Madison,* ed., Gaillard Hunt (Whitefish, MT: Kessinger Publishing, 2015 [1910]), Vol. 9:361. These words are inscribed in the Madison Memorial Hall, Library of Congress James Madison Memorial.

FOUR

Liberal Democracy

Wherever the real power in a Government lies, there is the danger of oppression. In our Governments the real power lies in the majority of the Community, and the invasion of private rights is chiefly to be apprehended, not from acts of Government contrary to the sense of its constituents, but from acts in which the Government is the mere instrument of the major number of the constituents. —James Madison[1]

There is no maxim . . . which is more liable to be misapplied . . . [than that] . . . the interest of the majority is the political standard of right and wrong." —James Madison[2]

The kind of political order established by the Constitution of the United States is conventionally classified as *liberal democracy*. Although the Founders themselves did not employ the term—they preferred such designations as "republic" or "representative democracy"—the modern classification has the advantage of pointedly distinguishing the two distinct but related elements of American constitutional order—the "liberal" element and the "democratic" element. The present chapter examines the meaning of the two discrete aspects of American constitutional design as well as the manner in which they jointly serve its overarching purpose.

We have seen that the political tradition of the United States, as of modern Western Europe more generally, is historically referred to as the liberal tradition. "Liberal," as we recall, derives from the Latin *liber* (free), highlighting the distinctive value of freedom characteristic of that tradition. The liberal tradition has a distinguished pedigree, shaped as it was by the contributions of numerous influential thinkers over the centuries.[3] Its precise origin is difficult to establish with certainty; scholars variously trace the genesis of liberal political conceptions to ancient Greek, Roman, Christian, or feudal sources. It is widely agreed, however, that the liberal tradition received major formative impetus in the early-modern era, especially in response to the religious conflict and political absolutism that followed in the wake of the Reformation and Renaissance. The writings of Locke are characteristic. Although pre-modern authors did not generally employ the term "liberal" in an expressly political sense, the term was gradually introduced to Anglo-American political discourse by leading thinkers such as Adam Smith and others. Smith, for instance, described the application of the principle of liberty to issues domestic and foreign as the "liberal system," and the term was adopted by early nineteenth-century political movements in Sweden and Spain.[4] Usage of the term in this sense spread throughout European and American society; well into the twentieth century "liberalism" was widely identified with principled advocacy of individual freedom of thought and action. We previously noted the transformation of the meaning of liberalism in modern American society and subsequent distinction between classical and modern liberalism.

The various thinkers who contributed to the liberal tradition over the course of its development were unified by a particular common concern. They were all concerned, in one way or another, to answer what, indeed, may be called the "liberal question," namely, *what is the proper role of government in society?* The tradition's preoccupation with the role of government stems from its preoccupation with freedom. Freedom and government, as we have seen, are inextricably linked within Western political thought and practice, a linkage especially pronounced within the Anglo-American tradition. On the Lockean and American view, as we recall, the central purpose of government is to secure the individual's natural and unalienable rights, including the right to liberty. Law is conceived as the means whereby such rights are secured and government as the organization established to declare, adjudicate, and enforce the law that secures them. The linkage between freedom and government that arises from their mutual relation to law ensures that considerations of freedom are inseparable from considerations of government. Such a conclusion is clearly evidenced by the institutional structure of liberal society previously discussed, that is, the necessarily inverse relation between the voluntary or private sector (freedom) and the involuntary or public sector (governmental coercion). The concern for freedom within the liberal tradition has, for good cause, led to its characteristic concern to identify the proper role of government in society.

Indeed, the only members of society who can avoid reflection upon the liberal question so conceived are those willing to embrace totalitarian government of one form or another. Any person, on the other hand, who rejects totalitarianism, who denies the moral right of government to control the totality of human experience, is more or less forced to consider the limits of legitimate governmental power, that is, more or less forced to address the liberal question. Although the proper role of government in society may not be susceptible of definitive resolution, the issue must be explored by every generation and, indeed, every individual alive to the larger social and political context of his personal existence. Every individual must reach his own conclusion regarding the proper limits of political power, but such deliberation does not demand reinvention of the wheel. Those who seek guidance have recourse to a wealth of philosophical reflection on this characteristically Western moral and political concern, the cumulative wealth that constitutes the liberal tradition.

LIBERALISM

Classical Liberalism

There are two chief responses to the liberal question in the modern era, conventionally designated as classical liberalism and modern liberalism. We have previously encountered the classical-liberal view in the influential formulation articulated by Locke and later adapted and adopted by Americans of the revolutionary and founding period. Neither Locke nor the Americans would have anachronistically described their political philosophy as "liberal." Such thinkers nevertheless shared a coherent political philosophy that spoke to the liberal question, namely, common and deeply held political principles proximately derived from their English forebears and contemporaries, in particular, the so-called Whigs or Old Whigs. Seventeenth-century Whigs, as we recall, were united by opposition to arbitrary political power, especially the exercise of discretion or will on the part of government. Their solution to the problem of arbitrary power was establishment of the rule of law. Locke of course was a major carrier of Whiggish beliefs and values, but he was far from their only source. Whig principles and convictions were widely disseminated in the American colonies, popularized, as mentioned, by the pamphlets of Trenchard and Gordon, as well as political sermons of the era.[5] The widespread embrace of Whiggish ideals in the colonial and revolutionary era ensured their formative influence on early American constitutional thought and practice. The transmission of eighteenth-century Anglo-American political thought to subsequent generations led in turn to the development of an explicitly "liberal" political philosophy in the following century. Thus, Old-Whig principles and doctrines, articulated in the seventeenth century by Locke, restated in the eighteenth century by Edmund Burke, and implicit in traditional American political thought and practice, would form the basis of the nineteenth-century liberalism that developed in their wake.[6] Whiggish ideals and principles constitute the proximate antecedent of the political philosophy that came to be known as classical liberalism.

The Old-Whig or classical-liberal answer to the liberal question—the question of the proper role of government in society—was previously elaborated in our discussion of Locke. The proper role of government is to protect the unalienable rights of the individual, his natural rights to life, liberty, and property, as well as pursuit of happiness. We recall Locke's celebrated response to the liberal question: "the great and chief end . . . of men's uniting into commonwealths, and putting themselves under government, is the preservation of their property." Individuals mutually agree to form a government in order to provide better security for their property broadly conceived, that is, their natural rights to life, liberty, and estate. "[T]o secure these rights," as Jefferson elegantly and succinctly restated the Lockean view, "governments are instituted among men." Madison elaborated the identical conviction:

> It is sufficiently obvious, that persons and property are the two great subjects on which Governments are to act; and that the rights of persons, and the rights of property, are the objects, for the protection of which Government was instituted. These rights cannot be separated. . . . Government is instituted to protect property of every sort; as well that which lies in the various rights of individuals, as that which the term particularly expresses. This being the end of government, which impartially secures to every man, whatever is his own.[7]

Madison's remarks specify both the purpose of government (protect the rights of "persons" and "property") and his conception of justice ("securing to every man, whatever is his own"), which, indeed, turn out to be one and the same. The purpose of government, as he elsewhere says, is precisely to secure justice: "Justice is the end of government." We recall in this context that government, on the Lockean Principle embraced by the Founders, is intrinsically limited by the ends for which it is created. The proper role of government is thus limited to securing justice, which means securing the rights of persons and property. Such is identical to the classical-liberal response to the liberal question advanced throughout the nineteenth century to the present day. Classical liberalism carries forward into the modern era the conviction shared by Locke, Jefferson, Madison, and other Old Whigs: the proper role of government is to secure the rights of person and property. Such a formulation, as we have seen, implies that both the individual's "person" (life and liberty) and "property" (estate) are to be protected against arbitrary coercion, whether exercised by private individuals or government.

On the classical-liberal or Old Whig view, then, government has a well-defined but limited role in society, namely, the administration of justice, which principally involves the protection of individual rights. Government so conceived is considered essential to society, but its power must not extend beyond constitutionally defined boundaries. The classical-liberal view of government was widely embraced by members of American society, regardless of party affiliation, well into the twentieth century and, moreover, continues to be embraced by many Americans to the present day. Its deep-rooted penetration of American consciousness is indicated by various commonplace epithets historically attached to the traditional American conception of government. Government is said to play the role of "night watchman" or "umpire," metaphors that clearly point to the traditionally limited sphere of governmental authority in American society. The role of a "night watchman" is important but limited; his responsibility is to secure the property under his watch, to prevent its violation by thieves and other criminals. Old Whigs and their classical-liberal descendants regard the role of government in precisely such a manner, important but limited. Its responsibility is to secure the life, liberty, and estate of the citizens under its watch, to prevent its violation by predators, aggressors, and other criminals, domestic and foreign. Such a view conceives a largely negative role for government. That is, government, like a night watchman and like law itself, fulfills its purpose by securing the absence of certain conditions, in its case, actions that would violate the rights of individual members of society. Its role is not to provide positive (material) goods and services to the American people but rather to administer the law that protects their unalienable (and negative) rights.

Government as Umpire

For the Founders and classical liberals, then, the central purpose of government is to secure justice, which requires protection of individual rights to life, liberty, property, and pursuit of happiness. Government is to secure "equal justice under law"—*isonomia*—the universal application of the same rules of just conduct to all persons in society, high and low, including those persons organized as government. Locke refers to this function as the "umpirage" of government.[8] It is worth exploring the conception of government as umpire in some depth, for the metaphor sheds considerable light on the traditional American or classical-liberal view of the proper role of government in society which, as we shall see and as Madison's remarks clearly indicate, is indeed inseparable from the traditional American conception of justice.

It is not coincidental that the American people have customarily regarded the game of baseball as their national pastime: this characteristically American sport perfectly embodies the customary American sense of justice. The correspondence between baseball and justice in the American mind is clearly demonstrated by a cursory analysis of the game. Baseball, of course, involves two teams that complete to win the game, as well as an umpire, an impartial official unaffiliated with either team. The winner is the team that scores the highest number of runs at the end of the game. The members of both teams, as well as the umpire, play the game within an established legal framework—the "rules of the game." Neither the players nor the umpire make the rules, which rather have developed over time independent of the preferences of players and umpire. The rules are given, a kind of man-made "higher law" which structures the activities of all participants and which no one at the time of the game has power to alter. The function of the umpire, then, is not to make but only enforce the rules, to ensure that all players adhere to the recognized rules of the game. The winning team must not only earn the highest number of runs but do so within the confines of such rules. Cheating is prohibited and penalized, and the umpire's role is to prevent such illegal (unfair) action on the part of the players. The umpire, in other words, is the impartial judge whose task is to secure justice or fairness. Fair play is of the essence of baseball, as of all sports, and fairness in this context means playing according to the rules of the game. A team that scored the highest number of runs by cheating or violating the rules in some fashion would not be considered a legitimate winner. People would cry, "Foul!" A winner is considered legitimate, a game considered fair and just, if and only if the winner succeeds while playing within the established rules. Such a conclusion is central to the American sense of justice within the context of baseball.

The sense of justice that informs the game of baseball, however, is not unique to that game but rather a particular expression of the more general sense of justice that has traditionally informed American society at large. The game of baseball, played by competing teams, may be analogized to the "game of life" played by individual members of American society at large. The goal of the game of life, it might be said, is to "win," if winning is taken to mean success in achieving one's personal goals or realizing one's life plans. Individuals in society, like players in a baseball game, are required to pursue their goals within the confines of an established set of rules, the customary moral and legal framework of society. An individual whose personal goal is, say, to possess a new automobile must obtain that object within the bounds of such rules. He is not permitted, for instance, to steal an automobile from its owner but rather must acquire it through a peaceful, voluntary, and legal transaction, whether purchase, trade, or gift. Theft is in violation of the rules, prohibited by law. Human law and the ethical injunctions from which it derives ("do not steal") constitute, so to speak, the rules of the game of life, which every person is expected to honor as he goes about the business of "winning"—achieving his personal goals.

A general rule of law, as we recall, does not direct persons to pursue particular goals but rather structures the means they may use to achieve their self-chosen ends. Such holds true for both baseball and social existence more generally. The game of life, like the game of baseball, thus requires an "umpire," an impartial agent who ensures that all players are actually pursuing their goals within the given rules of the respective games. The "umpire" in the "game of life" is, of course, "government." The function of government in traditional American society is identical to the function of the umpire in the game of baseball. Their mutual role is to ensure that all players, whether participating in the game of life or baseball, are pursuing their goals in accord with the established framework of law (the moral and legal rules of society and the rules of baseball, respectively). The function of the umpire in the game of baseball is thus perfectly analogous to the traditional function of government within society at large. The purpose of both entities is to secure the rule of law, that is, secure justice, and this in a particular sense mutually shared by baseball and American society more generally.

The analogy between baseball and society, then, extends beyond the particular role of government as umpire to the general American sense of justice. The outcome of a baseball game is regarded as fair if and only if a team has secured the highest number of runs and done so playing within the rules. A team that cheated to achieve the highest score would not be regarded as the legitimate winner. The American sense of justice further demands that the umpire act *impartially* with respect to the enforcement of rules. An umpire who displays favoritism toward one team or who is selective in his enforcement of the rules would be universally condemned as corrupt. People would again cry, "Foul!" Justice requires a disinterested and impartial umpire. The American people, moreover, have historically shown little resentment toward successful teams who beat their competitors time and again, even if their sympathies lie with beloved underdogs. Americans traditionally accept the success of the superior teams without rancor so long as they have won by fair means, that is, by playing according to the rules: "It's not whether you win or lose, but how you play the game."

By the same token, the American people have traditionally accepted the success of their "competitors" in the game of life without resentment or rancor so long as the more successful "players" have achieved their goals ethically, legally, justly, that is, within the bounds of established moral and legal rules. Such is characteristic even of those Americans who identify winning the game of life with financial success. The American people have not typically begrudged the accumulation of wealth by their fellows who have "won" their wealth justly and fairly. They have customarily regarded economic success as fair or just so long as it has been achieved within the bounds of law and morality. Indeed, so long as people gain financial success in an ethical manner, it has generally been applauded rather than condemned. This is only to say that Americans traditionally regard justice or fairness not as an attribute of the outcome of individual pursuits (success or failure; wealth or poverty) but rather as an attribute of the means by which individuals pursue their ends ("fair means or foul"): what matters is not whether one wins or loses, but how one plays the game. More formally, the traditional American sense of justice is a type of justice conventionally referred to as procedural and deontological justice, in contrast to a rival conception known as outcome-based or consequentialist justice.

Finally, the analogy between traditional American views of government and the baseball umpire holds in yet other respects. Justice requires that government, like the umpire, scrupulously avoid favoritism in its treatment of persons or groups. Government, like the umpire, is also forbidden to enforce the rules selectively. Justice, whether enforced by government or umpire, is to be "blind"—impartial and disinterested, no "respecter of persons." We have seen that the American sense of justice is partially but profoundly informed by the concept of equal treatment under the law; every person is to be judged in accordance with identical rules. Nor is government any more permitted to influence the outcome of the game of life than the umpire the outcome of a baseball game. Both government and umpire are to be strictly and solely concerned with the means employed by the players—the pre-established rules or procedures that structure their striving for success. A government that "throws" the game of life to preferred persons or groups is indistinguishable from an umpire who "throws" the game to his preferred team. On the traditional American standard of justice, any such action, whether by government or umpire, must be roundly condemned. Government's proper role, like that of the umpire, does not involve determining the outcome of the game of life but rather establishing, as is said, a "level playing field"—one on which every person is impartially judged by the same rules.

The classical-liberal answer to the liberal question, then, may be summarized as follows: the proper role of government in society is to secure justice, which means to secure the rights of person and property, broadly conceived as life, liberty, and estate. It exercises its role by acting as "umpire" or "night watchman." Its principal responsibility is to secure the rule of law, the moral and legal means that persons may legitimately employ in pursuing their self-chosen purposes. Government declares the law (legislature); adjudicates the law (judiciary); and enforces the law (executive) in the interest of securing and protecting the natural, unalienable, and negative rights of the individual. Such, according to Old Whigs such as Locke and the Founders, as well as their classical-liberal descendants, is the proper role of government, and such is the general conception that informed the development of American political order from the founding to the twentieth century.

Modern Liberalism (Progressivism)

Classical liberalism is not the only response to the liberal question offered in contemporary American society. A competing conception of the proper role of government, conventionally termed modern liberalism or Progressivism, has become increasingly influential over the course of the past century. Perhaps no other terms better illustrates the dramatic transformation of the meaning of key terms of Anglo-American moral and political discourse than the words "liberal" and "liberalism." In contemporary American society, "Liberalism" is widely understood to mean advocacy of Big Government and "Liberals" to represent in some fashion the political "Left." Such contemporary American meanings, as previously remarked, stand in stark contrast to the meaning of the terms prior to the early decades of the twentieth century. The liberal tradition is a tradition of limited, not expansive, government; Big Government, on the classical view, is not and can never be liberal. The semantic confusion caused by redefinition of the term liberal has necessitated, as we have seen, the modern scholarly distinction between classical and modern liberalism.

The first task is to define, so far as possible, the modern-liberal answer to the liberal question concerning the role of government in society. The classical-liberal answer, as we have seen, is clear and straightforward—the role of government is limited to securing the rights of person and property in service of freedom and justice. The modern-liberal position is not as clearly defined. According to the nineteenth-century philosopher John Stuart Mill, a pivotal figure in the transition from classical to modern liberalism, the proper role of government is not limited to securing the rights of person and property but rather encompasses the "improvement of mankind."[9] His predecessor and mentor, Jeremy Bentham, regarded government's task as securing the "Greatest Happiness of the Greatest Number." Perhaps the least controversial formulation is to say that modern-liberalism advocates extensive governmental direction of the social process, typically in service of equality and welfare, the major values championed by that school of thought.

Modern liberalism tends to dismiss the Founders' concerns regarding potential abuse of political power, which it rather regards as both necessary and competent to create the good society. Toward that end, it endorses far-reaching governmental regulation of social life, from so-called "trans-fat" intake to the minimum wage a worker may legally be paid. Modern liberalism qualifies or relativizes the Founders' conception of firmly established limits to governmental intervention in the individual's private sphere. As we have seen, the Founders conceived limited government as inseparable from other traditional American political values, such as the rule of law and negative rights to life, liberty, and property. Such conceptions are antithetical to the extensive role for government advocated by modern-liberal progressivism. It thus chafes under the restraints imposed on governmental action by the "charter of negative liberties" and rights that is the U.S. Constitution. In place of such constitutional restraints and negative rights, modern-liberal progressivism proposes, implicitly if not explicitly, a system of positive government that aims to secure positive liberty and positive rights.[10] Positive liberty, as we recall, involves the ability or power to achieve one's goals and such is said to require the possession of adequate wealth, income, or other material resources. The corresponding conception of positive rights entitles individuals to certain material goods and services ("entitlements") regarded as necessary to the realization of liberty so conceived. We have discussed the inherent conflict between the negative rights of the Founders' Constitution and the positive rights advocated by modern liberalism and various other collectivist ideologies. Such is a specific instance of a more general "conflict of visions" underlying the classical- and modern-liberal points of view.[11] The two "liberalisms" have little in common beyond their name.

The comprehensive and detailed picture of how the word "liberalism" came to be applied to the advocacy of Big Government has not yet been painted. A partial sketch of that process can nevertheless be drawn and may shed further light on the values and aspirations of modern liberalism. Well into the 1930s, the term liberal was usually although not invariably employed in its classical sense: to be "liberal" was to defend the principle of individual liberty of thought and action and the limited government correlative to that value.[12] A liberal, moreover, was understood to be a person of clear and firm political principle and liberalism the philosophy of principles par excellence. A person who holds a principled politics thinks and acts in a consistent manner, always in accord with his core principles and values. A traditional or classical liberal consistently upholds the principle of individual liberty in any and all circumstances. With respect to politics, this means that the first consideration in evaluating either candidates for office or legislative and policy proposals is their relation to individual liberty. A classical liberal will support a candidate or policy that promotes liberty but oppose those that undermine or violate individual liberty. What matters is not the particular benefits that may result from particular elections or legislation but rather upholding the general principle of liberty.[13] This is the meaning of a principled politics, whose foremost representatives in the American experience are the Founders themselves. As the North Carolina State Constitution expressed their common view, "A frequent recurrence to fundamental principles is absolutely necessary to preserve the blessings of liberty."[14] A principled politics of this nature is relatively rare in contemporary American society. Candidates and voters are more likely to campaign or vote on discrete "issues" detached from a guiding framework of overarching philosophical principles. The decline of classical liberalism has meant the decline of a principled American politics.

In any event, traditional morality generally held persons of principle in high esteem, and to be a Liberal was to be a person of principle. The term thus had tremendous positive resonance within American culture, as did the corresponding term liberty or freedom. In the nineteenth century, however, various political doctrines emerged as direct competitors to Liberalism, individual liberty, and limited government, including such collectivist ideologies as communism, socialism, Comtean positivism,

British Fabianism, and American Progressivism. Modern American liberalism is a hybrid doctrine resulting from a wedding of traditional liberal symbolism with certain moral and political aspirations derived from such collectivist movements.

Perhaps the chief such movement with respect to American political development is the Progressive movement of the late nineteenth and early twentieth century. Influential Progressive leaders embraced a radically relativistic philosophy of history that conceives linear movement through time as leading invariably and inevitably to Progress. On such a view, traditional values and institutions, such as the U.S. Constitution and Judeo-Christian morality, cannot be regarded as eternal or absolute truths but rather merely provisional stages on the road to Progress. Progress, accordingly, was said to demand adaptation of inherited American values and institutions to the flow of history. History, in turn, was said to be moving inexorably beyond the putatively antiquated individualism of the eighteenth and nineteenth centuries and toward the putatively advanced collective or social values of the future. Progress, then, was conceptualized as movement toward greater socialization or collectivization of society, which itself required greater governmental direction of the social process.

The Progressives were not alone in such convictions. Theirs was the era of so-called hot socialism, a time when many "advanced" Western thinkers were convinced of the failure of the free society, and especially its economic dimension—the order of competitive capitalism. Progress was said to require the replacement of capitalism with a "planned" or rationally organized economy of one form or another. All forms of planned economy require extensive governmental control of resources. The rejection of capitalism thus meant simultaneous rejection of its correlative constitutional framework, that is, limited government. The Constitution of the Framers was uncongenial to the expanded role for government envisioned by Progressives and other self-styled intellectuals of the era. The achievement of their goals thus required transformation of American constitutional order. One way to facilitate such change, as the Progressives seem to have realized, is redefinition of various concepts and symbols central to the American political tradition.

A reaction against Progressivism followed in the wake of World War I (1914–1918), into which America had been led by arch-Progressive President Woodrow Wilson. The term Progressive fell into disfavor among the general public, and Progressives were reluctant to overtly identify their positions with the now-discredited word. Americans were also traditionally hostile to the various "isms" or ideologies derived from Europe or at least the terms associated with them—socialism, communism, fascism, and so forth.[15] Thus Progressives and fellow travelers who advocated greater collectivization of American life had to choose their words carefully if they were not to alienate American voters. One strategy appears to have involved appropriation of the time-honored term liberal for various Progressive or collectivist proposals. The American people, as mentioned, generally warmed to the term "liberal." Thus they could potentially be swayed to support Progressive proposals labeled as such, even if they were not actually liberal in the classic sense. The appropriation of the term liberal by Progressives and socialists seems to have been well established by the 1920s. At that time, the *New York Times* criticized "the expropriation of the time-honored word 'liberal'" and demanded that "the radical red school of thought . . . hand back the word 'liberal' to its original owners."[16] By some means, however, perhaps endless repetition, the strategy took hold, and by 1954 the transformation of the meaning of liberal was a fait accompli. As economist Joseph Schumpeter remarked at the time, "[a]s a supreme, if unintended compliment, the enemies of the system of private enterprise have thought it wise to appropriate its label."[17] The details of the process may be somewhat murky but its end is clear—Progressive or socialistic legislation and policy came to be regarded in the United States as "liberal," a state of affairs that exists to the present day.

The Progressive roots of modern liberalism are further evidenced by contemporary American political discourse. The term Progressive, as we have seen, fell into disfavor after World War I, leading to its replacement by the term liberal. Ironically, almost a century later the same fate would befall the term liberal. Beginning in the 1980s, a reaction against the growth of government in the United States, a growth identified with "liberalism," caused the term liberal to fall into disfavor, indeed to become more or less a term of abuse. The liberal identification with Big Government became a liability for modern-liberal political actors. One response was to employ in reverse the tactic of modern liberalism's ideological ancestor, Progressivism, that is, to replace the term "liberal" with the term "Progressive."[18] The assumption seems to be that few Americans are aware of the historic connection between early Progressivism and modern liberalism, and, accordingly, that socialistic policies advanced by modern-liberal-politicians will be better received in the current cultural climate if labeled "Progressive" rather than "liberal." Such an approach is quite appropriate on historical grounds, mirroring, both substantively and strategically, the original substitution of liberal for Progressive in the early twentieth century.

The transformation of the meaning of liberalism, moreover, necessarily influenced the semantic fate of the traditional philosophy of liberalism, classical liberalism. The term liberal having been arrogated by a movement hostile to classical liberalism, advocates for the latter creed were more or less forced to find another label for their philosophy. In the United States, they are usually known as "Conservatives." Conservatism, however, is yet another term that requires clarification. To be "conservative" is, of course, to seek to "conserve" or preserve. In the American political context, contemporary Conservatism thus represents the desire to conserve in some fashion the pre-Progressive American political tradition deriving from the Founders and embodied in the U.S. Constitution, the tradition of the Old Whigs. As we have seen, Old Whig principles and convictions constitute the proximate source of the classical liberalism that emerged in the nineteenth century, which means that many (but not all) American Conservatives are Liberals in the classical sense. These are sometimes referred to as the "Old Right" in distinction to other partisans who claim the contemporary banner of Conservatism, such as so-called Neoconservatives. The latter group consists largely of former modern-liberals disaffected by the radical leftward shift of Liberalism in the 1960s.[19] All of this is confusing and complex but such is the state of modern American political discourse.[20]

We previously stated that there are essentially two modern answers to the liberal question, conventionally classified as classical and modern liberalism. This is true so long as one remains within the liberal tradition. There is, however, a third modern answer to the liberal question, one that arose from without that tradition and that is, moreover, profoundly significant for modern political development. This is the answer given by advocates of totalitarian or quasi-totalitarian government. Totalitarianism is, of course, not liberal in any sense of the word. It is nevertheless an answer to the liberal question regarding the proper role of government in society. Those who espouse totalitarianism claim, explicitly or implicitly, that government is morally and legally entitled to control or direct every aspect of social existence, without limits or boundaries of any kind. Totalitarianism means total political control of society and thus necessarily rejects the view that there are, or should be, limits to the power of government. Totalitarian government, in other words, is unlimited government.

The word itself (*totalitario*) is believed to have been coined by the Italian Fascist dictator Benito Mussolini in the early 1920s. His era was marked by widespread belief in the superiority of conscious governmental control to the spontaneous social process of the free society, as previously noted in the discussion of American Progressivism. Totalitarianism, said Mussolini, means "all within the state, none outside the state, none against the state."[21] We have seen that totalitarian government necessarily eliminates civil society, the voluntary, free, or private sector, as well as the corresponding conception of individual rights against government. Every aspect of life, from a person's religious convictions to the profession he practices, is in some fashion influenced if not directly controlled by government (the "state," in the terminology of Continental Europe). Totalitarianism is certainly an answer to the liberal question but one that demolishes in toto the conception of a liberal or free society. Millions upon millions of human beings nevertheless suffered under totalitarian rule, the utter absence of freedom, throughout the course of the twentieth century, the epoch now known to history as the tragic Age of Totalitarianism. No discussion of the free society can neglect a treatment of the modern phenomenon of totalitarianism and the ideological movements that engendered it.

Modern Liberalism, Progressivism, and totalitarianism are usually classified as perspectives of the political Left, while Classical Liberalism and Conservatism are usually classified as perspectives of the Right. The terms Left and Right derive from the French Revolution (1789–1799); they refer to seating arrangements in the National Assembly—the most radical deputies sat to the left of the president's chair.[22] In modern usage, the terms are typically employed to designate the political positions of individuals and groups. More particularly, they refer to the position taken with respect to the liberal question regarding the proper role of government in society. Various possible positions are conventionally represented by their placement along a continuum:

<LEFT Mussolini	Founders	RIGHT>
Totalitarianism/ Total Governmental Control		No Government/ Anarchy

The left-most position represents advocacy of complete governmental control of society—perfect or ideal totalitarianism. The right-most position represents advocacy of complete and utter absence of government—perfect or ideal anarchy. Every political thinker, actor, and philosophy can in principle be placed somewhere along such a continuum according to the degree of governmental control advocated by the person or doctrine. Mussolini and other infamous totalitarian dictators such as Joseph Stalin, Adolph Hitler, Mao Tse-tung, Castro, and Kim Jong-un would be positioned on the left-most position of the scale. The American Founders, advocates of limited government, could arguably be positioned, say, three-quarters toward the right of the continuum. Such designations are of course merely rough generalizations that can never be pinpointed with mathematical accuracy.

Moreover, it should be noted that philosophical or ideological positions of Left and Right can only with difficulty be correlated with the platforms and positions of the major political parties in the United States. In other words, contrary to popular misconceptions, not all Democrats are necessarily people of the Left, advocates for Big Government, and not all Republicans are necessarily people of the Right, advocates of limited government. The actual situation is more complex. For historical reasons (especially the Civil War and Reconstruction), the Republican Party was for decades anathematized in many sections of the Old South. Old Right or limited-government Conservatives in those regions thus tended to vote with the Democratic Party, and such Conservative Democrats exist in parts of the Old South to this day. Similarly, many Republicans in the Northeastern states and elsewhere actually lean very far Left in their support of extensive governmental involvement in society. The American political landscape is full of landmines for the unwary.

To this point, we have discussed the two chief expressions of liberalism in the American tradition, classical and modern. We conclude our discussion of the liberal element of American liberal democracy by emphasizing that the word liberal is therein employed in its classical or traditional sense—as relating to freedom and limited government. A liberal democracy is a particular kind of political order, a particular kind of democracy—a *liberal* or *limited* or *constitutional* democracy. The three terms are synonymous, highlighting the fact that liberalism traditionally honors individual freedom, which requires limits on government, which are established by the fundamental law of the Constitution. "Constitutionalism," as has been said, "means limited government."[23] Thus a liberal democracy is a limited democracy is a constitutional democracy. The Founders were proto-classical liberals, not modern liberals, and traditional American liberal democracy embodies the values of classical, not modern, liberalism. The democratic elements of the American political order, to which we now turn, are intended to serve the values of the qualifying liberal element—constitutional limits on government in the interest of securing freedom and justice. The Founders, as we shall see, did not conceive democracy as an end-in-itself but rather as a means toward fulfillment of the overarching end of American liberal democracy—the establishment of constitutional limits on the power of government in the interest of securing the unalienable rights of the people.

DEMOCRACY

Democracy is yet another significant term of Western political discourse whose meaning has become obscure or ambiguous over the course of modernity. The word is often employed carelessly and without clear definition, for instance, to suggest the identity of democracy and freedom or merely connote praise or approbation.[24] Indeed criticism of democracy in contemporary society treads on hallowed ground. Few ideas encounter greater resistance than the claim that the American Founders were not champions of democracy but rather somewhat hostile to that form of government. Such, however, is the case. To understand their position in this regard, we first examine the meaning of democracy and then its anticipated role in the political order established by the U.S. Constitution.

We have seen that American constitutional order consists of two distinct but related elements—liberalism and democracy. The liberal element is concerned with establishing limits to political power, with bounding the *range* or *extent* of legitimate political authority. The democratic element relates to a different political concern and answers a different question. Its concern is not the liberal concern—identifying the proper role of government and thus limits to political power—but rather establishing *who* shall wield political power. The question to which democracy is an answer is the question *"Who shall rule?"* Who is to establish and administer the laws, control the reins of government, wield the secular sword? Such a question is important but distinct from the liberal question regarding the legitimate range of political power. Liberalism is not concerned with identifying the particular persons or groups who should rule but rather the extent of governmental power regardless of who wields it. Democracy, on the other hand, is not concerned with the extent of political power as such but rather the identity of those who will exercise it.

The classic response to the question "Who shall rule?" was formulated by the ancient Greeks, the originators of political philosophy. The Athenian polis is conventionally honored as the "birthplace of democracy," the first democratic society in Western history. Greek thinkers of the era formulated the classification of rule that would endure for millennia in Western civilization. There are three possible answers, they said, to the question of "Who is to rule": one person, several persons, or "the many." The Greeks called a political constitution in which one person rules a monarchy (*mono,* one; archon, ruler); in which several persons rule, an aristocracy (rule of the *aristos,* the "best" or most virtuous); and in which "the many" rule, a democracy (rule of the *demos,* the people at large). These three possibilities represent three possible answers to one and the same question—who is to rule, who is to participate in the determination of law and policy and direct their administration? The answer to this question, said the Greeks, determines the form of a society's government, that is, whether monarchy, aristocracy, or democracy.

The Greeks further classified political constitutions as either good or corrupt forms of rule. A good constitution is concerned with the common good of society, that is, aims to secure justice. A bad or corrupt constitution, by contrast, rules in the interest of the ruler(s) or certain privileged groups at the expense of the common good, that is, fails to secure justice. Monarchy, aristocracy, and polity (*politeia,* usually translated as a "mixed regime" or constitutional republic) are the good constitutional forms, ruling in the interest of justice and the common good. Each of these constitutions has a corresponding bad or corrupt form, which the Greeks termed tyranny, oligarchy, and democracy, respectively. A single ruler or monarch who rules not for the common good but rather to further his own power or interest, or that of his friends and supporters, is not a true king but a tyrant. An aristocracy that becomes corrupt in this manner degenerates into an oligarchy, and a degenerate democracy is nothing more than mob rule.

The question *who shall rule?* is obviously conceptually distinct from the liberal question—*what is the proper role of government in society?* Accordingly, the two discrete elements of political order—persons entitled to rule and extent of rule—may be combined in various manners. Different combinations of the two elements produce different kinds of political regimes. A few concrete examples will serve as illustration. In the United States, liberalism (constitutional limits on government) is combined with democracy (officeholders are elected by the people at large and the people, through their elected representatives, indirectly participate in the determination of law and policy). The American form of government is thus known as "liberal democracy." It is possible, by contrast, to combine liberalism with one of the two other possible forms of government, monarchy or aristocracy. Liberalism when combined with monarchy, for instance, results in the form of government known as "constitutional monarchy" (liberal or limited monarchy). A liberal or constitutional monarchy is a regime wherein the monarch achieves his position in some manner other than election by the people, as in a democracy. The king (or queen) possesses exclusive authority to govern but the range of his or her power is limited by the constitutional or liberal element of the regime. The monarch is not democratically elected but nevertheless bound by established laws (constitutional, statutory, or customary) that circumscribe the extent of his power. History yields various examples of constitutional monarchy, for instance, the English monarchy following the Glorious Revolution of 1688 and the Austro-Hungarian Empire during the latter half of the nineteenth century.

Another possible combination of the two elements of political order—the extent of rule and the persons entitled to rule—results in the modern phenomenon known as "totalitarian democracy." The term was popularized by Jacob Talmon in his path-breaking work *The Rise of Totalitarian Democracy.*[25] Totalitarian democracy refers to a political regime in which rulers and elites assert a universal and common purpose that all members of society are expected to serve. Even if also entitled to participate in the election of rulers, voters have little if any influence on the actual determination of law and policy. The government aims to maintain totality of control over society, even if justified in the name of majority rule. Recall that the modern doctrine of totalitarianism, in certain respects, is a response to the liberal question regarding the proper limits to government. The totalitarian answer is to assert the moral right of government to control every aspect of human life and society. It rejects the liberal conception of absolute or permanent limits to the reach of governmental power and claims instead the right of total or unlimited authority over social existence. Totalitarianism, like liberalism, relates to extent of rule and not the question of participation in government. Thus, it can be, and has been, combined with the distinctly democratic element of political order. Various modern totalitarian regimes have permitted, and even compelled, the people at large to participate in election of their rulers (however contrived the electoral process) or to voice their approval of governmental policy, for instance, through the plebiscite.[26]

According to Talmon, the first modern example of totalitarian democracy was the French regime that emerged in the aftermath of the Revolution of 1789. Another classic example is the German regime formed by Adolph Hitler in the 1930s. Germany became a democratic republic after World War I, and Hitler came to power in 1933 through perfectly legitimate—democratic—means. It is often forgotten that Hitler did not impose himself on the German people by force but was duly and democratically elected to office. A more contemporary example of totalitarian democracy is the regime established by Hugo Chavez in Venezuela. Chavez came to power in 1999 by winning the support of the majority of voters in legal, and democratic, elections. He was widely perceived as attempting to establish totalitarian control over the Venezuelan people. His government engaged in ongoing and far-reaching intervention in society, including nationalization of key industries and the suppression of free speech and a free press. The crucial issue with respect to the present discussion, however, is the fact that Chavez and other modern totalitarian or quasi-totalitarian rulers came to power through legal and democratic elections. They did not seize power through force or violence but through legitimate democratic procedure. Once elected, aspiring totalitarian rulers in democratic states tend to follow a similar general strategy. Upon assumption of office, they begin to gradually dismantle existing constitutional limitations on the power of the elected ruler, whether through executive decree or other legal or quasi-legal means. The result is a democratically elected dictator who recognizes no limits to his power, that is, totalitarian democracy. The people may continue to participate in elections but these are readily manipulated by power-holders to ensure little real choice of candidates or policy. Indeed, voting in totalitarian or quasi-totalitarian societies is typically encouraged or even compelled, providing as it does a politically valuable appearance of popular consent. The compatibility of totalitarianism and democracy is well understood by enemies of the free society. Socialists, communists, and fellow travelers all hailed the Chavez revolution as the "democratic revolution."[27]

Democracy per se provides little guarantee for freedom, that is, little safeguard against the potential violation of individual rights or other abuse of power by government. Such a conclusion follows from the fact that democracy does not address the question that is central to freedom and other traditional American rights—the liberal question regarding the proper limits of governmental power. Contrary to certain popular misconceptions, democracy is not a substantive political doctrine that embodies definite values, principles, or ideals that can serve as guides to determining the legitimacy of governmental power. The operative principle of democracy is majority rule, a more or less utilitarian procedural device that allows collective decisions to be made in the absence of unanimity. People agree to vote their preference with respect to certain issues and abide by the decision of the majority. Majority rule is a useful convention that enables decision-making when some agreement must be reached and unanimity is not possible. Democratic procedure, as such, is appropriate in certain situations. There is no harm, for instance, in resorting to majority rule in the case of a family unable to reach unanimous agreement concerning the movie they will jointly watch on Saturday evening. Each family member casts a vote and agrees to abide by the decision of the majority. Democratic procedure can lubricate the wheels of political life in the same manner. Unanimity is not always possible in situations where some conclusive choice is desired or required; under such circumstances, it makes sense to agree to majority rule.

It is important to recognize, however, that the principle of majority rule is not a moral principle but rather a mere expediency. The opinion of the majority, whether of family members or the political electorate, is neither intrinsically moral nor immoral. Traditional American moral and political convictions do not regard right and wrong as determined by majority decision but rather by a higher and objective source beyond human preference. As Madison cautioned, "There is no maxim . . . which is more liable to be misapplied . . . [than that] . . . the interest of the majority is the political standard of right and wrong. . . . In fact it is only reestablishing under another name and a more specious form, force as the measure of right."[28] The operative principle of democracy, majority rule, is simply a neutral procedural tool, a device that elicits the opinion of voters and grants authority to the numerically powerful. The tool of democratic procedure, like any tool, can be employed for good or ill. Numerical might no more makes right than physical might.

Kinds of Democracy

The nature of democracy may be further clarified by identifying the various kinds of democracy that have existed and continue to exist in human society. We have previously encountered the first and most important distinction in this regard—the distinction between liberal democracy (constitutional or limited democracy) and unlimited democracy of one form or another (majoritarian, plebiscitary, or totalitarian democracy). A liberal or constitutional democracy, like all forms of democracy, establishes certain important democratic procedures. Within such a regime, however, such procedures, like all other aspects of government, are constrained to operate within the bounds of law, the fundamental law established by the constitution. The American political order, as said, is a classic instance of liberal or constitutional democracy. To illustrate the manner in which liberal constitutionalism constrains democracy or majority rule, assume a hypothetical scenario in which the American people unanimously declare their desire to eliminate freedom of speech. The

American people have spoken with one voice, and such is their will. They instruct their elected representatives in Congress to enact legislation to that end. Despite their unanimous desire to suppress free speech, however, the American people will be unable to achieve their goal if they also wish to remain within the law. Such action is expressly prohibited by the First Amendment to the U.S Constitution: "Congress shall make no law . . . abridging the freedom of speech." In order to eliminate freedom of speech and remain within the law, the American people would have to amend the Constitution, to repeal or revise the First Amendment.

Within liberal democracy, democratic procedure, like all actions of government, is qualified or controlled by the higher law of the constitution. In the case of the U.S. Constitution, democratic majorities are authorized to prevail in certain situations, for instance, voting in the House of Representatives. Various other actions, however, whether supported by a democratic majority or even the unanimous opinion of the citizens, are completely prohibited to the federal government. The purpose for so restricting majority rule is identical to the purpose of the U.S. Constitution more generally—to protect the natural and constitutional rights of each and every individual. The Founders regarded neither individual rights nor the morality implicitly informing them as the product of majority opinion. As we have seen, they regarded certain rights as inherent in human nature itself, deriving from a source higher than mere human decision—the "Laws of Nature and of Nature's God." As such, they are unalienable—beyond the reach of government in any form, monarchy, aristocracy, or democracy—and their protection the very reason the people agreed to establish formal government in the first place. Rights, as discussed, are protected by the rule of law, including the law of the Constitution. Thus, the overarching purpose of American government—the security of unalienable rights—is inseparable from its liberal or constitutional dimension, that is, the limits established on all governmental action, whether supported by a majority or not. Moreover, as we shall see, the Framers intended the democratic element of American liberal democracy to serve the same purpose.

Liberal or constitutional democracy is not the only type of democracy to prevail in the modern world. As previously mentioned, democracy can also exist in various illiberal or unlimited forms, including totalitarian, majoritarian, and plebiscitary democracy. Totalitarian democracy has been discussed in a prior context. So-called majoritarian and plebiscitary democracy are similar to the totalitarian form insofar as they too fail to establish firm limits to the range or extent of legitimate governmental power. The key feature of such regimes is that the power of the numerical majority is not limited by prior constitutional constraints. Majoritarian democracies are often based on universal suffrage (every citizen possesses the right to vote), but the opinion, interests, or desires of the majority triumph in every instance. The opinions and interests of the numerical majority within such regimes are typically valorized as the putative "will of the people," the "general will," or perhaps the exercise of "popular sovereignty."

Regardless of the particular expression employed, the crucial fact is that majoritarian democracy makes no provision for the protection of individual or minority rights. Regimes in which the "will of the majority" determines the outcome of every election or legislative proposal offer no security for the rights of those who hold a minority view, let alone those of the individual. As a result, majoritarian democracy routinely issues in the violation of individual rights, that is, the violation of justice as traditionally conceived in the American experience. For that reason the great majority of the American Founders regarded majoritarian democracy as the worst possible forms of government. Historical experience, including that of the Greek poleis and earlier republican forms of government, led Madison to conclude that majoritarian democracy is prone not only to instability and social unrest but outright oppression and injustice.[29] The Americans perceived no difference between subjection to the will of a majority and subjection to the will of a single dictator. Tyranny is tyranny, whether exercised by a sole ruler or a majority of the people (the "tyranny of the majority" later apprehended by Alexis de Tocqueville and others). As Thomas Jefferson remarked,

> One hundred and seventy-three despots [the number of contemporary congressional representatives] would surely be as oppressive as one. . . . An elective despotism was not the government we fought for; but one which should not only be founded on free principles, but in which the powers of government should be so divided and balanced among several bodies of magistracy, as that no one could transcend their legal limits, without being effectually checked and restrained by the others.[30]

The classic example of majoritarian democracy in the modern era is the political order advocated by Jean-Jacques Rousseau in *The Social Contract* (1762).[31] Rousseau therein argues for an unlimited democracy in which the "general will"—the will of the numerical majority—is to prevail in each and every instance, without constitutional constraints of any kind. Rousseau's thought influenced the development of the post-revolutionary French Constitution which, in turn, has been the model for numerous modern democratic governments in Europe, Latin America, and elsewhere.

A second important distinction regarding democracy is that between a pure (direct) and a representative (indirect) democracy. A pure or direct democracy is a form of government in which every proposed law or policy measure (a "bill" in American terminology) is submitted to the entire body of the citizens without mediation of any kind. The citizens are to discuss the proposal, engaging, ideally, in extensive debate and deliberation concerning its virtues and flaws. They then vote on the proposal, and majority decision determines whether or not it becomes law. In other words, every proposed law in a pure democracy is submitted directly to the electorate, and simple majority rule governs in each and every case. The Athenian polis is a classic example of this type of democracy, as is the aforementioned constitution advocated by Rousseau. The town hall meetings of colonial Massachusetts are generally regarded as another example of pure or direct democracy. These may have been important instruments of local government in the colonial period but such experience did not overcome the Founders' mistrust of democracy in general and pure democracy in particular.

Athens was regarded not as an inspiration but rather an example of what should at all costs be avoided. Pure or direct democracies, said Madison, ". . . have ever been spectacles of turbulence and contention: have ever been found incompatible with personal security, or the rights of property: and have in general been as short in their lives as they have been violent in their deaths."[32] As he further remarked, "Had every Athenian citizen been a Socrates, every Athenian assembly would still have been a mob."[33] Elbridge Gerry claimed that "the evils we experience [during the years between independence and ratification of the U.S. Constitution] flow from the excess of democracy."[34] The insecurity of individual rights in a pure or direct democracy was especially troubling. In such a democracy, as we have seen, the opinions or interests of the majority always and necessarily defeat other opinions or interests; all proposals are decided on the basis of mere numerical superiority. The rights and interests of the individual and the minority are ever at the mercy of the majority; the former readily become victims and tools of the latter. Madison expressed the leading idea with typical understatement: "in Republics, the great danger is, that the majority may not sufficiently respect the rights of the minority."[35] For Madison and other Founders, there could be no greater injustice. "Justice is the [very] end of government." said Madison, and justice entails the security of each and every individual's unalienable rights to life, liberty, and property. Pure or direct democracy, the most extreme form of majoritarian democracy, thus poses threats to such rights at every turn. We have previously encountered Madison's warning in this regard: "There is no maxim . . . which is more liable to be misapplied . . . [than that] . . . the interest of the majority is the political standard of right and wrong."

The Framers never considered the establishment of pure or direct democracy in the United States. They established instead what they called a representative democracy (which they sometimes referred to as a "republic"). In a representative or indirect democracy, citizens do not vote directly on each proposed law or legislative act. Instead they vote for individuals who are to represent their opinions and interests in Congress as members of the House of Representatives and U.S. Senate. The representatives of the people are expected to exercise the deliberative function, to discuss and debate legislative proposals, taking into account the opinions and interests of their constituents, and, finally, vote on the proposed measures. The passage of a bill into law, moreover, requires more than simple majorities in both Houses. It further requires the cooperation of the executive branch (the presidential signature or veto) as well as the ability to pass constitutional muster (that is, legislation must not conflict with the higher law of the U.S. Constitution). All such constitutional roadblocks to majority rule speak to the Founders' great fear of majoritarian tyranny. Such a concern was addressed not only by specific aspects of constitutional construction but, more generally, by the establishment of liberal or constitutional rather than majoritarian democracy. The potential for majoritarian tyranny, as any form of governmental tyranny, was to be limited by establishing constitutional boundaries to the power of government in general as well as a Bill of Rights that binds its power in particular respects. As Albert Gallatin explained, "The whole of the Bill [of Rights] is a declaration of the right of the people at large or considered as individuals. . . . It establishes some rights of the individual as unalienable and which consequently, no majority has a right to deprive them of."[36]

The Founders were leery of democratic or "popular" government not only for the threat it poses to individual and minority rights but for additional reasons as well. In particular, they mistrusted the passions of the people at large and sought to erect a buffer between their immediate desires and the enactment of law. Human beings, they realized, always make better decisions when calm than emotionally aroused; passion can lead to action that individuals may later regret. What is true for the individual applies to majorities in the political process as well. High emotion may lead the majority to advocate legislation that will ultimately prove averse to its own or the nation's long-term good. Moreover, citizens can be led astray by demagogues, whipped into frenzy by the manipulative arts of unscrupulous politicians. Wisdom, on the contrary, calls for reason and deliberation, for a cool head. Prudence and not passion should govern human action, including legislative action, which, moreover, should be concerned not with fulfillment of the people's immediate or short-term desires but rather the long-term common good of society.

For such reasons, the Founders advocated the principle of representation, the purpose of which, according to Madison, is to "enlarge and refine the public opinion."[37] Deliberation by elected representatives of the people was regarded as a means to check unwise or hasty legislation springing from emotion and not rational reflection. The Founders believed that the American people were capable of choosing representatives of superior character and integrity, statesmen genuinely concerned with the long-term good of American society. The people themselves may not personally possess the virtue requisite to wise legislation but they possess sufficient virtue to recognize statesmanlike qualities in their potential representatives. As Madison said,

> Is there no virtue among us? If there be not, we are in a wretched situation. No theoretical checks—no form of government can render us secure. To suppose that any form of government will secure liberty or happiness without any virtue in the people, is a chimerical idea, if there be sufficient virtue and intelligence in the community, it will be exercised in the selection of these men. So that we do not depend on their virtue, or put confidence in our rulers, but in the people who are to choose them.[38]

The Founders' Constitution, however, does provide one mechanism for the immediate or direct expression of majority opinion: direct or unmediated election of members of the House of Representatives, the most "democratic" branch of the federal government. The election of U.S. senators, by contrast, was to be achieved only indirectly. These were to be chosen by the legislatures of the several states (whose members, however, were directly elected by the people of the respective states).[39] The Founders believed, moreover, that ultimately and over time the opinion of the people would and must prevail, if for no other reason than their electoral power to remove members of Congress with whom they disagreed. They did not, however, believe that the people should be directly involved with crafting or enacting particular legislation. The art of legislation requires knowledge, statesmanship, and genuine concern for the nation's long-term and common good, qualities they believed the people could recognize in others but did not themselves necessarily possess. It should also be noted that the U.S. Constitution does not allow for the direct election of the president by a national majority. The president is elected by the people of the several states through the mechanism of the Electoral College, yet another device intended to prevent straightforward rule by a numerical majority.

The Movements of Liberalism and Democracy

Liberalism and democracy are often confused if not conflated in the popular mind. Such is due, in part, to the fact that the liberal movement and the democratic movement developed historically in similar regions over similar periods of time. While certain scholars trace the origins of both democracy and liberalism as far back as ancient Greece, the liberal tradition, as previously discussed, received its characteristically modern form—the explicit demand for individual freedom and limited government—in the encounter with several landmark events in the early-modern and modern eras. First and foremost among them is the Protestant Reformation, particularly the emphasis placed by Luther and other reformers on the inviolability of individual conscience. Protestantism does not recognize a need for spiritual mediation in the relationship between the individual and God. Its principle of *sola scriptura* implies individual responsibility for forging such a relation, a process in which the exercise of individual conscience is paramount. It is not coincidental that the very first natural right claimed by the Puritans in America was the natural right of conscience. Such a right stakes a moral claim at the boundary of individual conscience—"thus far and no farther"—establishing limits to the coercive force of government in the realm of the inner or spiritual life.

The religious conflicts that emerged in the aftermath of the Reformation led to a second crucial aspect of liberal freedom—freedom of religion. We recall that during this era governments in Europe generally asserted the right to control the religious belief and practice of their subjects, a claim that led to a series of violent struggles that lasted well into the seventeenth century. The solution to such violence would prove to be the principle of religious liberty. The cherished liberal value of religious freedom, conceived as a negative freedom realized by the absence of governmental coercion of religious belief and practice, would not be graciously granted by human authority in a spirit of charity and tolerance. It was rather the fruit of long and bitter struggle, a struggle which culminated in the exhaustion of all parties to the conflict and whose ultimate resolution would be greatly indebted to the genius of Locke.

Locke's pathbreaking *Letter Concerning Toleration* (1689) articulated what would become *the* liberal solution to intra-Christian religious conflict, namely, prohibition of governmental intervention in matters of religion.[40] The proper sphere or jurisdiction of government, Locke says, is strictly limited to worldly or temporal concerns, such as material property, inheritance, and establishment of rules essential for peace and order in this world. The inner or spiritual life of man, his religious belief and practice, is beyond both its jurisdiction and its competence. Religion, Locke maintains, does not lie within the legitimate sphere of governmental power or authority because coerciveness, the defining attribute of secular rule, has no place in the spiritual life of the human person. Religion and the church belong not to the realm of force but rather of voluntariness or freedom, the private sphere of civil society. Religion and the church, Locke pointedly says, are "voluntary" associations, the term, as we have seen, attached to the institutions of civil society to the present day.[41]

Locke was among the first major thinkers explicitly to define the church as a "voluntary" society but he did not originate the views underlying such a designation. Such views rather derive from English and American religious dissenters who subscribed to so-called Covenental Theology. Calvinists, Presbyterians, and other dissenting groups rejected the episcopal structure of the Church of England and conceived of church membership as a voluntary act that bound members within a solemn covenant. Locke himself grew up in a dissenting household. Nor did

Locke originate the conception of religion and government as two distinct spheres of social existence, which rather is as old as Christianity itself. Locke, however, was the first major theorist explicitly to differentiate religion and government on the grounds of voluntariness and coercion. The church, he maintained, is a voluntary or free society that must therefore be sharply distinguished from government, the communal agent of coercive force. Religion, argues the Protestant dissenter, must by its very nature be accepted voluntarily or not at all. For that reason, coercion has no place in religion, which means that government, whose essence is coercion, has no place in religion. Such Lockean views on the proper relation between religion and government were widely embraced in the American colonies and, as we shall see, eventually informed the First Amendment to the U.S. Constitution.

Another step in the development of the liberal movement—enlarging the range of individual freedom—was taken upon publication of John Milton's *Aereopagitica* in 1644. Milton argued for the elimination of governmental censorship of written publications, that is, for the establishment of what is conventionally termed a "free press." Prior to such an establishment, governments claimed the right to grant or deny permission to publish or disseminate written material, including and especially material that criticized government and its policies. The demand for a free press, like the demand for any right, is a moral demand, based on the conviction that human beings are morally entitled to express and disseminate their views without prior permission of governmental authority. The right to a free press so conceived is crucial to the overarching goal of Old-Whig and classical-liberal philosophy—the prevention of absolute and arbitrary government. Whigs such as Locke and the Americans not only claimed the moral right to resist such government but further recognized its dependence upon the related right to disseminate one's views without prior governmental permission or fear of post-publication penalties imposed by government.

A free press is considered essential to free government for the additional reason that an informed electorate depends upon access to reliable and accurate knowledge and information, which is only possible in the absence of governmental censorship or control of communication. In societies that do not enjoy the security of a free press, available information is generally confined to that which the ruling authorities wish to have disseminated among the people. Such political control of knowledge and opinion routinely degenerates into mere propaganda and even outright lies. A free press is thus fundamental to a free people who believe, with Jefferson, that legitimate government must be based on consent of the governed.[42] Free government is to be shaped in accord with the settled opinion of the people, an opinion that is not itself shaped by government but independent of it. Genuine consent must be based on genuine knowledge and information, which can only be achieved by means of a free press that permits access to every opinion and point of view, not merely those approved by political authorities. As Jefferson cautioned,

> If a nation expects to be ignorant and free, in a state of civilization, it expects what never was and never will be. The functionaries of every government have propensities to command at will the liberty and property of their constituents. There is no safe deposit for these but with the people themselves; nor can they be safe with them and never will be without information. Where the press is free, and every man able to read, all is safe.[43]

The liberal movement continued to advance, further extending the range of individual freedom, by calling into question the government's right to restrict or control trade, exchange, and commerce. The call of the eighteenth century was rather for "free trade" or economic freedom—the ability to engage in voluntary market transactions, that is, buy and sell at terms mutually agreed upon by buyer and seller, without the approval or intervention of governmental authority. The pivotal work in the battle to extend the principle of freedom or voluntariness to economic affairs was Adam Smith's celebrated *An Inquiry into the Nature and Causes of the Wealth of Nations*, published in 1776. Smith made the case for the individual and social benefits of free trade and provided one of the first systematic accounts of the market process. Classical liberals were also a powerful force in the abolitionist movement of the early nineteenth century, which culminated in the elimination of chattel slavery in the United States. Thus, little by little, battle after battle, freedom after freedom—freedom of conscience, freedom of religion, freedom of the press, economic freedom, the abolition of slavery—the modern Western liberal tradition took form. Such was the inheritance of the American colonists and Founders, who would contribute their own world-historical chapters to the ongoing story of freedom in the modern world.

The liberal movement over the centuries was paralleled at certain stages by the related but distinct movement of *democratization*—the demand for broader participation in the political process. The latter movement received major impetus with the French Revolution of 1787, and the nineteenth century witnessed ever-growing insistence on greater inclusiveness in political life. We have seen that the overarching aim of liberalism was to extend the range of individual freedom. The aim of democratization, by contrast, was to enlarge the electorate, to permit ever greater numbers of people to participate in the determination of law and election of public officials, in other words, to have greater say in the way they are governed. The English Reform Bill of 1832 was a milestone in this regard. Voting rights were gradually extended over the course of the nineteenth and twentieth centuries, both in Europe and the United States, culminating in the achievement of universal suffrage in the twentieth century. At present, all United States citizens eighteen years of age or older possess the right to vote, with certain qualifications. The process of democratization in most Western societies is more or less complete.

At the time of the American Founding, by contrast, democracy, that is, the opportunity for the people at large to elect government officials and representatives, was relatively limited, by contemporary if not present standards. There were strict qualifications for voting. Suffrage was generally restricted to white males who owned a requisite amount of property, a group estimated to have been about 25 percent of the contemporary population. Moreover, despite their general mistrust of democracy, the Founders did hold a distinct theory of voting rights, sometimes described as the "stake-in-society" theory.[44] The basic idea is that voting should be restricted only to permanent and established members of the community, as evidenced by ownership of requisite property. Such a restriction aims, among other purposes, to ensure greater rationality and discipline in the political process by establishing a close connection between advocacy and funding of policy measures. In other words, the aim is to ensure that those persons who participate in the determination of various policy measures (by voting for their representatives in state or federal legislatures) will be the same persons who must pay the requisite taxes to fund them. The assumption is that such an arrangement will cause voters to carefully consider their support for various policy proposals and demonstrate such support by their willingness personally to pay for them.

The Founders did not regard such restrictions on democracy as a violation of individual rights. For one thing, they did not regard voting as a right in the same sense as the unalienable rights proclaimed in the Declaration. These, as we have seen, are not regarded as products of human convention, preference, or volition but rather constituent of human nature that originates in a source beyond human opinion. Voting was not regarded as a right of this stature but more or less a convention based on expediency and prudence. Voting rights were governed by state law and thus varied among the several states. Moreover, the right to vote was not regarded as essential to securing the unalienable rights of the individual. Individual rights to life, liberty, and property were guaranteed by federal and state constitutions and bills of rights, as well as other laws protecting person and property. Property rights, like voting rights, were governed by state law and thus also varied from state to state. Such protection as was granted by state law, however, extended to the individual whether granted the privilege of voting or not.[45] We have seen that constitutionalism (liberalism) and democracy (the right to vote) are distinct aspects of a political order. Thus, the relatively qualified democracy of the period did not significantly affect federal and state constitutional commitments. Security for individual rights to life, liberty, and property, including constitutionally protected rights against government, was to be provided chiefly by the rule of law, not the franchise. In principle, the rule of law, including both the public law of the Constitution and the rules of just conduct embodied in the private law, protects every citizen equally, whatever the form of government, democratic or otherwise. On the traditional American view, the protection of individual rights and equality under law are neither dependent upon nor ensured by democratic participation in government.

Despite the lack of intrinsic connection between security of rights and democracy, the Founders nevertheless conceived an important relation between them, that is, between liberalism and democracy. Such accounts for the significant democratic elements incorporated within their constitutional design. First and foremost, the president and Congressional representatives in the United States government are elected, that is, selected on the basis of democratic participation. The American Republic, in contrast to monarchical or aristocratic forms of government, is not ruled by a hereditary political class that claims the right to govern on grounds of birth, wealth, intellect, or social superiority of any kind. The U.S. Constitution expressly forbids the granting of titles of nobility on the European model.[46] America was founded as a republic. This means not only that rulers are chosen by the people, directly or indirectly, but, perhaps even more important, also *accountable* to the people, an accountability to be secured by the principle of election. America would have an elected president and not a hereditary king, an elected Senate and not a hereditary House of Lords, and the people (those with a "stake in society") would ultimately decide who would hold such offices and hold them accountable to their trust.

On the Founders' view, democratic participation, while not insuring the preservation of American constitutional values such as freedom and limited government, is nevertheless an essential instrument toward that end. Democracy, one might say, is a necessary but not sufficient condition of free government on the American model. The liberal and democratic dimensions of American liberal democracy are related in a kind of means-end nexus: liberalism is the end and democracy the means. The overarching end or purpose of American constitutional order, as we have seen, is the protection of the natural and unalienable rights of the individual. Such of course is different from the end or purpose of democracy—widespread if not universal participation in voting. Democracy, however, plays a crucial role in realizing the end of liberal constitutionalism in several important ways. First, as previously mentioned, democratic election of government officials holds them accountable to the people. The provision that American officeholders remain in office only upon the good will of the electorate aims to ensure they govern in the interests of their constituents and not in their own interest or that of the ruling class. A democratically elected government that acts in a tyrannical or despotic fashion, that violates the individual rights it was entrusted to protect, can be voted out of office. In this way, democratic election provides an additional safeguard to the rights of the people, beyond the primary safeguards of the constitutions, bills of rights, and rule of law more generally. This aspect of American liberal democracy has been characterized as a kind of "preventative measure, like a sanitary measure meant to guard against the plague," the plague of arbitrary and tyrannical government.[47] The Founders assumed that the people would defend their individual freedom and other rights, stand guard against abuse of power by government, and employ the means of democratic election toward that end.

The importance of democracy for the preservation of liberal constitutionalism is further clarified by considering the alternatives to democratic election of rulers. Prior to the modern rise of democracy, the most common form of government in Western society was hereditary monarchy. The monarch was not usually elected by the people but rather acquired his or her position by birth. Political thinkers, including Christian philosophers such as Thomas Aquinas, struggled for centuries with the question of how the people should respond to a king who degenerates into a tyrant. On the classical-Christian view that informed Western political development for millennia, a king, by definition, secures justice and the common good.[48] A corrupt monarch—a ruler who abuses the power of his office for his own gain or that of his friends and allies or otherwise engages in acts of injustice—"unkings" himself and becomes a mere tyrant.[49] The question faced by former generations living under hereditary monarchy was whether the people must suffer passively under such a tyrant or whether there is a remedy for his abuse of power. Passive acquiescence to tyranny is, of course, one option. If this is rejected, however, there are only two possible ways to end the tyranny, that is, remove the tyrant—either assassination (tyrannicide) or revolution. Aquinas and others could only conclude that tyrannicide may be morally justified under certain circumstances.[50] The Americans of the eighteenth century chose the second option—armed revolt against the king of England, whom, they believed, had become a tyrant.

Both options, tyrannicide and revolution, are undesirable in that both involve violence. Democracy in this context provides an alternative to such awful choices. If rulers become tyrannical, the people do not have to choose between assassination and armed revolt but can simply vote them out of office at the next election. The benefits of democracy in this regard should not be underestimated. Many nondemocratic governments, those in which rulers are not subject to legitimate elections, exist in the contemporary world. If such governments become despotic, the choices of the people are limited to passive acquiescence or violence of one form or another (military coups, popular uprisings, and so forth). There are few alternatives beyond the force of arms in societies whose rulers are not subject to election. Democracy, then, not only serves to ensure the ultimate accountability of rulers to the people but also possesses another quality crucial to the preservation of a civilized society: it is the only method yet devised that permits the peaceful transition of political power. As Hayek put it, "Though democracy itself is not freedom . . . it is one of the most important safeguards of freedom. As the only method of peaceful change of government yet discovered, it is one of those paramount though negative values, comparable to sanitary precautions against the plague, of which we are hardly aware while they are effective, but the absence of which may be deadly."[51]

Liberal constitutionalism and democratic procedure, then, are distinct but related aspects of American political order. Both elements are essential to safeguarding the blessings of liberty. Liberal constitutionalism establishes the boundaries of legitimate governmental authority and democratically elected government encourages both its accountability to the people and the peaceful transition of power. Democracy, however, is not an end-in-itself. It is simply one of the means developed to secure the overarching end of American liberal or constitutional democracy—the establishment of a limited government that secures the unalienable rights of the individual. Democracy is also an important procedural device that allows for collective decision-making when needed. The principle of majority rule, however, is simply an instrumental convention devoid of substantive moral content. Majority decision-making is neither good-in-itself nor bad-in itself, neither intrinsically moral nor intrinsically immoral. It is a neutral tool that can be employed for good or ill—to protect rights or violate rights, to support freedom or destroy freedom.

Such a fact is widely recognized by would-be totalitarians and other persons and groups who desire greater political control over society. Socialists, communists, and fellow travelers have long understood that their goals can be realized not only through violent revolution, as Karl Marx anticipated, but also the peaceful means of democratization. History clearly demonstrates that people can vote, have voted, and continue to vote for socialist, fascist, communist, and other illiberal forms of rule in democratic elections. It is not coincidental that the constitution of the former Soviet Union guaranteed democratic rights, that the official name of former communist East Germany was the German Democratic Republic, and that of totalitarian North Korea the Democratic People's Republic of Korea. Nor is it surprising, as previously remarked, that the contemporary socialist revolution in Venezuela is hailed by the Left as the "democratic revolution."

NOTES

1. James Madison, Letter to Thomas Jefferson, October 17, 1788, Kurland and Lerner, eds, *Founders Constitution* 1:477–78.
2. James Madison, Letter to James Monroe, October 5, 1786. https://founders.archives.gov/documents/Madison/01-09-02-0054

3. A (very) short list would include Cicero; Augustine; Aquinas; Hobbes; Locke; Burke; Madison, Jefferson, and other Americans such as John Adams; de Tocqueville; Acton; Hayek; and others.

4. Daniel B. Klein, "A Plea Regarding Liberal," *Modern Age*, Summer 2015.

5. Ellis Sandoz, *Political Sermons of the Founding Era* (Indianapolis: Liberty Fund, 1991).

6. The term "Old Whig" is employed to differentiate the earlier doctrine of Locke and Burke from the later doctrine of the "New Whigs," who came to embrace the novel British doctrine of "parliamentary sovereignty" after the Glorious Revolution of 1688.

7. James Madison, Speech at the Virginia Convention, December 2, 1829; James Madison, *National Gazette*, March 1792, in *The Papers of James Madison*, ed R. A. Rutland (Chicago: University of Chicago Press, 1976), Vol. 14:266.

8. Locke, *Second Treatise*. 114.

9. John M. Robson, *The Improvement of Mankind: The Social and Political Thought of John Stuart Mill* (London: Routledge and Kegan Paul, 1968). See also Linda C. Raeder, *John Stuart Mill and the Religion of Humanity* (Columbia, MO: University of Missouri Press, 2002).

10. Gillis Harp, *Positivist Republic: Auguste Comte and the Reconstruction of American Liberalism, 1865–1920* (University Park, PA: Penn State University Press, 2005).

11. Thomas Sowell, *A Conflict of Visions: Ideological Origins of Political Struggles* (New York: William Morrow & Co., 1987). Hereinafter cited as *Conflict of Visions.*

12. In the latter part of the nineteenth century, Comtean Positivists (who were anything but liberal in a classic sense) and various radical secularists called themselves "liberals." By the early twentieth century, L. T. Hobhouse would publish a book entitled *Liberalism* that employs the term in the modern-liberal sense. Developments in the United States are undoubtedly related to such English precedents.

13. A principled person is thus predictable. One can infer his response to a variety of diverse circumstances, because what matters is upholding the principle, not whether he personally benefits from a particular situation or policy. Consequences or outcomes are more or less irrelevant; it is the principle that matters.

14. George Mason: "No free government, or the blessings of liberty can be preserved to any people, but by frequent recurrence to fundamental principles"; Benjamin Franklin: "a frequent recurrence to fundamental principles . . . is absolutely necessary to preserve the blessings of liberty and keep a government free" (Constitution of Pennsylvania, 1776, XIV).

15. Upton Sinclair to Norman Thomas: "The American People will take Socialism, but they won't take the label. I certainly proved it in the case of EPIC. Running on the Socialist ticket I got 60,000 votes, and running on the slogan to "End Poverty in California" I got 879,000. I think we simply must recognize the fact that our enemies have succeeded in spreading the Big Lie. There is no use attacking it by a front attack, it is much better to out-flank them." Letter to Norman Thomas (Norman Thomas Papers, microfilm, Series I, General Correspondence, reel 22, frame 1018 [Sept. 25, 1951]), cited in *The Family Letters of Victor and Meta Berger, 1894–1929*, ed, Michael E. Stevens (Madison: Wisconsin Historical Society Press, 2016), 26.

16. Cited in Ronald D. Rotunda, *The Politics of Language: Liberalism as Word and Symbol* (Iowa City: University of Iowa Press, 1986), 49.

17. Joseph Schumpeter, *A History of Economic Analysis* (New York: Oxford University Press, 1954), 394.

18. For instance, the Progressive Caucus within the contemporary U.S. Congress.

19. George H. Nash, *The Conservative Intellectual Movement in America since 1945* (Wilmington, DE: Intercollegiate Studies Institute, 2006).

20. To make matters even more confusing, the transformation of the meaning of liberalism that occurred in the United States did not occur in Europe. In Europe, the term "liberal" still carries its traditional, classical meaning—advocacy of individual liberty and limited government. Moreover, a European Conservative is not "liberal" in

the classical sense, as are many American Conservatives. European "conservatives" typically defend aristocracy and monarchy, neither of which are relevant to American society. The European counterparts of modern American liberals or Progressives are generally organized as the Labor Party (England) or Social Democrats (Continental Europe).

21. Benito Mussolini, "Speech to Chamber of Deputies" (December 9, 1928), cited in Marx Fritz Morstein, *Propaganda and Dictatorship* (Mahwah, NJ: Ramsey Press, 2007), 48.

22. From the perspective of the speaker addressing the assembly, the aristocracy (representing the "party of order" or "conservatism"—the monarchy and church) sat on the right and the commoners (representing the "party of movement" or "progress"— republicanism and secularism) on the left.

23. Hayek, *Rules and Order*, 1.

24. George Orwell, "Politics and the English Language," in *Politics and the English Language and Other Essays* (Oxford: Benediction Classics, 2010).

25. Jacob L. Talmon, *The Rise of Totalitarian Democracy* (Boston: Beacon Press, 1952).

26. Merriam-Webster defines plebiscite as "a vote by which the people of an entire country or district express an opinion for or against a proposal especially on a choice of government or ruler."

27. Irving Kristol, *Neo-Conservatism, Selected Essays 1949–1995* (Washington, DC: Free Press, 1995). The situation in Venezuela has deteriorated even further under rule of socialist President Nicolás Maduro. In April 2017 the Supreme Court of Venezuela stripped the country's National Assembly of its powers and transferred them to itself. The Court is stacked with Maduro's supporters.

28. James Madison, Letter to James Monroe, October 5, 1786, in Warren L. McFerran, *Birth of the Republic: The Origin of the United States* (Gretna, LA: Pelican Publishing, 2009). 435.

29. Madison, *Writings of James Madison*, ed. Hunt, vol. 5 (*Correspondence*, 1787–1790), 1904. Such unlimited democracies were characteristic of certain poleis in the ancient world. See Fustel De Coulanges, *The Ancient City: A Classic Study of the Religious and Civil Institutions in Ancient Greece and Rome* (New York: Doubleday and Company, Inc., 1955). Hereinafter cited as *The Ancient City*.

30. Thomas Jefferson, "Notes on the State of Virginia," in *Founders' Constitution*, Vol. 1:319–20.

31. Talmon, *Totalitarian Democracy*.

32. Madison, *Federalist* No. 10, *Federalist Papers*, 46.

33. Madison, *Federalist* No. 55, Ibid., 281.

34. Jonathan Elliot, ed., *The Debates in the Several States on the Adoption of the Federal Constitution, as Recommended by the General Convention at Philadelphia in 1787*, 5 volumes, 2nd edition. Reprinted from the 1845 edition (Buffalo, NY: William S. Hein & Co., Inc., 1996), 5:136.

35. James Madison, Speech at the Virginia Convention (1829). *The Mind of the Founder: Sources of the Political Thought of James Madison*, ed., Marvin Meyers (Indianapolis: Bobbs-Merrill, 1973), 512.

36. Albert Gallatin, New York Historical Society, October 7, 1789, ed. Henry Adams, *The Writings of Albert Gallatin, 1788–1816* (New York: Evergreen Review, 2011), Vol. 1.

37. Madison, Federalist No. 10, *Federalist Papers*, 46.

38. James Madison, Speech at the Virginia Ratifying Convention (1788), *Founders' Constitution*, Vol. 1:409–10.

39. The original Constitution was of course amended in 1913 to allow to direct election of Senators. The 17th Amendment states in part, "the Senate of the United States shall be composed of two Senators from each State, elected by the people thereof, for six years; and each Senator shall have one vote."

40. John Locke, *Two Treatises of Government and a Letter Concerning Toleration*, ed, Ian Shapiro (New Haven: Yale University Press, 2003). Hereinafter cited as *Letter Concerning Toleration*.

41. Ibid., 200.

42. Freedom of the press further requires the existence of private property, the private possession of the material means necessary to disseminate one's views publicly.

43. Thomas Jefferson, letter to Colonel Charles Yancey, January 6, 1816. *The Writings of Thomas Jefferson,* ed. Paul L. Ford (New York: G.P. Putnam, 2010 [1892–99]), Vol. 10:4.

44. For example, the famous Virginia Declaration of Rights, drafted by George Mason in 1776, explicitly defined those eligible for suffrage as all men "having sufficient evidence of permanent common interest with and attachment to the community," which generally meant sufficient property.

45. Women, slaves, native Americans, and persons suffering under various religious disabilities frequently excepted. In some states single women could own property but married women could not. In states like New Jersey, both women and blacks could own property and thus potentially meet the voting qualification.

46. Article I, Section 9, Clause 8: "No title of nobility shall be granted by the United States: and no person holding any office of profit or trust under them, shall, without the consent of the Congress, accept of any present, emolument, office, or title, of any kind whatever, from any king, prince, or foreign state."

47. F. A. Hayek, *The Political Order of a Free People, Law Legislation, and Liberty*, vol. 3 (Chicago: University of Chicago Press, 1979), 5. Hereinafter cited as *POFP*.

48. F. Schultz, "Bracton on Kingship," *English Historical Review* (1945) LX (CCXXXVII): 136–76.

49. Locke, *Second Treatise,* 119.

50. "He who kills a tyrant (i.e., an usurper) to free his country is praised and rewarded." Thomas Aquinas, *Commentary on the Sentences* (Rochester, NY: The Aquinas Institute, 2017), II. d.44.2.2.

51. Hayek, *POFP*, 5.

FIVE

Constitutional Considerations

Ambition and lust for power are the predominant passions in the breasts of most men. —Samuel Adams[1]

The freedom philosophy explored throughout this work is the traditional American response to the implicit question posed by all forms of political philosophy—*what are the rules that ought to govern human relations within society*? The American view, as we have seen, emphasizes the principle of individual liberty. The rules enforced by government should maximize the sphere of voluntary action, that is, minimize arbitrary coercion of the individual by both private individuals and government itself. We have seen that coercion neither can nor should be perfectly eliminated from human society. The traditional American conviction, however, is that governmental coercion should be employed with utmost caution and concern, in a manner limited by law and toward protection of the rights of peaceful and law-abiding persons. This is what it means to say, as does Jefferson, that the proper role of government is to secure the unalienable rights of the individual.

Such a view, however, raises an interesting and important question, namely, *why* should this be the purpose of government? Why should a political order aim to minimize coercive force, that is, maximize freedom? Such a question is simply another way of asking why freedom is important. There is no doubt that freedom has been important to Western society in general and American society in particular. It was important enough to inspire not only the birth of the American nation but the sacrifice of life and fortune—the "blood, toil, tears, and sweat"—of countless human beings over the centuries.[2] Why should this be? And why should the American people continue to cherish the freedom bequeathed at such cost by their forebears? Why should they care about the outcome of the "experiment" which, as George Washington believed, was ". . . entrusted to [their] hands: the preservation of the sacred fire of liberty."?[3]

The exploration of such questions leads beyond the bounds of political philosophy and even moral philosophy more generally. The American philosophy of freedom is, of course, a species of both kinds of philosophy; particular political convictions necessarily derive from more general moral convictions. With respect to individual freedom, traditional American political values and institutions presuppose the moral conviction that such freedom requires no justification. It is regarded, as the Declaration indicates, as self-evidently right, intrinsically right, right-in-itself, a moral entitlement inherent to every human being simply by virtue of his human nature. Because freedom is regarded as self-evidently and intrinsically right, unjustified or arbitrary coercion is regarded as self-evidently and intrinsically wrong, wrong-in-itself, and thus to be minimized so far as humanly possible. The traditional American assumption is that freedom *should* be maximized because permitting human beings to engage in voluntary action is inherently moral; coercion should be minimized because acts of arbitrary coercion are inherently immoral. Free or voluntary choice is an inherent quality of human being, and to deprive a person of freedom is to deprive a person of his humanity, to dehumanize him. The question of freedom is ultimately a moral and even spiritual question, as is the related question of coercion.

Such moral concerns, however, do not exist in isolation but ultimately relate to a more comprehensive set of assumptions regarding the very nature and meaning of human existence. For that reason, an inquiry into the value of freedom in human society necessarily leads to exploration of a deeper and wider level of human consciousness, that is, the "worldview" or *Weltanschauung* that informs moral and political convictions more narrowly conceived. All forms of political philosophy, including the systematic philosophy of freedom embraced by the Americans, are ultimately grounded in an overarching worldview—a complex of assumptions, beliefs, and values, both tacit and explicit, regarding the nature of existence. Political philosophy, as we have seen, is concerned with the specific question of how human beings should treat one another, given the inevitably social nature of human experience. Such a question can only be answered in light of a prior and more comprehensive view of both human nature and the nature of existence itself.

Traditional American convictions relating to individual freedom are far from universal. Indeed the achievement of freedom as historically conceived within American society has been among the rarest experiences in human history. The overwhelming majority of people who have lived on this earth have not enjoyed individual freedom-under-law. They have lived not at their own direction, voluntarily pursuing their own values and goals, but rather at the direction of some other person or persons wielding coercive power of one form or another. The vast majority of human beings throughout history have been oppressed as slaves, serfs, vassals, or otherwise under the thumb of arbitrary rule, whether exercised by emperors, pharaohs, warlords, caliphs, mullahs, military juntas, tribal chieftains, oligarchs, dictators, or other authoritarian rulers controlling human action through force and fear (perhaps under the guise of "law"). Such has been the human condition throughout the greater part of history and, moreover, remains the condition of countless human beings in the contemporary world. It has been estimated that only about 40 percent of the people currently alive on earth live under conditions that would be regarded as free by traditional American standards.[4]

The rarity of freedom in human experience is a curious fact from the American perspective. The American tradition, as we have seen, regards freedom as a universal unalienable right inherently possessed by every human being: "all men . . . are endowed by their Creator" with the unalienable right to liberty. Why, then, has the achievement of freedom remained beyond the reach of most human beings over the course of history? American assumptions readily lead to the contrary expectation, that freedom would be the universal condition of mankind and not a rarity among rarities. Such a puzzle is resolved by recognizing the exceptional nature of American presuppositions and values. The American conception of freedom as a God-given and universal natural right is not universally shared across cultures and peoples but rather unique and specific to its cultural inheritance. The quest for freedom and its institutional protection is a product of the particular worldview that definitively shaped the development of Western civilization in general and its American expression in particular, namely, the Judeo-Christian or biblical worldview transmitted to America by the earliest English settlers. The American commitment to freedom derives from its particular cultural heritage, and especially its spiritual and religious heritage. It is not coincidental that the free society first emerged in Western (Judeo-Christian) civilization. Nor is it coincidental that the only contemporary societies to uphold the value of freedom are those influenced by the Western heritage to one degree or another. One will search in vain for the institutional realization of freedom beyond the orbit of Western culture.[5] Other civilizations, formed on the basis of other cultural and religious presuppositions and values, do not revere individual freedom as Western and especially American civilization has historically revered it. The commitment to, and achievement of, individual freedom is the outgrowth of a unique cultural experience: the widespread assimilation of a unique and religiously inspired conception of existence conjoined, as we shall see, with a unique set of historical circumstances.

ON HUMAN NATURE: THE LUST FOR POWER

The American experiment in ordered liberty is incoherent without recognition of its spiritual and religious presuppositions. Both the demand for individual freedom and corollary demand for limited government are intimately related to the Judeo-Christian vision of existence in general (the biblical worldview) and human nature (so-called Christian anthropology). Such a relation is not surprising. The American Founders were heirs of Western civilization. Western civilization received not only its characteristic values but also its very identity from the decisive influence of biblical religion on its development. Indeed the inseparability of the Western from the biblical worldview is pointedly indicated by the traditional term for Western civilization, namely, Christendom. Americans of the founding era were carriers of a unique and religiously inspired worldview that informed their thought and action at every turn. The definitive role of biblical religion in shaping the development of Western civilization, including its characteristic quest for freedom, has been extensively explored by various scholars.[6] The present discussion focuses more narrowly on the manner in which certain biblically based assumptions informed the Founders' constitutional design. As we have seen, every form of political philosophy, and indeed every law and policy prescription, involves, explicitly or implicitly, a conception of human existence in general and human nature in particular. It is impossible to formulate any rule, including those that relate to political and legal institutions, without prior consideration of the nature of the being to be ruled. Any coherent rule always and necessarily takes into account the defining attributes of the ruled, whether animal, mineral, vegetable, or any conceivable type of entity; rules governing the cultivation of violets must take into account the nature of a violet. The rules that should govern human interaction in society—the subject of political philosophy, including the freedom philosophy—cannot be formulated without considering the nature of human being.

The American Founders held decided views in this regard. The vast majority presupposed a more or less conventional Christian conception of human nature, particularly its Augustinian expression. Human nature is given and universal ("all men are created equal") and, moreover, fallen or imperfect, so constituted that its propensity for darkness can never be dismissed. More particularly, Augustine maintained that every human being since the Fall is driven by three lusts—the lust for material things, the lust for sex, and, most significant for political order, the lust for power (*libido dominandi*). To possess a lust for power is not only to desire but also take positive pleasure in subjecting other people to one's own will. Every person carries within his mind a vision, however implicit or inchoate, of how the world *should* be and how other people *should* behave. Every person engages in ongoing inner commentary—"this is right; that is wrong." The inherent moral dimension of human nature means that no human being can avoid engaging in such discrimination and judgment. The political problem arises from the fact that human beings are driven by the lust for power and thus tempted to leap from such moral judgments to the conclusion that other people should be forced to conform to the former's particular conceptions of right and wrong. The universal lust for power thus poses a very real threat to the exercise of individual freedom. We have discussed the ubiquity of coercion in human existence.

The American Founders may have disagreed on various particulars of constitutional design but not on the general subject of human nature. On this matter, they were in universal agreement: acutely if not obsessively aware of the pleasure human beings take in exercising the lust for power. Indeed, they perceived lust for power lurking in the heart of every human being; no one is immune to its siren call. "Ambition and lust for power," claimed Sam Adams, "are predominant passions in the breasts of most men."[7] Such sentiments were a commonplace of the era and could be repeated almost indefinitely: "[I]t is natural for men to aspire to power—it is the nature of man to be tyrannical"; "Power was never given . . . but it was finally abused"; "Every man has a propensity to power."[8] The universal conviction among the founding generation of the dangers posed by the human lust for power is beyond dispute. One may nevertheless wonder how the Americans acquired such certitude. How did they know that all human beings are driven by the lust for power? Such a question is answered by their shared religious convictions. Political sermons of the colonial and revolutionary era were replete with emphatic warnings regarding the power-lust of man. As John Cotton (1585–1652), one of the foremost theologians of colonial Massachusetts, expressed the general view:

> Let all the world learn to give mortal men no greater power than they are content they shall use, for use it they will. . . . It is . . . most wholesome for magistrates and officers in church and commonwealth never to affect more liberty and authority than will do them good, and the people good; for whatever transcendent power is given will certainly overrun those that receive it. . . . It is necessary, therefore, that all power that is on earth be limited, church power or other. . . . It is counted a matter of danger to the state to limit prerogatives; but it is a further danger, not to have them limited.[9]

One suspects, moreover, that the Founders' firm conviction regarding the universal drive for power derived not only from such religious teaching but also the most compelling of all teachers, namely, personal experience. Individuals who acquire the habit of honest self-examination learn to recognize and acknowledge their personal motives, however unflattering these may be. The profound conviction of the universal lust for power so passionately asserted by the founding generation was surely rooted in knowledge above and beyond that acquired from sermons and books. Such conviction resonates with intimate knowledge of self. Americans of the era, like Augustine in this respect as others, seem to have demanded an unblinking moral realism that settles for nothing less than truth.

The lust for power is a curious phenomenon. The human capacity for imagination and propensity for self-love allows the drive for power to manifest itself in myriad fashions and mask itself in myriad guises, some of which are seemingly benign and even altruistic. To take a contemporary example, consider the controversy over the ingestion of so-called trans-fats, a type of fat commonly used in food preparation. Some people who regard trans-fats as unhealthy and "wrong" have leaped from such a judgment to the conclusion that the use of trans-fats in commercial restaurants should be banned by legislative action (as occurred in New York). Such persons do not want others to eat trans-fats and are displeased when they do so. Banning the intake of trans-fats, on the other hand, induces pleasure for such persons, the pleasure of having other people conform to their sense of right. Legislation banning trans-fats, like all human law, is a form of coercion, typically justified by an ostensibly high-minded concern for the welfare of others. Augustinian insight, however, penetrates beneath such appearance to a more probable reality, namely, that legislation of this nature is inspired not by selfless altruism but rather a far less flattering motive—the lust for power, the desire to dominate and control other people.

Persons in the habit of indulging such a lust may, of course, be blind to their actual motives. The human imagination is so constituted that human beings have the ability and even propensity to cast their personal intentions in self-flattering guises, in this case, as concern for the health of others. Such is only to recognize that human beings have a tremendous capacity for self-deception, the ability to convince themselves of the purity and nobility of their intentions in any and all instances. Individuals may be oblivious to the possibility that their actions are impelled not by altruism but rather the ignoble desire to force other people to live as they themselves think fit; in this case, abstaining from a diet that includes trans-fats.

Such self-styled altruism—forcing other members of society "for their own good"—is dramatically at odds with the manner in which Americans of the founding era generally conceptualized concern for the welfare of their fellows, even if they may have failed to honor such an ideal in practice. On the older view, concern for one's fellows should involve concern for the protection of their rights—the treatment to which they are morally entitled. Such rights include, of course, the unalienable right to liberty. The right to liberty, in the present case, means that an individual is morally entitled to consume unhealthy trans-fats if he voluntarily chooses to do so. Such so-called self-regarding behavior, which harms no one but the individual himself, traditionally falls within the private sphere carved out by his individual rights. Such indeed has been the view consistently upheld by Whigs and classical-liberals from John Locke through the American Founders to John Stuart Mill. As Mill elaborated the traditional view in his celebrated essay "On Liberty" (1859):

> The object of this Essay is to assert one very simple principle, as entitled to govern absolutely the dealings of society with the individual in the way of compulsion and control, whether the means used be physical force in the form of legal penalties, or the moral coercion of public opinion. That principle is, that the sole end for which mankind are warranted, individually or collectively, in interfering with the liberty of action of any of their number, is self-protection. That *the only purpose for which power can be rightfully exercised over any member of a civilized community, against his will, is to prevent harm to others. His own good, either physical or moral, is not sufficient warrant.* He cannot rightfully be compelled to do or forbear because it will be better for him to do so, because it will make him happier, because, in the opinion of others, to do so would be wise, or even right. . . . The only part of the conduct of anyone, for which he is amenable to society, is that which concerns others. In the part which merely concerns himself, his independence is, of right, absolute. Over himself, over his own body and mind, the individual is sovereign [emphasis added].[10]

Mill's so-called Harm Principle neatly summarizes the classical liberal view.[11] No one has the right to force another person to act in a prescribed manner "for his own good," in the case under discussion, for supposedly better health. The liberal tradition has long regarded an individual's physical body as his own possession. As Locke put it, each individual is "the absolute lord of his own person and possessions," including his "property" in his body. The Golden Rule is also relevant in this regard. No individual personally wants to be forced to eat what other persons think he should eat, and it is not difficult to realize that other individuals feel the same sense of resistance: "Do to others what you would want them to do to you" (Luke 6:31).[12] We have seen, moreover, that the American tradition regards the right to liberty as universal as well as unalienable. Every person possesses such a right and thus every other person bears the corresponding moral obligation to refrain from coercing his fellow men, especially from forcibly interfering with their merely self-regarding behavior ("for his own good").

The fact that every individual possesses an equal right to liberty means that members of a free society must often *tolerate* behavior of which they personally disapprove (such as eating trans-fats). Such toleration is in fact another traditional manifestation of concern for the welfare of other persons. One tolerates the choices of others, even when they conflict with one's own preferred choices, precisely because one honors the other person's right to liberty, conceived not only as a moral entitlement but a crucial aspect of his well-being. Toleration so conceived requires moral self-discipline, in particular, acquiring the habit of self-restraint. Individuals in a free society must learn to restrain themselves from forcible interference with the beliefs or self-regarding actions of their fellow men. They must learn, in other words, to restrain the lust for power. A free society is one that honors what might be called the "liberal" commandment: "thou shalt not force others to live as one personally thinks best." The American commitment to universal and unalienable individual rights can only be sustained by a people who honor the negative morality of self-restraint presupposed by such a commitment.

The crucial moral issue regarding the use of coercive force against an individual "for his own good" relates to its justification. Those who advocate legislation that violates the freedom of other persons "for their own good" must provide a moral defense of such action. With respect to the present example, they must explain the grounds of their assumed right to force other people to abstain from serving or ingesting trans-fats, that is, their assumed right to violate the freedom of individuals who voluntarily choose to sell or consume products made with that ingredient. The American political ideal, as we have seen, has invariably championed the principle of universal individual rights. It does not traditionally recognize rights that belong exclusively to a select group of persons, such as all people who wish to ban trans-fats. Such persons have no more right to violate the liberty of fellow citizens than does any other person or group, whether such violation is at gunpoint or by means of coercive legislation. The right to liberty is unalienable, individual, and universal, and no one is exempt from the obligation to refrain from arbitrary coercion, even if exercised with the best of intentions and in the name of another person's "own good." On the traditional American perspective there is no moral justification for legislation banning trans-fats (or similar legislation). Such is rather a clear violation of the individual right to liberty as traditionally conceived in American society, indeed a measure of the extent to which many members of contemporary society betray rather than honor their liberal inheritance.

Leaving aside the contemporary state of American political order, we return to the founding generation. We have seen that Americans of the era held a rather conventional Christian conception of human nature that stressed its imperfection. Such a conception was not, of course, original to the Founders but rather had shaped the development of Western political order for centuries. The Founders, however, advanced beyond previous thinkers who had also emphasized the human potential for lawless depravity. Such an emphasis had historically been a support of authoritarian rulers claiming the right of absolute rule. Fallen human nature, it was said, did not permit social order in the absence of the powerful controlling hand of government; Thomas Hobbes is representative. The American contribution in this regard was to turn the biblical conception of fallen human nature against authoritarian government itself. Augustine's celebrated admonition—rulers need to remember that they too are men—is everywhere implicit in the Founders' constitutional construction.[13] Government office holders, those who rule, are mere men and thus no less immune to the universal lust for power than those whom they rule.

Indeed the *libido dominandi* of political rulers is potentially far more dangerous than the lust for power that also drives private citizens. This is because government, as Augustine, Locke, and the Founders well understood, is the organized agent of coercive force in society. As such, it has at its disposal potentially dangerous power that can be employed by office-holders to indulge their power-lust in innumerable and far-reaching ways. The Founders did not regard such a threat as mere theoretical possibility. Government's propensity to abuse power, they believed, had been amply demonstrated by human history and, indeed, by the British government against which they rebelled. The danger of an unbridled exercise of governmental power was thus foremost in the minds of the Americans and, moreover, the basis of the constitutional limits on government they established. Indeed, a "mistrust of human nature armed with power," as M. Stanton Evan observed, implicitly informs not only the political thought of the American Founders but every coherent theory of limited government.[14]

Both their conception of human nature and the lessons of history, then, led the Founders to regard government with a wary eye. Yet while mistrustful of government, they were not anarchists; government may be a necessary evil but is nevertheless necessary. Such a conclusion also followed from their Christian or Christianized view of human nature. The universal lust for power requires a fundamental mistrust of government, organized and operated as it must be by flawed human beings, a mistrust that calls in turn for limits on its power. But the irremediable imperfection of human nature also means that private citizens will not always honor the rules of just conduct requisite to social existence in general and free government in particular. Human imperfection thus calls for a standing government ready and able to enforce the essential rules of civilized society as necessary. As Alexander Hamilton said,

> Why has government been instituted at all? Because the passions of men will not conform to the dictates of reason and justice without constraint. . . . [But, he cautioned] there is, in the nature of sovereign power, an impatience of control, that disposes those who are invested with the exercise of it, to look with an evil eye upon all external attempts to restrain or direct its operations. . . . [Conflict in the Confederation] has its origin in the love of power.[15]

Hamilton may have employed somewhat different language, but such a view is little different from Augustine's conviction that government is a necessary evil, the consequence of fallen human nature and sin.[16] Madison's variation on this theme has become nothing less than classic: "What is government itself, but the greatest of all reflections of human nature? If men were angels, no government would be necessary. If angels were to govern men, neither external nor internal controuls on government would be necessary." Such, however, is not the human condition; men are not angels and rulers are merely men. Madison thus concludes: "In framing a government which is to be administered by men over men, the great difficulty lies in this: you must first enable the government to control the governed; and in the next place oblige it to control itself."[17] Such is essential, he emphasizes, because "all men having power ought to be distrusted to a certain degree."[18]

Virtue and Free Government

The Founders were leery of human nature, especially when armed with political power. Their recognition of the human potential for evil, however, did not blind them to its simultaneous potential for goodness. Human beings, after all, are made in God's image, endowed with reason and free will, potentially capable of overcoming the "worse angels" of their nature and rising to genuine morality and virtue. The Founders, unlike Hobbes, did not condemn human beings to an endless pursuit of power-after-power. They perceived instead the possibility that human beings can acquire the moral self-discipline and self-restraint necessary to live in harmony with their fellow men, in other words, to honor and respect their rights. Indeed the Founders emphasized that free government depends precisely upon such a capacity for individual self-government. A society of human beings who are unable to restrain their lusts, their impulses to violate others, cannot know freedom but must rather live under an omnipresent police. The concept of free or limited government, by contrast, presupposes a moral people capable of both self-regulation and respect for the rights of other individuals. As Madison said, the hope for free government is based squarely on the possibility of such virtue: "To suppose that any form of government will secure liberty or happiness without any virtue in the people, is a chimerical idea."

It is obvious that every society must achieve some degree of order; chaos, Hobbesian or otherwise, is clearly undesirable. Edmund Burke observed that such requisite social order can be attained in two, and only two, ways—from without or from within. The first possibility, order from without, requires a powerful and absolute government. It requires something akin to the "mortal god" that is the Hobbesian Sovereign, a government charged with overseeing and controlling the putative immorality and lawlessness of human action. Such an externally ordered society offers little possibility of freedom and limited government but rather requires a ubiquitous coercive presence to enforce the wide-ranging law and legislation that must be imposed on a personally lawless people. The second possibility, order from within, allows, by contrast, for free government. The concept of limited government presupposes the existence of self-governing individuals, individuals who have internalized the rules of morality, personal and social, and formed the habit of doing what is right for-its-own-sake, not merely from fear of external punishment. It presupposes a society of individuals who are largely governed by their own conscience. Such individuals have no need of an omnipresent police or plethora of legislation, no need of Big Brother, of absolute or unlimited political power; they largely govern their own thoughts and actions. Free government demands precisely such an internally or self-governing people. Only a virtuous people so conceived can achieve order without external imposition and sustain the stringent moral demands required for the existence and preservation of limited government and a regime of universal individual rights.

The moral realism of the Founders, then, involved recognition of the dual moral potentialities of human beings—the potential for goodness and the potential for its opposite. Unlike political theorists who exaggerate one or the other such propensity—Hobbes's conviction of the utter depravity of human nature and Rousseau's equally unbalanced assertion that "man is naturally good"—the Americans perceived human beings whole and as they are, neither utterly evil nor utterly good.[19] They recognized the human potential for both good and evil, linked as it is to yet another assumption derived from their Judeo-Christian heritage—the existence of free will. Indeed, insofar as the dual moral potentialities of human beings hinge on the human capacity for moral choice, it might be said that the existence of free will is the very linchpin of the Founders' moral vision.

Such a dualistic view of human nature, moreover, is central to American constitutional construction, implicit in the design of the United States Constitution. On the one hand, the universal lust for power, in conjunction with the human capacity to choose evil, requires that permanent and "fixed" limits be placed upon the actions of government.[20] Angels do not govern men; it is and must always be administered by imperfect human beings prone to indulge the lust for power. Establishing such limits is, of course, the principal purpose of the U.S. Constitution and Bill of Rights. Human nature is so constituted that no one is competent to be entrusted with unlimited power. No human being, not even a Mother Teresa, is capable of resisting its temptations, and rulers need to remember that they are merely men. As the nineteenth-century historian Lord Acton succinctly expressed the traditional view, "Power tends to corrupt and absolute power corrupts absolutely."[21]

On the other hand, the existence of free will means that human beings are capable of choosing goodness. It means they are capable of moral self-government, of cultivating the virtue, self-discipline, and self-restraint necessary for the preservation of free government and security of individual rights. It means they are capable of caring for more than own personal desires and interests, caring for the rights of others as well as their own. Defense of one's rights is undoubtedly a virtue, but a free society also requires individuals who are capable of respecting and defending the rights of others. Such a moral achievement is utterly essential to a free society based on a conception of universal individual rights. Moreover, only a self-governing people can be permitted to enjoy a wide sphere of individual freedom, to follow their own conscience, to pursue their own goals and values. Freedom always implies responsibility for the consequences of one's choices, a burden not easily borne by the morally immature. A people incapable of self-government, those who cannot or will not discipline impulses or desires that would lead to a violation of other persons, or who will not consider the consequences of their actions, must be subjected to external compulsion, to human government. As Burke said, "society cannot exist, unless a controlling power upon will and appetite be placed somewhere; and the less of it there is within, the more there must be without. It is ordained in the eternal constitution of things, that men of intemperate minds cannot be free. Their passions forge their fetters."[22]

The human potential for virtue or goodness is further significant for American constitutional order insofar as it provides grounds for hope that the ideals it embodies may in fact be realized, however partially or imperfectly. In other words, it means that free government, like freedom itself, is not merely a beautiful ideal but also capable of actualization. The human capacity to choose the good means that the American people are capable of honoring the Constitution and rule of law, even when these impose constraints on the spheres of individual and collective action. Such a capacity is crucial to American constitutional order because only a people willing to honor the higher law of the Constitution, and the rule of law more generally, over and above their immediate personal desires can maintain such a form of government.

The importance of such willing acquiescence to constitutional values is readily illustrated by concrete example. To recur to an earlier example, suppose that a substantial majority of the people passionately desire to suppress the speech of an obnoxious group, say, neo-Nazis. The First Amendment establishes a constitutional obstacle to fulfillment of the majority's desires; it expressly forbids Congress from enacting law that abridges freedom of speech. Only a people prepared to recognize and honor the higher and enduring values of American constitutionalism, values that may conflict with the realization of immediate desires, can preserve such an order. No mere "parchment barrier," as Madison put it, can maintain American constitutional order in the absence of an underlying moral and political ethos predisposed to respect its provisions.[23] Limited or constitutional government requires adherence not only to written or positive law, such as the explicit law of the Constitution, but also to what has been called the "unwritten constitution," which includes the tacit or implicit morality of self-restraint upon which formal constitutional arrangements rest.[24] The existence of a written constitution cannot in itself restrain a people from violating its letter or spirit or the rights of their fellow men. With respect to American society, the people must first and foremost be *willing* to defer to both the higher law of the Constitution and the higher moral law, the law of nature, which establishes not only their personal unalienable rights but those of their fellow human beings as well. While free government is inherently fragile, the evidence provided by the historical experience of the American people clearly demonstrates that human beings have the capacity to honor and practice the rules of just conduct, written and unwritten, essential to its preservation. Free government may be difficult to sustain but is more than a chimera.

Statecraft as Soulcraft

The Founders' views on the relation between virtue and free government represent a sharp departure from a long-standing tradition of rule derived from classical political philosophy. Plato (c. 427–347 B.C.), generally regarded as the first political philosopher in Western history, famously argued in *The Republic* that the attainment of good government is only possible if the reins of power are exclusively held by the wisest and most virtuous members of society, the so-called philosopher-kings. A political order, he said, cannot achieve justice unless and until kings become philosophers or philosophers become kings. The American Founders would reject such a view. The Founders, unlike Plato, did not regard the achievement of good government as *ultimately* dependent on the personal qualities of those who rule. It would, of course, be best if only persons of the highest virtue and integrity were to attain political office. The Founders, however, did not expect the normal course of events consistently to produce such results; as Madison pointedly observed, "enlightened statesmen will not always be at the helm."[25] The Founders' hope for good government did not center on the selection of particular statesman or officeholders but rather on the virtue of the people at large and careful crafting of political institutions. The Founders, in contrast to Plato, did not believe that any human being, however great in knowledge or virtue, possesses qualifications that issue in a title to unlimited rule. Rulers need to remember that they are merely men, that is, congenitally prone to power lust and, moreover, constrained to "see through a glass, darkly."[26] In other words, the Founders, unlike Plato, were heirs of Judeo-Christian civilization and its fundamental assumption of fallen or imperfect human nature.

The American solution to the problem of good government in light of human nature so conceived is not the philosopher-king but rather limited government. No one is to be entrusted with the exercise of political power except within certain well-defined limits, for certain well-defined purposes, and in accordance with the higher law of the Constitution. We recall in this regard that American government was established as a "government of laws, not of men."[27] In a society ruled by such a government, as we have seen, no human being, philosopher-king or other, governs other human beings; rather *impersonal* law governs every institution and every person, ruled and rulers alike. American officeholders who take the oath of office swear not to obey some personal superior, president, king, or *Fuehrer* but rather "preserve, protect and defend the Constitution," that is, secure the impersonal rule of law, including the law that limits their own power.[28]

In this regard as in others, the Americans had more in common with medieval than pre-Christian thinkers such as Plato. For American as for medieval thinkers, no human being, whatever his personal qualities, social status, or political position, is above the law. The medieval jurist Bracton, as we recall, succinctly expressed the universal conviction of the Judeo-Christian tradition: "the king is under God, and under law." The Founders, as heirs to this tradition, utterly rejected any and all conceptions of *personal* sovereignty or *personal* government of any kind, whether rule by one person, several persons, or a collective majority of persons. A free society has no place for philosopher-kings entitled to rule solely on the basis of purportedly superior wisdom, virtue, or personal qualities of any kind. In a free society, rulers, like all other men, are governed by sovereign, impersonal, and universal law.

The Founders, as we have seen, believed that free government could only be secured by a virtuous people, both the people at large and statesmen, representatives, and leaders. The blessings of liberty and limited government could only be enjoyed by individuals who govern their own behavior in accord with the moral law. A lawless or degenerate people does not possess the requisite personal character and virtue, the internal moral discipline required to sustain constitutional government, the rule of law, and a regime of universal individual rights. The Founders well recognized the indispensability of moral self-government to free government and were thus concerned with its source or spring. Many of them concluded that one such source, perhaps the chief source, is religion, generally understood as Protestant Christianity of one form or another. For this reason—the perceived link among free government, moral self-government, and religion—statesmen such as George Washington thought it wise to ensure the vitality of religion in American society. His celebrated "Farewell Address" (1796) spoke directly to such a concern:

> Of all the dispositions and habits which lead to political prosperity, religion and morality are indispensable supports. In vain would that man claim the tribute of patriotism, who should labor to subvert these great pillars of human happiness, these firmest props of the duties of

> men and citizens. The mere politician, equally with the pious man, ought to respect and to cherish them. A volume could not trace all their connections with private and public felicity. Let it simply be asked: Where is the security for property, for reputation, for life, if the sense of religious obligation desert the oaths which are the instruments of investigation in courts of justice? And let us with caution indulge the supposition that morality can be maintained without religion. Whatever may be conceded to the influence of refined education on minds of peculiar structure, reason and experience both forbid us to expect that national morality can prevail in exclusion of religious principle.
>
> 'Tis substantially true, that virtue or morality is a necessary spring of popular government. The rule, indeed, extends with more or less force to every species of free government. Who that is a sincere friend to it can look with indifference upon attempts to shake the foundation of the fabric?[29]

John Adams also cautioned that "[o]ur Constitution was made only for a moral and religious people. It is wholly inadequate to the government of any other."[30] Religion, for Adams and the great majority of the Founders, meant Christianity. "The general principles upon which the Fathers achieved independence," he stated, "were the general principles of Christianity."[31] Such comments could be multiplied endlessly, expressing as they do the more or less general opinion of the era.

The Founders, then, conceived an intimate relation between virtue or morality and free government, on the one hand, and morality and religion, on the other, yielding, of course, the previously noted triadic relation among virtue, free government, and religion. Religion (Christianity) gives rise to a virtuous people, a people thus capable of sustaining free government. Free government, accordingly, is dependent on both virtue and religion. Such a conviction led various thinkers of the era to express support for religious institutions in America on both spiritual and utilitarian grounds. We have seen that the Americans rejected the Platonic conception of the philosopher-king. They further rejected a related concept characteristic of the Platonic and pre-Christian philosophical tradition, the view conventionally summarized as *statecraft as soulcraft*. The basic idea is that government ("statecraft") should be responsible for the moral and spiritual formation of the people ("soulcraft"). Such a view is characteristic of pre-Christian or pagan societies that had not yet differentiated the strictly political from the strictly religious dimensions of human existence. The pagan conception, however, has been rephrased and revived in modern society, even by certain self-proclaimed Christian writers.[32] In the language of contemporary American discourse, the issue is whether government should be involved in "legislating morality," that is, employ its coercive power to instill virtue in the people, to make them good. Such a view is implicit in contemporary governmental efforts at so-called social engineering, such as the stated intention of recent public officials to legally "nudge" or coerce people to make better choices by penalizing behavior the government deems wrong.[33] It similarly informs the contemporary concept of "hate-speech" and related constructs.[34]

For present purposes, we will leave aside the contentious issue of the substantive content of morality.[35] The question at hand is whether government has the right or indeed the ability to determine, or even encourage, the moral formation of the people. Plato and pagan culture more generally believed it did; such practice was not only commonplace in the ancient and classical world but the norm. "Statecraft as soulcraft" was more or less universally practiced in pre-Christian societies because, as mentioned, such societies did not sharply distinguish between religion and government, between the moral and the legal. Pagan society characteristically united religious and political ("secular") authority in the same hands; in contemporary language, "separation of Church and State" had not yet been conceived. Consequently, pagan rulers generally claimed authority over all aspects of social life, including moral and religious belief and practice. The laws in such societies served a dual function, secular and religious; they aimed not only to prevent wrongdoing but also to make men good.

Christianity overturned such pagan conceptions. It did so by conceptually differentiating religion and government as two distinct spheres of jurisdiction, "God" and "Caesar" ("Church" and "State"). The jurisdiction of government was henceforth to be limited to worldly concerns. The spiritual and moral life of the people was henceforth to fall under the jurisdiction, not of secular government but rather religious authority. Such Christian conceptions would have profound significance for the development of Western political order. The point at present is that the American Founders inherited and embraced the traditional Christian view of the distinction between religion and government. While the desirable degree of "separation" between Church and State was variously interpreted and the distinction at times violated in practice, Americans of the revolutionary and founding era did not generally regard government as either entitled or competent to instill virtue in the people. Indeed the Founders themselves would absolutely prohibit the federal government from intervening in spiritual or moral concerns; such religious regulation as did occur was reserved to the several state governments. We recall, moreover, that the first natural right claimed by American colonists was the right of conscience. Religion and morality were generally regarded as prior to and independent of government. The Founders established constitutional limits on its power precisely to ensure the moral and religious autonomy of the people, an issue of such importance as to be addressed in the very first clauses of the First Amendment to the U.S. Constitution.

Moreover, the Founders not only denied the new federal government constitutional authority to interfere with the spiritual life of the people but also implicitly denied its competence to do so. Rulers are just men, and mere election to political office does not endow a person with any special moral, spiritual, or religious insight. Locke, as we recall, explicitly asserted the utter impotence of government with respect to religious belief and conviction. The only tool possessed by government, he observed, is coercive force. Coercion, he argued, may influence a person's outward behavior but can never touch the inner man. The inner life of faith and the spirit is inherently immune to coercive pressure; it can be touched only by "inward persuasion" of mind and heart, by voluntary acceptance.[36] On such a view, defended not only by Locke but fellow Protestant dissenters as well, the conception of "statecraft as soulcraft" is nothing short of preposterous.

THE UNITED STATES CONSTITUTION

We have seen that all coherent philosophies of limited government, including and especially the philosophy of the American Founders, involve an implicit distrust of political power. The Founders' conception of human nature, in conjunction with the lessons of history, led them to conclude that no human being can be permitted to wield unlimited power. The central aim of their constitutional design was thus to limit the scope of government while simultaneously providing the means essential to fulfillment of its legitimate purposes. We have previously encountered Madison's characterization of the problem: "In framing a government which is to be administered by men over men . . . you must first enable the government to control the governed; and in the next place oblige it to control itself." The sword of government, as we have seen, is always dual-edged: its coercive power is necessary to constrain the wicked but also subject to abuse by those who wield it. The tool of coercion can be employed for good or ill. Government, as experience had painfully taught the American colonists, can prove as dangerous to the safety of individual rights as predatory actions of private individuals. The Founders' task was thus to devise a government strong enough to facilitate the good—liberty and justice—while simultaneously preventing, so far as humanly possible, the bad—abuse of power and consequent injustice. The problems involved in such a task were not exclusive to the founding generation but perennially confront every generation of Americans, stemming as they do from human nature itself.

The general aim of the Framers' Constitution, then, was simultaneously to establish the structure of the federal government and limit the range of its activity to the purposes specified in the Preamble to the Constitution: *We the People of the United States, in Order to form a more perfect Union, establish Justice, insure domestic Tranquility, provide for the common defence, promote the general Welfare, and secure the Blessings of Liberty to ourselves and our Posterity, do ordain and establish this Constitution for the United States of*

America. The U.S. Constitution not only establishes the institutional structure of the federal government but also the bounds, explicit and implicit, of its proper authority.[37] Such limits were established by various devices: the American invention of a *written* constitution; a Bill of Rights that imposes clear and specific limits on the power of the federal government; and various institutional constructs embedded in the structure of the government that were intended to serve as further obstacles to potential abuse of power, including federalism, separation of powers, and various so-called checks and balances.

We begin with the American invention of a written constitution. The colonial Americans, as we recall, unhappily discovered that the rights and liberties they traditionally enjoyed under the British constitution ultimately proved no barrier to aggrandizement of power by the British government of the era. Developments in England since the Glorious Revolution of 1688 had led to changes in the British constitution, in particular, the embrace of a novel political doctrine known as *parliamentary sovereignty.* Parliament, asserted the British, held an absolute (unconditional) right to legislate as it, and it alone, saw fit. Strenuous American objections to such a constitutional innovation were summarily dismissed by the British. The unwritten constitution of the British people—a collection of historical precedents, judicial rulings, custom, statutory and common law—had proved incapable of providing the security of rights demanded by the Americans. The conclusion drawn from such experience was that protection of their rights required an explicit *written* document specifying such rights with precision and also establishing institutional mechanisms to enforce them. Common sense recognizes that a formal written contract provides greater security than a handshake and a promise. The first written constitutions were established by the several newly established states in the period following the break with England.[38] The state constitutions drew on such precedents as the Mayflower Compact, the written colonial charters granted by the British crown, and even the Bible. The new federal constitution was a natural extension of such local experience and practice.

Federalism

Beyond the invention of a written constitution, the Founders also intended the intrinsic design of the new United States government, as prescribed in the Constitution, to provide further safeguards for their rights and against potential abuse of governmental power. One of the principal institutional devices to serve this purpose is *federalism* or *decentralization.* A *federal* government is one in which political power is divided and dispersed among various governmental entities, toward the end of preventing concentration of power in one center. In the United States, power and authority (jurisdiction) is divided, first, between the federal government and the fifty states, and further divided within the several states among counties, cities, townships villages, parishes, and other forms of local government. The division of political power between the federal and state governments is conventionally termed "dual sovereignty." We recall that sovereignty in political discourse refers to an ultimate governmental authority, beyond which there is no other. On the American conception, the new federal government was to be sovereign—the ultimate authority—within its legitimate constitutional sphere and the several state governments were to be sovereign—the ultimate authority—within their legitimate constitutional spheres.

The American conception of federalism thus refers to the various *levels* of government comprised by the political order of the United States—federal, state, and local. American government includes numerous and distinct entities, some of which are federal and some of which are state or local. Each such entity is established by law and bounded by its constitutionally defined area of jurisdiction (the area within which it is lawfully competent to operate). The U.S. Constitution establishes the structure and jurisdiction of the federal government in Washington, DC, and the fifty state constitutions establish the structure of the fifty state governments comprised by the Union. In addition to federal and state governments, the United States is also marked, as mentioned, by a wide variety of local governmental entities, each of whose authority is defined and limited by the constitutions or charters that establish them. "Government" in the United States is a complex entity that comprises all three levels—federal, state, and local.

The significance of a federal system of the American type may be grasped by comparing such a form of government to its opposite—a *unitary* or *centralized* government. A centralized government, as the name suggests, centralizes or concentrates all governmental authority and power in one entity. For purposes of illustration, assume that the government of the United States were constituted not as a federal but rather as a unitary or centralized government. If such were the case, the federal government would have exclusive and universal jurisdiction throughout the entire nation, that is, constitute the only authority legally entitled to declare, adjudicate, and enforce law. There would, of course, be no state or local laws or ordinances since there would be no state or local governments. Political representation would be limited to the members elected to the federal Congress in Washington, which would legislate for the entire nation en masse. There would be no state legislatures, no state congressmen or senators; no state executives (governors); no state judges or courts of law; no local government, no city councils or mayors, and so on. All government would be centralized in one overarching and universal power and, moreover, possess exclusive authority to make, interpret, and enforce the law to be uniformly imposed throughout the nation.

It is not difficult to understand why the American Founders rejected a system of centralized political power in no uncertain terms, indeed, condemned such government as the utmost extreme of despotism: "The accumulation of all powers in the same hands," said Madison, "whether of one, a few or many, and whether hereditary, self-appointed, or elective, may justly be pronounced the very definition of tyranny."[39] It is tyrannical precisely because such a centralized government encounters few, if any, "checks" to the potential abuse of power. There was thus no question of consolidating power exclusively in the newly created federal government, the danger of which, as we shall see, led so-called Antifederalists of the era to oppose ratification of the Constitution. The perils posed by "consolidated power" may have especially alarmed the Antifederalists, but they were not alone in such apprehensions. Both Antifederalists and their political opponents—the so-called Federalists—unanimously agreed that prevention of tyranny requires dispersal of political power and such must be achieved, in part, by establishment of a federal or decentralized government.

The Founders regarded federalism as essential to free government for various reasons. First and foremost, we have seen that decentralized government prevents the concentration of political power and thus lessens the possibility of its abuse. A federal system of government also allows for better representation of the people in political affairs and provides for greater accountability among officeholders. Decentralized government is vastly superior to a uniform and remote central government in this regard because state and local governments are necessarily closer to the people, in both a physical and cultural sense. Accordingly, they can better accommodate the diverse opinions of the people associated within the myriad local communities comprised by the United States. The proximity of state and local representatives to those who keep them in power—their constituents—further means that officeholders must attend far more closely to their constituent's concerns than if safely sequestered in a distant national capital. Political accountability is facilitated for the same reason. Federalism, then, is one of the major devices the Founders employed to limit the power of the new federal or "general" government. Its purpose is to prevent governmental despotism or tyranny, regarded as the inevitable consequence of centralized or consolidated political power. A remote, unaccountable, centralized government that can legislate, adjudicate, and enforce the law as it sees fit must lead to the destruction of republican liberty and the trampling of justice, precisely the ends the U.S. Constitution aims to prevent.

Federalism is also essential to free government insofar as the Founders regarded the several states comprised by the United States both as bulwarks against violation of the people's unalienable rights and guarantees for the existence of republican self-government. The newly established federal government was to have limited jurisdiction that encompassed only those powers specifically enumerated in the U.S. Constitution itself. The Tenth Amendment clearly states that all other powers are reserved "to the States respectively, or to the people."[40] The sovereignty of the several states within their legitimate jurisdiction was intended to prevent the imposition of a uniform national agenda and thus allow for the existence of vibrant and diverse moral and cultural communities, that is, authentic self-government. For that reason, the sovereign state governments were regarded as crucial elements of American constitutional order, the first line of defense against the perennial danger of encroaching centralized power.

Separation of Powers

Similar fears of governmental tyranny informed the second constitutional device the Founders employed to prevent abuse of power by the new federal government—so-called separation of powers. Federalism, as we have seen, refers to the distinct *levels* of government comprised by American political order (federal, state, and local). Separation of powers, by contrast, refers to the distinct *branches*—legislative, executive, and judicial—characteristic of both the federal and state governments in the United States. The purpose of institutionally separating the three main functions or powers of government is identical to the purpose of establishing a federal structure of government—to divide and disperse political power in order to prevent its abuse. The Founders regarded separation of powers, like federalism, as an essential attribute of free government. We have previously encountered their firm and universal conviction, famously articulated by Jefferson and restated by Madison: "[a]ll the powers of government, legislative, executive, and judiciary . . . concentrat[ed] . . . in the same hands is precisely the definition of despotic government."[41]

The concept of separation of powers was briefly discussed in Locke's account of the rise of government in the *Second Treatise*. As we recall, the three "inconveniences" of the Lockean state of nature were remedied by the creation of three branches of government, each of which is assigned a specific and distinct function. The legislative branch declares the law; the judicial branch adjudicates the law; and the executive branch enforces the law. By the time of the American Founding, there was more or less universal agreement that free government requires the division of governmental functions in such a manner. The alternative, of course, would be a unified governmental entity simultaneously exercising the three functions of government. A government that simultaneously possesses the power to make, interpret, and enforce the law renders the people helpless before its designs.

Such tyranny arises from the lack of obstacles or "checks" to the potential abuse of power inherent in such a system. To provide a concrete illustration of the dangers involved, imagine that the Constitution of the United States provides not for separation or independence of the three branches of the federal government but rather consolidates all three functions in a single entity. Further suppose that the unitary power in this hypothetical system enacts a law that compels citizens to pay 90 percent of their earned income in taxes to the government. There are no institutional obstacles to such a law, for instance, no independent executive with the power to veto such legislation. Nor is there an independent judiciary that can review the law for its constitutionality or otherwise challenge its interpretation; the unitary power can interpret the law as it sees fit and with impunity. The same power can then employ the executive or coercive force it simultaneously wields to enforce the law—a law which it has made and which it alone interprets—as it chooses. In short, a consolidated governmental entity that can make, adjudicate, and enforce the law offers absolutely no security for the rights and liberties of the people, which are ever at its mercy; it is rather, as Jefferson said, the very definition of despotism. The separation of powers, like the federal structure also established by the U.S. Constitution, aims precisely to prevent such dictatorial oppression.

Further Checks and Balances

The Founders' overarching concern with potential governmental tyranny, then, was addressed by the establishment of a written constitution, federalism, and separation of powers. The separation of powers was further reinforced by the design of various Constitutional mechanisms that aim to provide members of the three independent branches of the federal government with both the means and the incentive to enforce the division of power. Each of the three branches is provided with institutional authority to "check" an encroachment of power by one or both of the other branches. Such institutional devices include a bicameral legislature; the executive veto; impeachment of executive and judicial officeholders; Senate confirmation of executive appointments and treaties; and an independent judiciary.[42] By such means, members of one branch are constitutionally empowered to resist another branch that is perceived to abuse its power or violate the Constitution in some fashion.

To illustrate the significance and operation of such constitutional checks, assume a scenario in which both houses of Congress, the House of Representatives and Senate, are dominated by the influence of unscrupulous "special interests" ("factions" or "sinister interests," in the language of an older tradition).[43] The two houses jointly enact legislation that benefits such interests at the expense of the rights of individuals, minorities, or taxpayers in general. Every American school child knows the procedure whereby a bill becomes law in the United States, that is, it must be independently passed by both houses of Congress and also signed by the president. The executive branch, represented by the president, is provided with the constitutional means to check such abuse of power by the legislative branch: the president can exercise the executive veto. Or suppose that the president is as corrupt as Congress and both branches jointly enact legislation that violates the Constitution or the rights of the people. The Founders' remedy was to establish an independent judiciary that possesses constitutional means to check such abuse of power by the other two branches. Early in the American experience, Chief Justice John Marshall established the legitimacy of so-called judicial review, that is, the authority of the U.S. Supreme Court to strike down or invalidate federal legislation that violates the fundamental or higher law of the Constitution. Such authority provides the Court with institutional means to thwart abuse of power by a renegade or corrupt Congress and president by declaring federal legislation unconstitutional. Additional such checks, as mentioned, include the provisions for impeachment of the president and federal judges by joint Congressional action and the requirement for Senate confirmation of certain executive appointees, treaties, and nominees, such as to the Supreme Court. Such devices enable the legislative branch to restrain a corrupt executive or judiciary.

The Founders further relied upon the self-interest of political actors as an additional support for preserving the constitutional separation of powers. That is, they believed that the personal ambition of congressional representatives, presidents, and judges would align itself with defense of the constitutional authority of their respective branches. They did not anticipate passive submission of any of the three independent branches to attempts by other branches to grasp illegitimate power. If nothing else, the Founders believed, mere personal self-interest would lead the several members of the respective branches to defend the authority and autonomy of their branch against encroachment by the others, thereby defending, however inadvertently, the Constitution itself. As Madison famously summarized the underlying theory, "Ambition must be made to counteract ambition. The interest of the man must be connected with the constitutional rights of the place."[44] We have previously discussed the Founders' view of human nature and their moral realism. "Self-interest rightly understood," as Alexis de Tocqueville famously characterized the Founders' conception, was regarded as a sure spring of human action, for political actors as for every human being.[45] Human nature cannot be changed; neither the lust for power nor the propensity to act on the basis of self-interest can be eradicated from the human heart. The Founders believed, however, that proper institutional design can ameliorate or constrain certain of their more harmful manifestations and perhaps even channel such propensities in beneficial directions. The hope was that various constitutional mechanisms—checks and balances—united with personal ambition and self-interest, would provide additional safeguards against the ever-likely abuse of power in a government "administered by men over men."

Another such check on the potential abuse of power, one whose significance is frequently misrepresented in contemporary American political discourse, involves the so-called gridlock that may result from the federal legislative process. The term gridlock, of course, refers to a situation in which action comes to a standstill, as in a traffic jam. With respect to federal legislation, it refers to a situation in which congressional representatives are unable to reach sufficient agreement to pass legislation through the House or Senate or both. The legislative process comes to a standstill; it is gridlocked. Political commentators often bemoan this consequence of American constitutional design, suggesting that the potential for gridlock is a flaw that stands in need of correction. From the perspective of the American Founders, on the contrary, such a possible outcome of the legislative process is highly desirable. Accordingly, they deliberately created a complex process that establishes numerous roadblocks to the enactment of federal legislation. These include, first, a bicameral legislature consisting of two houses. Federal legislation requires passage in both the House and Senate, whose members, moreover, are elected at different times and for different durations of tenure. One of the purposes of the latter provisions is to avoid complicity between the two houses of Congress by establishing electoral distance between them. Legislation further requires the signature of the executive and the ability to pass constitutional muster. Federal legislation may thus be blocked from passage at various points in the political process, congressional, executive, and judicial. When such occurs, when agreement cannot be reached among the requisite constitutional actors, a bill cannot be passed into law; gridlock arises.

Such was precisely the intention of the Framers. The complexity of the legislative process, and thus potential for gridlock, was deliberately designed to prevent the passage of unwise or hasty legislation, rammed through Congress by zealous majorities and signed into law by a president perhaps eager for popular approval or desirous of fulfilling some nefarious purpose. The Founders, as we have seen, mistrusted not only political officeholders but also popular majorities and public policy driven by emotion. They were acutely aware of the propensity of political majorities to consider only their own interest and disregard either the rights of those who hold a minority interest or the long-term welfare of the nation. Madison's perceptive comment is worth repeating in this context: "In Republics, the great danger is, that the majority may not sufficiently respect the rights of the minority." The Founders further understood that the electorate is easily swayed by both emotion and immediate concerns, often blinding majorities to reason and long-term considerations. As has been discussed, every individual understands that he should not make important decisions under sway of strong emotion but rather upon calm and rational deliberation. Individuals also know they should consider the long-term consequences of their actions, not merely their immediate or short-run gratification. Political majorities, constituted as they are by individual human beings, are no different.

The Framers thus aimed to ensure that any legislation passed by Congress was actually in accord with the deliberate, considered opinion of the people and not a reckless response to narrow self-interest or mere emotion, so easily whipped into frenzy by the arts of politicians and demagogues. Constitutional hurdles to the passage of legislation aim to ensure sufficient time for reflection on the wisdom of every act or policy measure, including its long-term consequences. Toward that end, the Framers crafted the potential for gridlock within their constitutional design. Such potential is not a flaw in the U.S. Constitution but, on the contrary, one of its great strengths. Far better, on the Framers' view, to reach a standstill than pass unwise or unjust legislation that fails to provide for the long-term good of American society or protect the rights of individuals or the minority. The latter possibility was of special concern. Madison is again worth repeating in this context: "There is no maxim . . . which is more liable to be misapplied . . . than that the interest of the majority is the political standard of right and wrong." We have discussed the Founders' great concern regarding the possibility of majoritarian tyranny. The purpose of government is not to realize the will of the majority but rather, as Madison said, to secure justice, conceived as an objective standard of right and wrong that may or may not conform to majority opinion. Justice entails, among other obligations, majority respect for the rights of the individual and the minority. It entails the exercise of moral restraint, both individual self-restraint and institutional restraint on the part of majorities. A mere political majority is no more entitled to violate the rights of others than is the individual. Gridlock is yet another institutional device intended to assist imperfect human beings in restraining the lower propensities of their dual nature.

It cannot be too often repeated that the Founders were leery of human nature armed with power. "Power," they believed, "is of an encroaching nature," and their unflagging aim was to constrain its exercise within proper boundaries.[46] Political power, they realized, can be abused not only by individual dictators or tyrants but also political majorities acting through their elected representatives. Jefferson's admonition is worth repeating in this regard: "One hundred and seventy-three despots [the number of contemporary congressional representatives] would surely be as oppressive as one. . . . An *elective* despotism was not the government we fought for; but one . . . in which the powers of government should be so divided and balanced . . . as that no one could transcend their legal limits, without being effectually checked and restrained by the others." Meticulous constitutional construction—a written constitution, federalism, separation of powers, and the various institutional checks under discussion, including the potential for gridlock—aimed precisely to prevent transgression of the legal limits to power so carefully crafted by the American Framers.

The Antifederalists and the Bill of Rights

It might be said that two chief groups were instrumental in framing the U.S. Constitution—those concerned with restraining the human lust for power, on the one hand, and those obsessed with restraining that lust, on the other. The former are usually called Federalists and the latter Antifederalists. The conventional labels, however, are somewhat misleading, even ironic, a product of the propaganda wars of the period. The self-styled Federalists tended to support ratification of the new Constitution; the Antifederalists, probably characterized as such by their Federalist opponents, tended to oppose ratification. The irony is that the Antifederalists' grounds for such opposition largely stemmed from their concern to establish a truly federal government, the system of dual sovereignty previously discussed. The proposed Constitution, they argued, threatened to "consolidate" power in the new government, establishing a national and not an authentically federal system. Their particular fear was that certain ambiguous language in the document would be manipulated by officeholders toward the end of concentrating power in the new federal government, thus threatening the sovereign rights of the several states and the citizens thereof. Several well-known constitutional phrases were of special concern in this regard, for instance, the "General Welfare" clause; the "Necessary and Proper" clause; the "Supremacy" clause; and the "Commerce" clause.[47] On the Antifederalist view, the universal lust for power all but ensured that such phrases would be stretched far beyond their intended meaning to justify an illicit expansion of power by the (nominally) federal government. By such means, they feared, the new American government would be transformed over time from a truly federal system into a national or centralized government that would "destroy the state governments," that is, absorb into itself functions that properly belong to the several states. Such, said Patrick Henry, would not only destroy republican liberty, self-government by the states, but also "swallow the liberties of the people."[48]

To such Antifederalist apprehensions do Americans owe the Bill of Rights, the first ten amendments to the U.S. Constitution. The Antifederalists refused to support ratification of the Constitution unless and until they were given explicit guarantees of the strictly limited jurisdiction of the proposed federal government. Like the demand for a written constitution more generally, the Antifederalists demanded specific written prohibitions on the reach of federal power. Such prohibitions, enumerated in the Bill of Rights, circumscribe, so to speak, a sphere of sovereignty for both the states as such and the individual as such. The former are guaranteed autonomy with respect to their constitutionally reserved powers, and the latter is guaranteed a constitutionally bounded private sphere wherein he is free to pursue his values and goals unimpeded by arbitrary coercion on the part of the federal government. In this context, we recall the general meaning of a right as held by the architects of American constitutional order: a moral claim that involves a corresponding obligation on the part of another agent to refrain from certain action. The majority of rights enumerated in the Bill of Rights are rights in precisely this sense. They are negative rights against the government (originally the federal government, later applied to the state governments as well) that oblige it to refrain from certain specified actions ("Thou shalt not"). There are certain actions the federal government simply may not take, certain negative prohibitions it is morally and legally obliged to honor. The purpose of such prohibition ("Congress shall make no law . . .") is to protect both the corporate liberty of the sovereign states and the unalienable rights of the individual.

The Bill of Rights, then, enumerates the particular rights and liberties asserted against the federal government on behalf of both individuals and the several states. The Antifederalists regarded such constitutional guarantees as essential to free government and demanded their inclusion as a condition of ratifying the U.S. Constitution.

1. The *First Amendment* (freedom of religion, speech, press, assembly): *Congress shall make no law respecting an establishment of religion, or prohibiting the free exercise thereof; or abridging the freedom of speech, or of the press; or the right of the people peaceably to assemble, and to petition the Government for a redress of grievances.*

> The First Amendment safeguards some of the most cherished and celebrated American rights and liberties—freedom of religion (prohibition of governmental control of religious belief and practice); freedom of speech and the press (prohibition of governmental control of speech and other forms of communication); freedom of assembly (prohibition of governmental restriction on the free association of the people ("right to assemble") or their right to "petition" for justice ("redress of grievances")). Its original purpose is to forbid the federal government from enacting any legislation, for or against, pertaining to the specified areas. The U.S. Congress is to make "no law" with respect to religion, speech, press, or assembly; these are immune to the reach of federal power.

2. The *Second Amendment* (right to bear arms): *A well regulated Militia, being necessary to the security of a free State, the right of the people to keep and bear Arms, shall not be infringed.*

> The Second Amendment forbids the federal government from interfering with the right of the people to possess firearms.[49]

3. The *Third Amendment* (quartering of soldiers): *No Soldier shall, in time of peace be quartered in any house, without the consent of the Owner, nor in time of war, but in a manner to be prescribed by law.*

> The Third Amendment prohibits the federal government from forcing citizens to quarter soldiers in their homes, as had been the much-resented practice of the British government in the American colonies.

4. The *Fourth Amendment* (search and seizure): *The right of the people to be secure in their persons, houses, papers, and effects, against unreasonable searches and seizures, shall not be violated, and no Warrants shall issue, but upon probable cause, supported by Oath or affirmation, and particularly describing the place to be searched, and the persons or things to be seized.*

> The Fourth Amendment forbids the federal government from harassing citizens through arbitrary searches or seizure of their person or possessions. In its conduct of criminal investigations, the federal government must obtain what is popularly known as a "search warrant" from a member of the independent judiciary, who must be shown evidence sufficient to convince him or her that the government has "probable cause" to justify such a search. The warrant must also be specific, indicating the particular place, person, and items to be searched.

5. The *Fifth Amendment* (trial and punishment; compensation for "takings"): *No person shall be held to answer for a capital, or otherwise infamous crime, unless on a presentment or indictment of a Grand Jury, except in cases arising in the land or naval forces, or in the Militia, when in actual service in time of War or public danger; nor shall any person be subject for the same offense to be twice put in jeopardy of life or limb; nor shall be compelled in any criminal case to be a witness against himself, nor be deprived of life, liberty, or property, without due process of law; nor shall private property be taken for public use, without just compensation.*

> The Fifth Amendment, popularized by movies and television, forbids the government from charging a defendant with a capital crime (a crime eligible for the death penalty) unless he or she has been indicted by a Grand Jury (a group of private citizens assembled by the government to hear evidence against an accused person and determine whether it is sufficient to justify criminal indictment). The Amendment also prohibits so-called double jeopardy, that is, the prosecution of a person twice for the same crime, even if additional evidence is discovered subsequent to the conclusion of the first trial. It further prevents the government from forcing individuals to testify against themselves ("taking the Fifth") and requires that proper legal procedure ("due process of law") be followed before any person can be deprived of life, liberty, or property. Finally, it establishes the government's traditional power of "eminent domain." Such a power permits government to appropriate or "take" the property of private citizens, so long as two

conditions are met—the taking is for "public use" and "just compensation" is paid to the owner.

6. The *Sixth Amendment* (rights to speedy trial and trial by jury in criminal cases; confrontation of witnesses; right to counsel): *In all criminal prosecutions, the accused shall enjoy the right to a speedy and public trial, by an impartial jury of the State and district wherein the crime shall have been committed, which district shall have been previously ascertained by law, and to be informed of the nature and cause of the accusation; to be confronted with the witnesses against him; to have compulsory process for obtaining witnesses in his favor, and to have the Assistance of Counsel for his defence.*

The Sixth Amendment establishes a defendant's rights to a "speedy and public trial" as well as the ancient British right to trial by an "impartial jury," conducted in the place where the crime was committed. The defendant has the further right to be informed of the charges against him, confront the testimony of witnesses against him, and also compel the testimony of witnesses in his favor (subpoena). He is further entitled to an attorney; if the defendant cannot afford legal fees, he or she has been adjudged a constitutional right to a public defender paid for by taxpayers.[50]

7. The *Seventh Amendment* (trial by jury in civil cases): *In Suits at common law, where the value in controversy shall exceed twenty dollars, the right of trial by jury shall be preserved, and no fact tried by a jury, shall be otherwise reexamined in any Court of the United States, than according to the rules of the common law.*

The Seventh Amendment secures to American citizens the right to a trial by jury in certain civil cases. It also establishes the finality of the jury's verdict.

8. The *Eighth Amendment* (cruel and unusual punishment): *Excessive bail shall not be required, nor excessive fines imposed, nor cruel and unusual punishments inflicted.*

The Eighth Amendment prohibits "excessive" bail and fines and also "cruel and unusual punishment."

9. The *Ninth Amendment* (construction or interpretation of Constitution): *The enumeration in the Constitution, of certain rights, shall not be construed to deny or disparage others retained by the people.*

The Ninth Amendment acknowledges that the American people may possess rights that have not been specifically enumerated in the text of the Constitution. The Constitution should not be presumed to contain an exhaustive list of individual rights.

10. The *Tenth Amendment* (powers of the states and people): *The powers not delegated to the United States by the Constitution, nor prohibited by it to the States, are reserved to the States respectively, or to the people.*

> The Tenth Amendment states that the legitimate powers of the federal government include only those powers specifically delegated to it by the Constitution (the doctrine of "enumerated powers"). It further establishes that the several state governments retain all their traditional powers with the exception of those specifically prohibited to the states by the Constitution (for instance, the power to coin money). Any powers not specifically delegated to the federal government or specifically forbidden to the States "are reserved to the States respectively, or to the people."

The purpose of the Bill of Rights, as discussed, is to establish permanent and precise limits on the power or jurisdiction of the federal government. Many of the secured rights, such as the right to trial by jury, were either restatements or elaborations of the historical rights and liberties of the English people reaching back to Magna Carta of 1215 and beyond.[51] Others addressed specific violations of the colonists' rights that occurred during the recent conflict with England (for instance, quartering of soldiers; trials of Americans held in England; lengthy imprisonment of defendants awaiting trial). The Americans, however, moved beyond their British forebears in various and significant ways, including, as we have seen, the demand for a written constitution. For the same reason, the Antifederalists demanded specific enumeration of the rights of the people and specific enumeration of the powers both delegated and prohibited to the new federal government. The conflict with England had made them acutely aware of the myriad threats posed by overreaching government to the political order of a free people; and they demanded that the fruits of such experience be incorporated into the U.S. Constitution.

The ideal of the rule of law has traditionally been among the most hallowed of American political values. Throughout most of their history, the American people have held the fundamental law of the Constitution in the highest esteem, an esteem bordering on reverence. The U.S. Constitution was long regarded as the lodestar of America's unique and exceptional political order, its authors and signers as the brightest stars in its heavens. Every schoolchild once knew that "George Washington never told a lie" and marveled at his heroic band of ragtag soldiers trudging barefoot through the snow to win American freedom. Contemporary American students, by contrast, are taught little if anything of the valor of the revolutionary generation or the "miracle at Philadelphia" that established the first government in history dedicated to the cause of liberty and justice for all.[52] The typical student's knowledge of the founding era, as previously remarked, is confined to such facts as the slaveholding of Thomas Jefferson or absence of female suffrage. To acknowledge the present state of American education is, of course, merely to acknowledge the obvious—the temper of American society has significantly changed over the course of the past hundred years and especially the past fifty years. Extensive curricular revision has led to a generation relatively ignorant of American history, including the substantive content of the Constitution and other American founding documents. The neglect of American history in the schools, moreover, is often accompanied by an implicit or explicit disparagement of traditional American values in general and American reverence for the Constitution in particular. Lingering patriotism or pride in the American achievement are typically reproached by Progressive and Multicultural educators as mere "ethnocentrism" or worse ("right-wing extremism," "racism," "homophobia," "Islamophobia," and so on). Defense of the Constitution seems more and more a partisan political position than the common commitment of every American citizen.

NOTES

1. Bernard Bailyn, *The Ideological Origins of the American Revolution* (Cambridge: Cambridge University Press, 1973), 97.
2. Winston Churchill, speech given to House of Commons, May 13, 1940.
3. Washington, n2.
4. "Freedom in the World 2015." Freedom House (Washington, DC) https://www.aei.org/publication/measuring-freedom-around-the-world/
5. Which is not to say that individuals have not personally conceived and valued individual freedom but that the desire for individual freedom did not become a self-conscious and socially significant ideal in societies beyond Western influences.
6. See, for instance, the numerous influential works by historian Christopher Dawson.
7. Bailyn, *Ideological Origins,* 97.
8. Jackson Turner Main, *The Anti-Federalists* (New York: Quadrangle, 1964), 127–28.
9. John Cotton, cited in Perry Miller and Thomas Johnson, eds., *The Puritans* (New York: Harper, 1963), 212–13.
10. John Stuart Mill, *Utilitarianism, On Liberty and Considerations on Representative Government,* ed., H. B. Acton (London: J. M. Dent & Sons Ltd., 1972), 78.
11. Mill did restate in his "Harm Principle" the long-standing liberal view that the proper function of law is to restrain harm to others but that does not mean he himself was a consistent advocate of such a view.
12. Matthew 7:12.
13. Augustine, *City of God,* Bk. XIX: 7, 447.
14. M. Stanton Evans, *The Theme Is Freedom: Religion, Politics, and the American Tradition* (Washington, DC: Regnery Publishing, 1994), 98. Hereinafter cited as *Theme Is Freedom.*
15. Alexander Hamilton, *Federalist* No. 15, *Federalist Papers,* 72–73.
16. Linda C. Raeder, "Augustine and the Case for Limited Government" (*Humanitas,* Winter 2004).
17. Madison, *Federalist* No. 51, *Federalist Papers,* 251.
18. Cited in George Seldes, ed., *The Great Quotations,* 1st edition (New York: L. Stewart, 1960), 460.
19. Jean-Jacques Rousseau, "Man is naturally good and it is by their institutions alone that men become wicked." *Hobbes and Rousseau,* ed., Maurice Cranston and Richard S. Peters (New York: Doubleday, 1972), 297.
20. ". . . [I]n all free states, the constitution is fixed." Sam Adams, "Massachusetts Circular Letter to the Colonial Legislatures," February 11, 1768.

21. John Emerich Edward Dalberg-Acton, 1st Baron Acton (1834–1902), Lord Acton, "Letter to Bishop Mandell Creighton," April 5, 1887, in *Historical Essays and Studies*, eds, J. N. Figgis and R. V. Laurence (London: Macmillan, 1907).

22. Edmund Burke, "A Letter from Mr. Burke to a Member of the National Assembly of France" (1791), in *The Writings and Speeches of Edmund Burke*, Vol. IV (New York: Cosimo Classics, 2001 [1791]).

23. Madison, *Federalist* No. 48, *Federalist Papers*, 250.

24. Ryn, "The Unwritten Constitution." The morality implicit in American constitutionalism is, of course, the inherited morality of the Judeo-Christian tradition and, in particular, its emphasis on the virtue of self-restraint ("thou shalt not"). This is the morality that largely informed the Founders' understanding of virtue and that is presupposed in their constitutional design.

25. Madison, *Federalist* No. 10, *Federalist Papers*, 45.

26. I Corinthians 13:12.

27. Article XXX of the Massachusetts Constitution of 1780: "In the government of this Commonwealth, the legislative department shall never exercise the executive and judicial powers, or either of them: The executive shall never exercise the legislative and judicial powers, or either of them: The judicial shall never exercise the legislative and executive powers, or either of them: to the end it may be a government of laws and not of men."

28. "I do solemnly swear (or affirm) that I will faithfully execute the Office of President of the United States, and will to the best of my Ability, preserve, protect and defend the Constitution of the United States."

29. George Washington, "Farewell Address," September 19, 1796. *Founders' Constitution*, Vol. 5:684.

30. John Adams, Letter from John Adams to Massachusetts Militia, October 11, 1798. National Archives, last modified December 6, 2016.

31. The quote continues, ". . . I will avow that I believed and now believe that those general principles of Christianity are as eternal and immutable as the existence and the attributes of God." Letter from John Adams to Thomas Jefferson, June 28, 1813, in *The Adams-Jefferson Letters: Complete Correspondence between Thomas Jefferson and Abigail and John Adams*, 1st edition (Chapel Hill: University of North Carolina Press, 1988).

32. Francis J. Beckwith, *Politics for Christians: Statecraft as Soulcraft* (Downers Grove, IL: IVP Academic, 2012).

33. Richard H. Thaler and Cass Sunstein, *Nudge: Improving Decisions about Health, Wealth, and Happiness* (New York: Penguin Books, 2009); George F. Will, *Statecraft as Soulcraft: What Government Does* (New York: Touchstone, 1984).

34. "Micro-aggressions," "trigger-warnings," and the like.

35. Traditional Judeo-Christian morality, unlike certain contemporary views, does not, for instance, regard the ingestion of trans-fats, salt, or sugar or opposition to abortion, euthanasia, and homosexual marriage as moral evils.

36. Locke, *Letter Concerning Toleration*, 219.

37. Indeed, every authentic constitution implies limits on government—if there were no such limits, if government could do whatever it wants by any means it chooses, there would be no need for a constitution of any kind. "Constitutionalism means limited government." (Hayek, *Rules and Order*, 1).

38. The honor of creating the first written Constitution in human history belongs to Virginia. Kevin R. C. Gutzman, *Virginia's American Revolution* (Lanham, MD: Lexington Books, 2007), 7.

39. Madison, *Federalist* No. 47, *Federalist Papers*, 244.

40. Tenth Amendment: "The powers not delegated to the United States by the Constitution, nor prohibited by it to the States, are reserved to the States respectively, or to the people."

41. Jefferson, *Founders' Constitution*, Vol. 1: 319. Madison, as we have seen, expressed the identical belief.

42. It might also be argued that the later development of such doctrines as interposition, nullification, and secession represent further implicit "checks and balances" that aim to prevent the abuse of power by the U.S. government. While such doctrines quickly reared their heads in the course of early American political development and played a significant role in the nineteenth century, they were not explicitly advanced in the decades leading up to American independence.

43. Hayek, *POFP*, 15; James Mill, "Government," Supplement to the 1825 edition of the Encyclopedia Britannica.

44. Madison, *Federalist* No. 51, *Federalist Papers*, 262.

45. Alexis de Tocqueville, *Democracy in America,* ed. and trans., Harvey C. Mansfield and Delba Winthrop (Chicago: University of Chicago Press, 2000), 500–1.

46. James Madison, *Federalist* No. 48, *Federalist Papers*, 250.

47. The *Preamble* to the Constitution states: "We the people of the United States, in order to form a more perfect union, establish justice, insure domestic tranquility, provide for the common defense, promote the general welfare, and secure the blessings of liberty to ourselves and our posterity, do ordain and establish this Constitution for the United States of America."

The *Necessary and Proper Clause*: Article One of the U.S. Constitution, section 8, clause 18: "The Congress shall have Power—To make all Laws which shall be necessary and proper for carrying into Execution the foregoing Powers, and all other Powers vested by this Constitution in the Government of the United States, or in any Department or Officer thereof."

The *Commerce Clause* is an enumerated power listed in the United States Constitution. Article I, Section 8, Clause 3 states that the United States Congress shall have power "To regular Commerce with foreign Nations, and among the several States, and with the Indian Tribes."

The *Supremacy Clause* (Article VI, Clause 2) reads as follows: "This Constitution, and the Laws of the United States which shall be made in Pursuance thereof; and all Treaties made, or which shall be made, under the Authority of the United States, shall be the supreme Law of the Land; and the Judges in every State shall be bound thereby, any Thing [*sic*] in the Constitution or Laws of any State to the Contrary notwithstanding."

48. Patrick Henry, *The Debates in the Several State Conventions on the Adoption of the Federal Constitution,* ed. James McClellen and M. E. Bradford (Richmond: James River Press, 1991), 52.

49. In his popular edition of *Blackstone's Commentaries on the Laws of England* (1803), St. George Tucker, a lawyer, Revolutionary War militia officer, legal scholar, and later a U.S. District Court judge (appointed by James Madison in 1813), wrote of the Second Amendment: "The right of the people to keep and bear arms shall not be infringed, and this without any qualification as to their condition or degree, as is the case in the British government." In the appendix of the *Commentaries,* Tucker elaborates further: "This may be considered as the true palladium of liberty. . . . The right of self-defense is the first law of nature; in most governments it has been the study of rulers to confine this right within the narrowest limits possible. Whenever standing armies are kept up, and the right of the people to keep and bear arms is, under any color or pretext whatsoever, prohibited, liberty, if not already annihilated, is on the brink of destruction." St. George Tucker, *Blackstone's Commentaries: with Notes of Reference to the Constitution and Laws, of the Federal Government of the United States, and of the Commonwealth of Virginia,* five volumes (Clark, NJ: The Lawbook Exchange, Ltd., 1996 [1803].

50. As previously noted, certain scholars dispute the modern Court's reading of the Sixth Amendment as equivalent to a positive right to counsel. It has been argued, on the contrary, that the Amendment was originally intended to prohibit the federal government from interfering in the relation between lawyer and defendant.

51. Leonard W. Levy, *Origins of the Bill of Rights* (New Haven: Yale University Press, 1999).

52. Catherine Drinker Bowen, *The Miracle at Philadelphia* (New York: Little, Brown, and Co., 1966).

Bibliography

Acton, H. B. 1972. ed. John Stuart Mill, *Utilitarianism, On Liberty and Considerations on Representative Government*. London: J.M. Dent & Sons Ltd.

Adams, Charles Francis. ed. 1851. *The Works of John Adams*. Boston: Charles Little & Brown.

Adams, Henry. 2011. ed. *The Writings of Albert Gallatin, 1788–1816*. New York: Evergreen Review.

Adler, Mortimer. 1958. *The Idea of Freedom: A Dialectical Examination of the Conceptions of Freedom*. New York: Doubleday.

Aquinas, Thomas. 2017. *Commentary on the Sentences*. Rochester, NY: The Aquinas Institute.

Aristotle. 1947. *The Politics*, vol. 1, trans. Benjamin Jowett, in *Introduction to Aristotle*, ed Richard McKeon. New York: McGraw-Hill.

Ashcraft, Richard. 1962. *Revolutionary Politics and Locke's Two Treatises of Government*. Princeton: Princeton University Press.

Augustine. 1962. ed. Henry Paolucci. *The Political Writings of St. Augustine*. Washington, DC: Regnery Gateway.

Bailyn, Bernard. 1973. *The Ideological Origins of the American Revolution*. Cambridge: Cambridge University Press.

Barker, Ernest. 1960. *Social Contract*. Oxford University Press.

Beckwith, Francis J. 2012. *Politics for Christians: Statecraft as Soulcraft*. Downers Grove, IL: IVP Academic.

Berlin, Isaiah. 1969. "Two Concepts of Liberty." In *Four Essays on Liberty*, by Isaiah Berlin. Oxford: Oxford University Press.

Berman, Harold J. 1983. *Law and Revolution: The Formation of the Western Legal Tradition*. Harvard.

Bingham, Tom. 2011. *The Rule of Law*. London: Penguin UK.

Bowen, Catherine Drinker. 1966. *The Miracle at Philadelphia*. New York: Little, Brown, and Co.

Bracton, Henry of. 1903. ed. W. S. Holdsworth, *A History of English Law*. London: Methuen & Co., Ltd.

Brent, Allen. 2009. *A Political History of Early Christianity*. London: T&T Clark.

Burke, Edmund. 1907. *Thoughts and Details on Scarcity*, in *The Works of the Right Honorable Edmund Burke*. Vol. VI. London: Oxford University Press.

Carey, George W. 1995. *In Defense of the Constitution*, revised and expanded. Indianapolis: Liberty Fund.

Carter, Stephen L. 1993. *The Culture of Disbelief: How American Law and Politics Trivializes Religious Devotion*. New York: Anchor Books.

Cicero. 1998. *The Republic and The Laws*. Translated by Niall Rudd. New York: Oxford University Press.

Cogliano, Francis D. 2017. *Revolutionary America 1763–1815*. 3rd ed. New York: Routledge.

Corwin, Edward S. 2008. *The Higher Law Background of American Constitutional Law*. Indianapolis: Liberty Fund.

Coulanges, Fustel De. 1955. *The Ancient City: A Classic Study of the Religious and Civil Institutions in Ancient Greece and Rome*. New York: Doubleday and Company, Inc.

Cranston, Maurice and Peters, Richard S. 1972. eds. *Hobbes and Rousseau*. New York: Doubleday. 297.

Dalberg-Acton, John Emerich Edward. 1907. eds. J. N. Figgis, and R. V. Laurence, *Historical Essays and Studies*. London: Macmillan.
Diaz, Howard. 2012. *A Charter of Negative Liberties: Defining the Bill of Rights and Other Commentary*. Bloomington, IN: Westbow Press.
Dicey, A. V. 1915. *Introduction to the Study of the Law of the Constitution*. London: Macmillan and Co.
Dreisbach, Daniel L. and Hall, Mark David. 2009. eds. *The Sacred Rights of Conscience*. Indianapolis: Liberty Fund.
Ekirch, Arthur A., Jr. 1976. *The Decline of American Liberalism*. New York: Atheneum.
Elliot, Jonathan. 1996. ed. *The Debates in the Several States on the Adoption of the Federal Constitution, as Recommended by the General Convention at Philadelphia in 1787*. 5 volumes, 2nd edition. Reprinted from the 1845 edition. Buffalo, NY: William S. Hein & Co.
Evans, M. Stanton. 1994. *The Theme is Freedom: Religion, Politics, and the American Tradition*. Washington, DC: Regnery Publishing.
Fontana, Biancamaria, ed. 1988. *Constant, Political Writings*. Cambridge: Cambridge University Press, 1988.
Ford, Paul L. 2010. ed. *The Writings of Thomas Jefferson*. New York: G. P. Putnam.
Frohnen, Bruce. ed. 2008. *The American Nation: Primary Sources*. Indianapolis: Liberty Fund.
———. ed. 2002. *The American Republic: Primary Sources*. Indianapolis: Liberty Fund.
———. ed, 1999. *The Antifederalists: Selected Writings and Speeches*. Washington, DC: Regnery Publishing, Inc.
Glendon, Mary Ann. 1991. *The Impoverishment of Political Discourse*. New York: The Free Press.
Gutzman, Kevin R. C. 2007. *Virginia's American Revolution: From Dominion to Republic 1776–1840*. Lanham, MD: Lexington Books.
Hall, Daniel L. Dreisbach and David Mark, ed. 2009. *The Sacred Rights of Conscience*. Indianapolis: Liberty Fund.
Hamowy, Ronald, ed. 1995. *Cato's Letters*. Indianapolis: Liberty Fund.
Harp, Gillis. 2005. *Positivist Republic: Auguste Comte and the Reconstruction of American Liberalism, 1865–1920*. University Park, PA: Penn State University Press.
Hayek, F. A. 1978. *Law, Legislation and Liberty, Rules and Order*. Vol. 1. 3 vols. Chicago: University of Chicago Press.
———. 2012. *Law, Legislation, and Liberty, The Mirage of Social Justice*. Vol. 2. 3 vols. Chicago: University of Chicago Press.
———. 1981. *Law, Legislation, and Liberty, The Political Order of a Free People*. Vol. 3. 3 vols. Chicago: University of Chicago Press.
———. 1960. *The Constitution of Liberty*. Chicago: University of Chicago Press.
———. 1979. *The Counterrevolution of Science: Studies on the Abuse of Reason*. Indianapolis: Liberty Fund.
———. 2007. *The Road to Serfdom*. ed. Caldwell, Bruce. Chicago: University of Chicago Press.
———. 1945. "The Use of Knowledge in Society." *American Economic Review* (American Economic Association) XXXV (4): 519–30.
Henry, Patrick. Speech given at St. John's Church, Richmond, VA, March 23, 1775. Avalon Project, Documents in Law, History and Diplomacy (New Haven: Yale Law School).
Hobbes, Thomas. 1996. ed. John Gaskin. *Leviathan*. Oxford: Oxford University Press.
Holdsworth, W., ed. 1903. *A History of English Law*. London: Methuen & Co. Ltd.
Howard, A. E. Dick. 1964. *Magna Carta: Text and Commentary*. Charlottesville: University of Virginia Press.
Hunt, Baillard, ed. 2015. *The Writings of James Madison*. Whitefish, MT: Kessinger Publishing.

Jefferson, Thomas. 1904. eds. Lipscomb, Thomas and Bergh, Albert. *The Writings of Thomas Jefferson*. Vol. 10. 20 vols. Monticello: The Thomas Jefferson Memorial Association of the United States.
Kirk, Russell. 2003. *The Roots of American Order*. Wilmington, DE: Intercollege Studies Institute.
Kristol, Irving. 1995. *Neo-Conservatism, Selected Essays 1949–1995*. Washington, DC: Free Press.
Laslett, Peter. 1956. "The English Revolution and Locke's 'Two Treatises of Government'," *Cambridge Historical Journal* 12.
Lehmann, Winfred P. 1986. *A Gothic Etymological Dictionary*. Leiden, Netherlands: Brill Publishers.
Leoni, Bruno. 1991. *Freedom and the Law*. Indianapolis: Liberty Fund.
Lerner, Ralph and Kurland, Philip B., eds. 1987. *The Founders' Constitution*. 5 vols. Indianapolis: Liberty Fund.
Levy, Leonard W. 1999. *Origins of the Bill of Rights*. New Haven: Yale University Press.
Locke, John. 1980. ed. Macpherson, C. B. *Second Treatise of Government*. Indianapolis: Hackett Publishing
———. 2003. *Two Treatises of Government and a Letter Concerning Toleration*. New Haven: Yale University Press.
Looney, J. Jefferson, ed. 2012. *The Papers of Thomas Jefferson*. Princeton: Princeton University Press.
Lutz, Donald S. ed. 1998. *Colonial Origins of the American Constitution: A Documentary History*. Indianapolis: Liberty Fund, Inc.
———. 1988. *The Origins of American Constitutionalism*. Baton Rouge: Louisiana State University Press.
Main, Jackson Turner. 1964. *The Anti-Federalists*. New York: Quadrangle.
Marsilius of Padua. 2001. Alan Gewirth, trans. *Defensor Pacis*. New York: Columbia University Press.
McDonald, Forrest M. 1979. *E Pluribus Unum: The Formaton of the American Republic 1776–1790*. Indianapolis: Liberty Fund.
McFerran, Warren L. 2009. *Birth of the Republic: The Origin of the United States*. Gretna, LA: Pelican Publishing.
McIlwain, Charles Howard. 2010. *Constitutionalism: Ancient and Modern*. Indianapolis: Liberty Fund.
Meyers, Marvin, ed. 1973. *The Mind of the Founder: Sources of the Political Thought of James Madison*, Indianapolis: Bobbs-Merrill.
Miller, John Chester. 1959. *Origins of the American Revolution*. 2nd ed, Stanford: Stanford University Press.
Miller, Perry and Johnson, Thomas, eds. 1963. *The Puritans*. New York: Harper.
Mises, Ludwig von. 2010. *Human Action*. Auburn, AL: Ludwig von Mises Institute.
Moots, Glenn A. 2010. *Politics Reformed: the Anglo-American Legacy of Covenent Theology*. Columbia: MO: University of Missouri Press.
Morley, Felix. 1978. *Freedom and Federalism*. Indianapolis: Liberty Fund.
Morstein, Marx Fritz. 2007. *Propaganda and Dictatorship*. Mahwah, NJ: Ramsey Press.
Murray, Charles. 2013. *American Exceptionalism: An Experiment in History*. Washington, DC: AEI Press.
Nash, George H. 2006. *The Conservative Intellectual Movement in America since 1945*. Wilmington DE: Intercollegiate Studies Institute.
Neusner, Jacob, ed. 2006. *Religious Foundations of Western Civilization: Judaism, Christianity, and Islam*. Nashville: Abingdon Press.
Nisbet, Robert. 2010 [1953]. *The Quest for Community: A Study in the Ethics of Order and Freedom*. Wilmington, DE: Intercollegiate Studies Institute.
Opitz, Edmund A. 1996. *Religion: Foundation of the Free Society*. Irvington-on-Hudson, NY: Foundation for Economic Education, Inc.
Orwell, George. 2010. *Politics and the English Language and Other Essays*. Oxford: Benediction Classics.

Paine, Thomas. 2000. ed. Slaughter, Thomas P. *Common Sense: and Related Writings*. New York: Bedford/St. Martin's Press.
Raico, Ralph. 2012. *Classical Liberalism and the Austrian School*. Auburn, AL: Ludwig von Mises Institute.
———. 1985. *Liberalism in the Classical Tradition*. 3rd. Cobden Press.
Robinson, J. H., ed. 1905. *Readings in European History*. Boston: Ginn.
Robson, John M. 1968. *The Improvement of Mankind: The Social and Political Thought of John Stuart Mill*. London: Routledge and Kegan Paul.
Rutherford, Samuel. 1998. *Lex, Rex, or The Prince and the Law*. Berryville, VA: Hess Publications.
Rutland, R. A., ed. 1976. *The Papers of James Madison*. Chicago: University of Chicago Press.
Ryn, Claes G. 1990. *Democracy and the Ethical Life*. 2nd edition. Washington, D.C.: The Catholic University of America Press.
———. 1992. "Political Philosophy and the Unwritten Constitution." *Modern Age* 303–9.
Sandoz, Ellis, ed. 1991. *Political Sermons of the Founding Era*. Indianapolis: Liberty Fund.
———, ed. 1993. *The Roots of Liberty: Magna Carta, Ancient Constitution, and the Anglo-American Tradition of Rule of Law*. Indianapolis: Liberty Fund.
Schumpeter, Joseph. 1954. *History of Economic Analysis*. New York: Oxford University Press.
Seldes, George, ed. 1960. *The Great Quotations*, 1st edition. New York: L. Stewart.
Shah, Timothy Samuel and Hertzke, Allen D., ed. 2016. *Christianity and Freedom*. Vol. I: Historical Perspectives. II vols. Cambridge: Cambridge University Press.
Shogimen, Takashi. 2010. *Ockham and Political Discourse in the Late Middle Ages*. Cambridge: Cambridge University Press.
Siedentop, Larry. 2014. *Inventing the Individual: The Origins of Western Liberalism*. Cambridge, MA: The Belknap Press of Harvard University Press.
Skinner, Quentin. 1978. *Foundations of Modern Political Thought*. Vol. II: the Age of Reformation. Cambridge: Cambridge University Press.
———. 1998. *Liberty Before Liberalism*. Cambridge: Cambridge University Press.
Sowell, Thomas. 1987. *A Conflict of Visions: Ideological Origins of Political* Struggles. New York: William Morrow & Co.
Stevens, Michael, ed. 2016. *The Family Letters of Victor and Meta Berger, 1894–1929*. Madison: Wisconsin Historical Society Press.
Storing, Herbert. 2008. *What the Antifederalists Were For: The Political Thought of the Opponents of the Constitution*. Chicago: University of Chicago Press.
Talmon, Jacob L. 1952. *The Rise of Totalitarian Democracy*. Boston: Beacon Press.
Thaler, Richard H. and Sunstein, Cass. 2009. *Nudge: Improving Decisions about Health, Wealth, and Happiness*. New York: Penguin Books.
Thucydides. 1993. *On Law, Power, and Justice*. Indianapolis: Hackett Publishing Company, Inc.
Tierney, Brian. 2008. eds. John Witte and Frank S. Alexander, *Christianity and Law*. Cambridge: Cambridge University Press.
———. 1988. *The Crisis of Church and State* 1050–1300. Toronto: University of Toronto Press.
Tocqueville, Alexis de. 2000. *Democracy in America*, ed. and trans., Harvey C. Mansfield and Delba Winthrop. Chicago: University of Chicago Press.
Treadgold, Donald W. 1990. *Freedom: A History*. New York: New York University Press.
Tucker, St. George. 1996 [1803]. *Blackstone's Commentaries: with Notes of Reference to the Constitution and Laws, of the Federal Government of the United States, and of the Commonwealth of Virginia*, five volumes. Clark, NJ: The Lawbook Exchange, Ltd.
Waley, Arthur, trans. *Analects*. New York: Vintage, 1989.
Walker, Graham. 2014. *The Moral Foundations of Constiutional Thought: Current Problems, Augustinian Prospects*. reprint. Princeton: Princeton University Press.

Watkins, William J., Jr. 2016. *Crossroads for Liberty: Recovering the Anti-Federalist Values of America's First Constitution*. Oakland, CA: Independent institute.
Will, George. 1984. *Statecraft as Soulcraft: What Government Does*. New York: Touchstone.
Wills, Garry, ed. 1982. *The Federalist Papers by Alexander Hamilton, James Madison and John Jay*. New York: Bantam Books
Witte, John, Jr. 2005. *Religion and the American Constitutional Experiment*. 2nd ed. Boulder, CO: Westview Press.

Index

About the Author

Linda C. Raeder is professor of politics at Palm Beach Atlantic University in West Palm Beach, Florida, where she teaches modern and American political philosophy. She is the author of numerous scholarly publications exploring the nature and development of the Western liberal tradition, including a monograph on the religious thought of J. S. Mill, chapters and articles on Hayek, Burke, Marx, Augustine, Voegelin, and related subjects. She received the PhD in politics and American government from The Catholic University of America and serves as both associate editor of the academic journal *Humanitas* (Washington, DC) and senior fellow at the James Madison Institute in Tallahassee. In 2017, she was recipient of the Charles and Hazel Corts Award for outstanding teaching.

www.ingramcontent.com/pod-product-compliance
Ingram Content Group UK Ltd.
Pitfield, Milton Keynes, MK11 3LW, UK
UKHW042037051026
476324UK00001BB/80

9 781498 56604